THE CONFLICT OF CONVICTIONS

THE CONFLICT

edited by Jack Lindeman
✿ Chilton Book Company
Philadelphia · New York · London

American writers report the Civil War—
A selection and arrangement from
the journals, correspondence and
articles of the major men and women
of letters who lived through the war

OF CONVICTIONS

ACKNOWLEDGMENTS

I would like to thank the Charles Henry Lea Library of the University of Pennsylvania, The Free Library of Philadelphia, and The Vail Memorial Library of Lincoln University for research facilities put at my disposal. I would also like to thank Nan Braymer for her valuable editorial suggestions and for her typing of the manuscript.

To WALTER LOWENFELS
who first conceived the idea for this book

and DORCAS
whose encouragement and patience never faltered

Preface

The Conflict of Convictions brings together, under chapter headings reflecting content and chronology, a selection of Civil War writings by seventeen great literary figures of the period. Although the separate pieces are products of widely divergent personalities—warrior Bierce, "wisest man" Emerson, poets Longfellow and Dickinson, to name a few—the impact of the "irrepressible conflict" on them emerges as the contemporary expression of a collective, creative conscience.

Of all the contributors, Walt Whitman alone had contemplated a book on the war: the others wrote deeply and extensively about it but much of the material was put down in letters, journals, notebooks, and speeches, not intended for publication in book form. All the more, the informal, personal tone of many of the passages results in a close-up of the "real war" that Whitman said "would never get into the books."

Lacking our own modern, widespread network of communication, the special insights of these writers were often expressed in their correspondence. *Hospital Sketches*, Louisa May Alcott's first popular book, was a collection of letters written to members of her family. The personal letters and diary entries in this collection reflect the everyday reality of how both the great and the humble reacted to the greatest cataclysm of their time.

We are all familiar with classic contributions to American literature of authors contemporary with the Civil War —*Moby Dick, Walden, Leaves of Grass, Uncle Tom's Cabin,* the list is almost endless—but few of us know how much and how well they wrote about the war. Living close to the origins of our nation (there were veterans of '76 still alive; the War of 1812 was just yesterday to them), 19th century writers were profoundly shaken by the threat to the Union. As thinkers, poets, philosophers, analysts, they pondered over underlying causes, deplored the war's agonies, considered its long-range effect on the fate of our country. The reflective picture they paint of these four crucial years deepens our understanding of the historical record.

Most of the writers were civilians, yet personally involved in the conflict in one way or another. Four of them —Sidney Lanier, Samuel Clemens, Ambrose Bierce, and Thomas Wentworth Higginson—were soldiers. Clemens and Lanier were in the Confederate Army and in this book represent the only spokesmen for the Southern point of view, and even Clemens was never a whole-hearted partisan of the Rebel cause.

Lanier was a signal officer stationed in Virginia and North Carolina, where, in addition to his military duties, he found time to write the first anti-war novel, *Tiger-Lilies.* He was eventually assigned to a blockade runner out of Wilmington, North Carolina, and was captured when a Union cruiser intercepted his ship. Of both these war experiences, he writes vivid accounts in letters to his family.

Ambrose Bierce, a topographical engineer in the Union Army, took part in many important battles before he was finally wounded and discharged. Thomas Wentworth Higginson, colonel of the first Negro regiment in the Union army, describes his experiences in terms of singular interest today.

Both Walt Whitman and Louisa May Alcott came in touch with the war through the wounded they tended. Whitman was a hospital aide, comforter and letter-writer, and Miss Alcott was a regular army nurse. Nathaniel Hawthorne, Oliver Wendell Holmes and Herman Melville at various times made unofficial tours of many of the battlefields and towns where fighting had occurred. Hawthorne has left us some of the most moving observations to come out of the war—most of them written shortly before he died, in 1864. Holmes, in searching for his wounded son, Oliver Wendell, Jr., was brought into contact with many of the most harrowing and revealing aspects of the war during the long journey. Melville, in 1866, in an epilogue to *Battle-Pieces and Other Aspects of the War,* a volume of his poems, wrote the masterpiece of sanity and tolerance on reconstruction that concludes this volume.

Ralph Waldo Emerson's writings seem to have been well known to Lincoln, though he was certainly also acquainted with Whittier, Longfellow, Lowell, Holmes and Bryant. Emerson (and perhaps this must be said of Bryant, too) seems to have exercised considerable influence over the President's policies—especially in relation to the Emancipation Proclamation. Both Emerson and Bryant exchanged views with Lincoln at the White House; in fact, it is reported that Lincoln attended one of Emerson's lectures in Washington.

William Cullen Bryant, editor-in-chief of the *New York Evening Post,* wrote many memorable editorials and many letters to friends expressing his thoughts and feelings as the conflict developed. James Russell Lowell, having completed his editorship of *The Atlantic Monthly* shortly before the war began, wrote essays reflecting his philosophic and political opinions. Henry Wadsworth Longfellow, the uncrowned poet laureate of America, was a prolific correspondent and diarist. John Greenleaf Whittier's prime concern remained the freedom of the slaves; he had joined the abolitionist movement as early as 1830, and had been an unremitting propagandist for emancipation. Whittier's fellow-Brahmins, including Bryant, formed a group espousing a higher morality that could not be dissuaded by any compromises for the sake of political expediency.

Thoreau died only a few weeks after the first anniversary of the fall of Sumter and his strong anti-slavery sentiments never slackened. Harriet Beecher Stowe, who had made her great contribution to the cause—*Uncle Tom's Cabin*—ten years before the outbreak of the war, continued to maintain her vigorous opposition to the enslavement of the Negro. Her "reply" to a group of English women at a time when English sympathies (among the upper classes especially) were largely pro-Confederate expresses ringing indignation. Emily Dickinson, when the war came to Amherst as a frightening epidemic might have come, expressed her profound feelings of sympathy for its victims and their kin.

Chronological sequence in this collection has been maintained as far as possible so that the reader might follow the changes in the feelings of the writers as they responded to the fortunes of battle and the shifting political tides. The period covered begins with the fall of Sumter and ends with the opening of the reconstruction era. A number of chapters are devoted to the important political and military personalities seen through the eyes of the authors, while other passages deal with Confederate prisoners of war, army hospitals, copperheadism, and so forth.

Much of the material contained in this book has been out of print for some time, or else buried in the moldering pages of century-old issues of magazines, and therefore is virtually unavailable to the public. It is interesting to note here that even exhaustive critical studies of the authors appear to have passed over most of the war pieces.

The nature of *The Conflict of Convictions* was determined from the beginning by the writers themselves, and reflects only those phases of the war that were of transcendent interest to men and women of their stature and humanity. I hope that the book can be looked upon as an enlightening study of the Civil War as it was seen, and felt, and recorded by some of the most distinguished minds in our American literary heritage.

JACK LINDEMAN

Contents

1 *Fort Sumter Falls*

Two days before the fall of Sumter, Thoreau (in Concord) "counterbalances" newspaper headlines by reading Herodotus.

As for my prospective reader, I hope that he *ignores* Fort Sumter, & Old Abe, & all that, for that is just the most fatal, and indeed the only fatal, weapon you can direct against evil ever; for as long as you *know* of it, you are *particeps criminis*. What business have you, if you are "an angel of light," to be pondering over the deeds of darkness, reading the New York Herald & the like? I do not so much regret the present condition of things in this country (provided I regret it at all) as I do that I ever heard of it.

I know one or two who have this year, for the first time, read a president's message; but they do not see that this implies a fall in themselves, rather than a rise in the president. Blessed were the days before you read a president's message. Blessed are the young for they do not read the president's message.

Blessed are they who never read a newspaper, for they shall see Nature, and through her, God.

But, alas, I have heard of Sumter, & Pickens, & even of Buchanan (though I did not read his message).

I also read the New York Tribune, but then I am reading Herodotus & Strabo, & Blodget's Climatology, and Six

Years in the Deserts of North America, as hard as I can, to counterbalance it.[1]

Samuel Clemens, from another part of the country, sees the opening of the war from a different point of view.

Out West there was a good deal of confusion in men's minds during the first months of the great trouble—a good deal of unsettledness, of leaning first this way, then that, then the other way. It was hard for us to get our bearings. I call to mind an instance of this. I was piloting on the Mississippi when the news came that South Carolina had gone out of the Union on the 20th of December, 1860. My pilot mate was a New Yorker, He was strong for the Union; so was I. But he would not listen to me with any patience; my loyalty was smirched, to his eye, because my father had owned slaves.

I said, in palliation of this dark fact, that I had heard my father say some years before he died that slavery was a great wrong and that he would free the solitary Negro he then owned if he could think it right to give away the property of the family when he was so straitened in means. My mate retorted that a mere impulse was nothing—anybody could pretend to a good impulse, and went on decrying my Unionism and libeling my ancestry. A month later, the secession atmosphere had considerably thickened on the Lower Mississippi, and I became a rebel; so did he.

We were together in New Orleans the 26th of January, when Louisiana went out of the Union. He did his full share of the rebel shouting, but was bitterly opposed to letting me do mine. He said that I came of bad stock—of a father who had been willing to set slaves free. In the following summer he was piloting a federal gunboat and shouting for the Union again, and I was in the Confederate Army. I held his note for some borrowed money. He was one of the most upright men I ever knew, but he repudiated that note without hesitation because I was a rebel and the son of a man who owned slaves.[2]

Longfellow enters a series of brief comments on the outbreak of the war in his journal for April.

April 12: News comes that Fort Sumter is attacked. And the war begins! Who can foresee the end?

April 15: The news only a repetition of yesterday's. We are in the beginning of a civil war. A very bitter thought!

April 16: Today two regiments muster on the Common for the Southern war.

April 17: Go to town. Faces in the streets are stern and serious. A crowd in the State House. At intervals drums are heard. . . . At the gateway of the State House two youths of twenty, with smooth, fair cheeks, stand sentry. Ah, woe the day!

April 20: In town. Dine . . . and we talk of war, war, war! Interesting but not agreeable nor instructive, as none of us know anything about it.

April 21: At chapel, a war sermon.

April 23: Weary days with wars and rumors of wars, and marching of troops, and flags waving, and people talking. No reading but reading of newspapers.

April 28: I was glad the pulpit did not thunder a war-sermon today. A "truce of God" once a week is pleasant. At present the North is warlike enough, and does not need arousing.

April 30: When the times have such a gunpowder flavor, all literature loses its taste. Newspapers are the only reading. They are at once the record and the romance of the day.[3]

Emerson, in nearby Concord, reflects the prevailing excitement, in a letter dated April 20.

You have heard that our village was all alive yesterday with the departure of our braves. Judge Hoar made a speech to them at the Depot; Mr. Reynolds made a prayer in the ring, the cannon which was close by us making musi-

cal beats every minute to his prayer. And when the whistle
of the train was heard, & George Prescott (the commander), who was an image of manly beauty, ordered his
men to march, his wife stopped him & put down his sword
to kiss him, & grief & pride ruled the hour. All the families
were there. They left Concord 45 men, but on the way recruits implored to join them, &, when they reached Boston,
they were 64.[4]

Walt Whitman was living in New York at the time.

News of the attack on Fort Sumter and *the flag* at
Charleston Harbor, South Carolina, was received in New
York City late at night (13th April 1861) and was immedi-
ately sent out in extras of the newspapers.

I had been in the opera in Fourteenth Street that
night, and after the performance was walking down Broadway around twelve o'clock on my way to Brooklyn, when I
heard in the distance the loud cries of the newsboys, who
came presently tearing and yelling up the street, rushing
from side to side more furiously than usual.

I bought an extra and crossed to the Metropolitan
Hotel, . . . where the great lamps were still brightly blazing, and, with a crowd of others who gathered impromptu,
read the news—which was evidently authentic.

For the benefit of some who had no papers, one of us
read the telegram aloud, while all listened silently and
intently.

No remark was made by any of the crowd, which had
increased to thirty or forty, but all stood a moment or two,
I remember, before they dispersed. I can almost see them
there now, under the lamps at midnight again. . . .[5]

*Louisa May Alcott, a neighbor of Emerson's, tells of the
Concord company's departure.*

War declared with the South, and our Concord company went to Washington. A busy time getting them ready,

and a sad day seeing them off; for in a little town like this we all seem like one family in times like these. At the station, the scene was very dramatic as the brave boys went away perhaps never to come back again.

I've often longed to see a war, and now I have my wish. I long to be a man; but as I can't fight, I will content myself with working for those who can.[6]

Lowell summarizes the state of affairs for his Atlantic Monthly *readers.*

The country had come to the conclusion that Mr. Lincoln and his cabinet were mainly employed in packing their trunks to leave Washington, when the "venerable Edward Ruffin of Virginia" fired the first gun at Fort Sumter which brought all the Free States to their feet as one man. That shot is destined to be the most memorable one ever fired on this continent since the Concord fowling-pieces said, "That bridge is ours, and we mean to go across it," eighty-seven Aprils ago. As these began a conflict which gave us independence, so that began another which is to give us nationality. It was certainly a great piece of good-luck for the Government that they had a fort which it was so profitable to lose. The people were weary of a masterly inactivity which seemed to consist mainly in submitting to be kicked. We know very well the difficulties that surrounded the new Administration; we appreciate their reluctance to begin a war the responsibility of which was as great as its consequences seemed doubtful; but we cannot understand how it hoped to evade war, except by concessions vastly more disastrous than war itself.

War has no evil comparable in its effect on national character to that of a craven submission to manifest wrong, the postponement of moral to material interests. There is no prosperity so great as courage. We do not believe that any amount of forbearance would have conciliated the South so long as they thought us pusillanimous. The only way to retain the Border States was by showing that we had the will and the power to do without them. The little Bo-peep policy of:

"Let them alone, and they'll all come home
Wagging their tails behind them"

was certainly tried long enough with conspirators who had shown unmistakably that they desired nothing so much as the continuance of peace, especially when it was all on one side, and who would never have given the Government the great advantage of being attacked in Fort Sumter, had they not supposed they were dealing with men who could not be cuffed into resistance.

The lesson we have to teach them now is that we are thoroughly and terribly in earnest. Mr. Stephens' theories are to be put to a speedier and sterner test than he expected, and we are to prove which is stronger—an oligarchy built *on* men, or a commonwealth built *of* them. Our structure is alive in every part with defensive and recuperative energies; woe to theirs, if that vaunted cornerstone which they believe patient and enduring as marble should begin to writhe with intelligent life.

We have no doubt of the issue. We believe that the strongest battalions are always on the side of God. The Southern army will be fighting for Jefferson Davis, or at most for the liberty of self-misgovernment, while we go forth for the defense of principles which alone make government august and civil society possible. It is the very life of the nation that is at stake. There is no question here of dynasties, races, religions, but simply whether we will consent to include in our Bill of Rights—not merely as of equal validity with our other rights, whether natural or acquired, but by its very nature transcending and abrogating them all—the Right of Anarchy. We must convince men that treason against the ballot-box is as dangerous as treason against a throne, and that, if they play so desperate a game, they must stake their lives on the hazard.

The Government, however slow it may have been to accept the war which Mr. Buchanan's supineness left them, is acting now with all energy and determination. What they have a right to claim is the confidence of the people, and that depends in good measure on the discretion of the press. Only let us have no more weakness under the plausible name of conciliation.

We need not discuss the probabilities of an acknowledgment of the Confederated States by England and France; we have only to say, "Acknowledge them at your peril." But there is no chance of the recognition of the Confederacy by any foreign governments, so long as it is without the confidence of the brokers.

The whole tone of Southern journals, so far as we are able to judge, shows the inherent folly and weakness of the secession movement. Men who feel strong in the justice of their cause, or confident in their powers, do not waste breath in childish boasts of their own superiority and querulous deprecation of their antagonists. They are weak, and they know it.

And not only are they weak in comparison with the Free States, but we believe they are without the moral support of whatever deserves the name of public opinion at home. If not, why does their Congress, as they call it, hold council always with closed doors, like a knot of conspirators? The first tap of the Northern drum dispelled many illusions, and we need no better proof of which ship is sinking than that Mr. Caleb Cushing should have made haste to come over to the old Constitution, with the stars and stripes at her masthead.

We cannot think that the war we are entering on can end without some radical change in the system of African slavery. Whether it be doomed to a sudden extinction, or to a gradual abolition through economical causes, this war will not leave it where it was before. As a power in the state, its reign is already over. The fiery tongues of the batteries in Charleston Harbor accomplished in one day a conversion which the constancy of Garrison and the eloquence of Phillips had failed to bring about in thirty years. And whatever other result this war is destined to produce, it has already won for us a blessing worth everything to us as a nation in emancipating the public opinion of the North.[7]

Whittier addresses a circular letter to his fellow Quakers, justifying their participation in the war effort.

We have no right to ask or expect an exemption from the chastisement which the Divine Providence is inflicting upon the nation. Steadily and faithfully maintaining our testimony against war, we owe it to the cause of truth to show that excited heroism and generous self–sacrifice are not incompatible with our pacific principles. Our mission is, at this time, to mitigate the sufferings of our countrymen, to visit and aid the sick and the wounded, to relieve the necessities of the widow and the orphan, and to practice economy for the sake of charity.

Let the same heroic devotion to duty which our brethren in Great Britain manifested in the Irish famine and pestilence be reproduced on this side of the water, in mitigating the horrors of war and its attendant calamities. What hinders us from holding up the hands of Dorothea Dix in her holy work of mercy at Washington? Our society is rich, and of those to whom much is given, much will be required in this hour of proving and trial.[8]

2 The Civil War Gathers

With the real battles of the war still ahead, Emerson strikes a note of optimism in his journal on May 3rd.

An affecting incident of the war occurred on the arrival of the Fifth Regiment (of Massachusetts) at Springfield, received with such enthusiasm by the people that a funeral procession, passing by, stopped and joined in the cheers with which the troops were hailed. The *National Intelligencer* says of the arrival and performance of the Massachusetts Eighth Regiment at Annapolis that probably no other regiment in the country could do what this regiment did—put a locomotive together, lay the rails on the broken railroad, and bend the sails of a man–of–war (the frigate *Constitution*), which they named.

Men delight in being well governed. When two men meet, one of them usually offers his vacant helm to the hands of the other.

The country is cheerful and jocund in the belief that it has a government at last. The men in search of a party, parties in search of a principle, interests and dispositions that could not fuse for want of some base—all joyfully unite in this great Northern party on the basis of Freedom.

What a healthy tone exists! I suppose when we come to fighting, and many of our people are killed, it will yet be found that the bills of mortality in the country will show a better result of this year than the last, on account of the general health: no dyspepsia, no consumption, no fevers, when there is so much electricity, and conquering heart and mind. So, in finance, the rise of wheat paid the cost of the Mexican war; and the check on fraud and jobbing, and the new prosperity of the West will pay the new debt.[1]

Miss Alcott records her earliest contribution to the war effort.

Spent our May-day working for our men—three hundred women all sewing together at the hall for two days.[2]

Longfellow writes in his journal for May.

May 2: The civil war grumbles and growls and gathers. But the storm-clouds do not yet break. Sumner comes out to tea. He seems rather depressed. It is indeed a heavy atmosphere to breathe—the impending doom of a nation!

May 9: In the afternoon went with Felton to the arsenal to see the students drill—a dress parade. As the major did not arrive, Felton and I were requested to review them!—which we did, by marching up and down, in front and rear.

May 11: In town. The "Corner" looks gloomy enough. Business at a standstill. So much for the war and books.

May 14: If South Carolina had not been so self-conceited and precipitate, this war might have been avoided. But the North could not stand the firing on the flag at Sumter.

May 20: Angry articles in the papers about England. John Bull is not behaving well about this rebellion. He chooses to put Civilization and Barbarism on an equality.

Everywhere in the air the warlike rumor of drums mingles discordantly with the song of birds.

May 21: A note from Curtis, urging me to write a national song. I am afraid the "go to, let us make a na-

tional song'' will not succeed. It will be likely to spring up
in some other way.

May 27: The days come and go, with a trouble in the
air, and in the hearts of men.[3]

*Hawthorne's son Julian recalls one of his father's out-
bursts not long after Sumter had fallen: "I hope that we
shall give them a terrible thrashing, and then kick them
out." On May 26, Hawthorne wrote to his friend Henry A.
Bright in a tone of exhilaration.*

The war, strange to say, has had a beneficial effect
upon my spirits, which were flagging woefully before it
broke out. But it was delightful to share in the heroic sentiment of the time, and to feel that I had a country—a consciousness which seemed to make me young again. One
thing as regards this matter I regret, and one thing I am
glad of. The regrettable thing is that I am too old to shoulder a musket myself, and the joyful thing is that Julian is
too young. He drills constantly with a company of lads,
and means to enlist as soon as he reaches the minimum
age.

But I trust we shall either be victorious or vanquished
before that time. Meantime, though I approve the war as
much as any man, I don't quite understand what we are
fighting for, or what definite result can be expected. If we
pummel the South ever so hard, they will love us none the
better for it; and even if we subjugate them, our next step
should be to cut them adrift. If we are fighting for the
annihilation of slavery, to be sure, it may be a wise object
and offer a tangible result, and the only one which is consistent with a future union between North and South.

A continuance of the war would soon make this plain
to us, and we should see the expediency of preparing our
black brethren for future citizenship by allowing them to
fight for their own liberties, and educating them through
heroic influences. Whatever happens next, I must say that
I rejoice that the old Union is smashed. We never were one

people, and never really had a country since the Constitution was formed. . . .[4]

Thoreau, who was traveling in the West during the late spring and early summer of 1861 to improve his failing health, comments on the effect the war was having at this stage on the people of Minnesota, especially in the small town in which he was staying.

I am not even so well informed as to the progress of the war as you suppose. I have seen but one eastern paper (that, by the way, *was* the *Tribune*) for five weeks. I have not taken much pains to get them; but, necessarily, I have not seen any paper at all for more than a week at a time.

The people of Minnesota have *seemed* to me more cold—to feel less implicated in this war—than the people of Massachusetts. It is apparent that Massachusetts, for one state at least, is doing much more than her share in carrying it on. However, I have dealt partly with those of Southern birth, & have seen but little way beneath the surface.

I was glad to be told yesterday that there was a good deal of weeping here at Redwing the other day, when the volunteers stationed at Fort Snelling followed the regulars to the seat of the war. They do not weep when their children go up the river to occupy the deserted forts, though they may have to fight the Indians there.

I do not even know what the attitude of England is at present.[5]

Walt Whitman looks back on the First Battle of Bull Run, which took place on June 21, and in which the North suffered its first great military defeat.

(All battles, and their results, are far more matters of accident than is generally thought; but this was throughout a casualty, a chance. One side had, in point of fact, just the same right to be routed as the other. By a fiction, or series of fictions, the national forces at the last moment exploded in a panic and fled from the field.) The defeated troops commenced pouring into Washington over the Long Bridge at daylight on Monday, 22nd—day drizzling all through with rain.

The Saturday and Sunday of the battle (20th, 21st) had been parched and hot to an extreme—the dust, the grime and smoke in layers, sweated in, followed by other layers again sweated in, absorbed by those excited souls —their clothes all saturated with the clay-powder filling the air, stirred up everywhere on the dry roads and trodden fields by the regiments, swarming wagons, artillery, etc.—all the men with this coating of murk and sweat and rain, now recoiling back, pouring over the Long Bridge—a horrible march of twenty miles—returning to Washington, baffled, humiliated, panic-struck.

Where are your banners and your bands of music and your ropes to bring back your prisoners? Well, there isn't any band playing, and there isn't any flag but clings ashamed and lank to its staff.

The sun rises but shines not. The men appear, at first sparsely and shamefaced enough, then thicker, in the streets of Washington; appear in Pennsylvania Avenue and on the steps and basement entrances. They come along in disorderly mobs; some in squads, stragglers, companies. Occasionally a rare regiment, in perfect order, with its officers (some gaps, dead—the true braves), marching in silence, with lowering faces—stern, weary to sinking, all black and dirty, but every man with a big musket and stepping alive; but these are the exceptions.

Sidewalks of Pennsylvania Avenue, Fourteenth Street, etc. crowded, jammed with citizens, darkies, clerks, everybody, lookers-on; women in the windows; curious expressions from faces, as those swarms of dirt-covered returned solders there (will they never end?) move by; but nothing said, no comments; (half our lookers-on, Secesh of the most venomous kind—they say nothing, but the devil snickers in their faces). During the forenoon Washington gets all over motley with these defeated soldiers—queer-looking objects—strange eyes and faces, drenched (the steady rain drizzles all day) and fearfully worn, hungry, haggard, blistered in the feet.

Good people (but not over-many of them either) hurry up something for their grub. They put wash-kettles on the fire for soup, for coffee. They set tables on the sidewalks, wagonloads of bread are purchased, swiftly cut in stout chunks. Here are two aged ladies, beautiful, the first in the city for culture and charm—they stand with store of eating and drink at an improvised table of rough plank, give food and have the store replenished from their house every half-hour of that day; and there in the rain they stand, active, silent, white–haired, and give food, though the tears stream down their cheeks almost without intermission the whole time.

Amid the deep excitement, crowds and motion and desperate eagerness, it seems strange to see many, very many of the soldiers sleeping—in the midst of all—sleeping sound. They drop down anywhere—on the steps of houses, up close by the basements or fences, on the sidewalk, aside on some vacant lot—and deeply sleep. A poor seventeen–or–eighteen–year old boy lies there on the stoop of a grand house; he sleeps so calmly, so profoundly. Some clutch their muskets firmly even in sleep. Some in squads—comrades, brothers, close together—and on them, as they lay, sulkily drips the rain.

As afternoon passed and evening came, the streets, the barrooms, knots everywhere—listeners, questioners, terrible yarns, bugaboo, masked batteries, "our regiment all cut up," and so on—stories and storytellers, windy, bragging, vain centers of street crowds. Resolution, manliness, seem to have abandoned Washington.

The principal hotel, Willard's, is full of shoulder-straps. (I see them and must have a word with them. There you are, shoulder straps!—But where are your companies? Where are your men? Incompetents! Never tell me of chance of battle, of getting strayed, and the like. I think this is your work, this retreat, after all. Sneak, blow, put on airs in Willard's sumptuous parlors and barrooms or anywhere—no explanation shall save you. Bull Run is your work; had you been half or one tenth worthy your men, this never would have happened.)

Meantime in Washington, among the great persons and their entourage, a mixture of awful consternation, uncertainty, rage, shame, helplessness, and stupefying disappointment. The worst is not only imminent but already there. In a few hours—perhaps before the next meal—the Secesh generals, with their victorious hordes, will be upon us. The dream of humanity, the vaunted Union we thought so strong, so impregnable—lo! it seems already smashed like a china plate.

One bitter, bitter hour—perhaps proud America will never again know such an hour. She must pack and fly—no time to spare. Those white palaces, the dome–crowned Capitol there on the hill, so stately over the trees—shall they be left, or destroyed first? For it is certain that talk among certain of the magnates and officers and clerks and officials everywhere for twenty-four hours in and around Washington after Bull Run was loud and undisguised for yielding out and out and substituting the Southern rule, and Lincoln promptly abdicating and departing.[6]

Emerson speaks out through a letter written on August 4.

The war—though from such despicable beginnings, has assumed such huge proportions that it threatens to engulf us all—no preoccupation can exclude it, & no hermitage hide us.—And yet, gulf as it is, the war with its defeats & uncertainties is immensely better than what we lately called the integrity of the Republic, as amputation is better than cancer. I think we are all agreed in this, and find it out by wondering why we are so pleased, though so beaten & so poor.

No matter how low down, if not in false position, if the abundance of heaven only sends us a fair share of light

& conscience, we shall redeem America for all its sinful
years since the century began.

At first sight, it looked only as a war of manners,
showing that the Southerner who owes to climate & slavery
his suave, cool & picturesque manners, is so impatient of
ours that he must fight us off. And we all admire them till a
long experience only varying from bad to worse has shown
us, I think finally, what a noxious reptile the green & gold
thing was.

Who was the French madame who said of Talleyrand,
"How can one help loving him, he is so vicious?" But
these spit such unmistakeable venom, that I think we are
désillusionnés once for all. There is such frank confession
in all they do, that they can have no secrets hereafter for
us. Their detestation of Massachusetts is a chemical description of their substance, & if a state more lawful, honest, & cultivated were known to them, they would transfer
to it this detestation. This *spiegato carattere* of our adver-
sary makes our part & duty so easy. Their perversity is
still focusing us into better position than we had taken.
Their crimes force us into virtues to antagonize them, and
we are driven into principles by their abnegation of them.

Ah, if we dared think that our people would be simply
good enough to take & hold this advantage to the end!
—But there is no end to the views the crisis suggests, &
day by day. You see I have been following my own lead,
without prying into your subtle hints of ulterior political
effects. But one thing I hope—that "scholar" and "her-
mit" will no longer be exempt, neither by country's per-
mission nor their own, from the public duty. The function-
aries, as you rightly say, have failed. The statesmen are all
at fault. The good heart & mind, out of all private corners,
should speak & save.

In dark days & amidst sinking men, we miss his
strength [Theodore Parker, who had died on May 10, 1860]
the more, and yet we cannot doubt his relief & joy in the
present pronounced state of the Republic over the so-called
"integrity of the Republic" six months ago.[7]

Emily Dickinson, writing to a friend in August, refers to her future plans.

I shall have no winter this year—on account of the soldiers—Since I cannot weave Blankets, or Boots—I thought it best to omit the season—Shall present a "Memorial" to God—when the maples turn—

Can I rely on your "name?"[8]

Emerson discusses the war as a "great teacher" in his journal for August 5.

The war goes on educating us to a trust in the simplicities, and to see the bankruptcy of all narrow views. The favorite pet policy of a district, the *épicier* party of Boston or New York, is met by a conflicting *épicier* party in Philadelphia, another in Cincinnati, others in Chicago and St. Louis, so that we are forced still to grope deeper for something catholic and universal, wholesome for all. Thus war for the Union is broader than any State policy, or Tariff, or Maritime, or Agricultural, or Mining interest. Each of these neutralizes the other.

But, at last, the Union Party is not broad enough, because of slavery, which poisons it; and . . . "emancipation with compensation to the loyal States," is the only broad and firm ground. . . .

The war is a great teacher, still opening our eyes wider to some larger consideration. It is a great reconciler, too, forgetting our petty quarrels as ridiculous:

"On such a shrine,
What are our petty griefs? Let me not number mine."

But to me the first advantage of the war is the favorable moment it has made for the cutting out of our cancerous slavery. Better that war and defeats continue, until we have come to that amputation. I suppose, if the war goes on, it will be impossible to keep the combatants from the extreme ground on either side. In spite of themselves, one army will stand for Slavery pure; the other for Freedom pure.[9]

Oliver Wendell Holmes attempts to set forth the significance of the war as a valuable experience.

The great war which is upon us is shaking us down into solidity as corn is shaken down in the measure. We are heaped up in our own opinion, and sometimes running over in expressions of it. This rude jostling is showing us the difference between bulk and weight, space and substance.

In one point of view we have a right to be proud of our inexperience, and hardly need to blush for our shortcomings. These are the tributes we are paying to our own past innocence and tranquillity. We have lived a peaceful life so long that the traditional cunning and cruelty of a state of warfare have become almost obsolete among us. No wonder that hard men, bred in foreign camps, find us too good–natured, wanting in hatred towards our enemies. We can readily believe that it is a special Providence which has suffered us to meet with a reverse or two, just enough to sting, without crippling us, only to wake up the slumbering passion which is the legitimate instrument of the higher powers for working out the ends of justice and the good of man.

There are a few far–seeing persons to whom our present sudden mighty conflict may not have come as a surprise; but to all except these it is a prodigy as startling as it would be if the farmers of the North should find a ripened harvest of blood-red ears of maize upon the succulent stalks of midsummer. We have lived for peace: as individuals, to get food, comfort, luxuries for ourselves and others; as communities, to insure the best conditions we could for each human being, so that he might become what God meant him to be. The verdict of the world was that we were succeeding. Many came to us from the old civilizations; few went away from us, and most of these such as we could spare without public loss.

We had almost forgotten the meaning and use of the machinery of destruction. We had come to look upon our fortresses as the ornaments rather than as the defences of our harbors. Our warships were the Government's yacht–squadron, our arsenals museums for the entertainment of peaceful visitors. The roar of cannon has roused us from this Arcadian dream. A ship of the line, we said reproachfully, costs as much as a college; but we are finding out that its masts are a part of the fence round the college. The Springfield Arsenal inspired a noble poem; but that, as we are learning, was not all that it was meant for. What poets would be born to us in the future without the *"placida quies"* which *"sub literate"* the sword alone can secure for our children.

It is all plain, but it has been an astonishment to us, as our war–comet was to the astronomers. The comet, as some of them say, brushed us with its tail as it passed; yet nobody finds us the worse for it. So, too, we have been brushed lightly by mishap, as we ought to have been, and as we ought to have prayed to be, no doubt, if we had known what was good for us; at this very moment we stand stronger, more hopeful, more united than ever before it our history.

Our early mishaps were all predicted, sometimes in formal shape, as in various letters dated long before the breaking out of hostilities, and very often in the common talk of those about us. But, after all, when the first chastisement from our hard schoolmaster, Experience, comes upon us, it is a kind of surprise, in spite of all our preparation.

. . . There is a complete literature of panics, not merely as occurring among new levies, but seizing on the best appointed armies, containing as much individual bravery as any that never ran away from an enemy. The men of Israel gave way before the men of Benjamin. . . . Their enemies did not lie still or run as fast the other way, like ours at Bull Run. . . . Yet "all these were men of valor."

A pleasing consequence of this war we are engaged in has hardly been enough thought of. It is a rough way of introducing distant fellow–citizens of the same land to each other's acquaintance.

"We shall learn to respect each other," as one of our

conservative friends said long ago. It is a great mistake to try to prove our own countrymen cowards and degenerate from the old stock. It is worth the price of some hard fighting to show the contrary to the satisfaction of both parties. The Scotch and English called each other all possible hard names in the time of their international warfare; but the day has come for them, as it will surely come for us, when the rivals and enemies must stand side by side and shoulder to shoulder, each proud of the other's bravery.

For three–quarters of a century we have been melting our several destinies in one common crucible, to mould a new and mighty empire such as the world has never seen. Our partners cannot expect to be allowed to break the crucible or mould, or to carry away the once separate portions now flowing in a single incandescent flood. We cannot sell and they cannot buy our past. Our nation has pledged itself by the whole course of its united action. There is one debt alone that all the cotton fields of the South could never pay: it is the price of our voluntary humiliation for the sake of keeping peace with the slaveholders. We may be robbed of our inalienable nationality, if treason is strong enough, but we are trustees of the life of three generations for the benefit of all that are yet to be. We cannot sell. We dare not break the entail of freedom and disinherit the first–born of half a continent.[10]

Bierce offers a military criticism of the budding Union Army.

. . . The war was young, and military camps entertained the error that while sleeping they were better protected by thin lines a long way out toward the enemy than by thicker ones close in. And surely they needed as long notice as possible of an enemy's approach, for they were at that time addicted to the practice of undressing—than which nothing could be more unsoldierly. On the morning of the memorable 6th of April, at Shiloh, many of Grant's men when spitted on Confederate bayonets were as naked as civilians; but it should be allowed that this was not because of any defect in their picket line. Their error was of another sort: they had no pickets.[11]

3   The Battle for Missouri

*At the outbreak of the war Samuel Clemens joined with his
fellow townsmen of Hannibal, Missouri, to form a company
to fight in the Confederate Army.*

You have heard from a great many people who did
something in the war, is it not fair and right that you
listen a little moment to one who started out to do something in it, but didn't? Thousands entered the war, got just
a taste of it, and then stepped out again permanently.
These, by their very numbers, are respectable and are
therefore entitled to a sort of a voice—not a loud one but
a modest one; not a boastful one but an apologetic. They
ought not to be allowed much space among better people—people who did something. I grant that, but they
ought at least to be allowed to state why they didn't do
anything and also to explain the process by which they
didn't do anything. Surely this kind of light must have a
sort of value.

In that summer of 1861, the first wave of war broke
upon the shores of Missouri. Our state was invaded by the
Union forces. They took possession of St. Louis, Jefferson
Barracks, and some other points. The Governor, Calib
Jackson, issued his proclamation calling out fifty thousand
militia to repel the invader.

I was visiting in the small town where my boyhood
had been spent, Hannibal, Marion County. Several of us

got together in a secret place at night and formed ourselves into a military company. One Tom Lyman, a young fellow of a good deal of spirit but of no military experience, was made captain; I was made second lieutenant. We had no first lieutenant; I do not know why; it was long ago. There were fifteen of us. By the advice of an innocent connected with the organization, we called ourselves the Marion Rangers. I do not remember that anyone found fault with the name. I did not; I thought it sounded quite well. The young fellow who proposed this title was perhaps a fair sample of the kind of stuff we were made of. He was young, ignorant, good–natured, well–meaning, trivial, full of romance, and given to reading chivalric novels and singing forlorn love–ditties.

Well, this herd of cattle started for the war. What would you expect of them? They did as well as they knew how, but, really, what was justly to be expected of them? Nothing, I should say. That is what they did.

We waited for a dark night, for caution and secrecy were necessary; then toward midnight we stole in couples and from various directions to the Griffith place, beyond the town; from that point we set out together on foot. Hannibal lies at the extreme southeastern corner of Marion County, on the Mississippi River; our objective was the hamlet of New London, ten miles away, in Ralls County.

The first hour was all fun, all idle nonsense and laughter. But that could not be kept up. The steady trudging came to be like work, the play had somehow oozed out of it, the stillness of the woods and the somberness of the night began to throw a depressing influence over the spirits of the boys, and presently the talking died out and each person shut himself up in his own thoughts. During the last half of the second hour nobody said a word.

Now we approached a log farmhouse where, according to report, there was a guard of five Union soldiers. Lyman called a halt, and there, in the deep gloom of the overhanging branches, he began to whisper a plan of assault upon that house, which made the gloom more depressing than it was before. It was a crucial moment; we realized with a cold suddenness that here was no jest—we were standing face to face with actual war. We were equal to the occasion. In our response there was no hesitation, no indecision: we said that if Lyman wanted to meddle with those soldiers, he could go ahead and do it, but if he waited for us to follow him, he would wait a long time.

Lyman urged, pleaded, tried to shame us, but it had no effect. Our course was plain, our minds were made up: we would flank the farmhouse—go on around. And that is what we did.

We struck into the woods and entered upon a rough time, stumbling over roots, getting tangled in vines and torn by briers. At last we reached an open place in a safe region and sat down, blown and hot, to cool off and nurse our scratches and bruises. Lyman was annoyed but the rest of us were cheerful; we had flanked the farmhouse; we had made our first military movement and it was a success; we had nothing to fret about, we were feeling just the other way. Horseplay and laughing began again; the expedition was become a holiday frolic once more.

Then we had two more hours of dull trudging and ultimate silence and depression; then about dawn we straggled into New London, soiled, heel-blistered, fagged with our little march, and all of us except Stevens in a sour and raspy humor and privately down on the war. We stacked our shabby old shotguns in Colonel Rall's barn and then went in a body and breakfasted with that veteran of the Mexican War.

Afterward he took us to a distant meadow, and there in the shade of a tree we listened to an old–fashioned speech from him, full of gunpowder and glory, full of that adjective–piling, mixed metaphor and windy declamation which were regarded as eloquence in that ancient time and that remote region; and then he swore us on the Bible to be faithful to the State of Missouri and drive all invaders from her soil, no matter whence they come or under what flag they might march. This mixed us considerably and we could not make out just what service we were embarked in, but Colonel Ralls, the practiced politician and phrase-juggler, was not similarly in doubt; he knew quite clearly that he had invested us in the cause of the Southern Confederacy. He closed the solemnities by belting around me the sword which his neighbor, Colonel Brown, had worn at Buena Vista and Molino del Rey; and he accompanied this act with another impressive blast.

Then we formed in line of battle and marched four miles to a shady and pleasant piece of woods on the border of the far-reaching expanses of a flowery prairie. It was an enchanting region for war—our kind of war.

We pierced the forest about half a mile and took up a strong position, with some low, rocky, and wooded hills behind us and a purling, limpid creek in front. Straightway half the command were in swimming and the other half fishing. The ass with the French name gave this position a romantic title, but it was too long, so the boys shortened and simplified it to Camp Ralls.

We occupied an old maple sugar camp, whose half-rotted troughs were still propped against the trees. A long corncrib served for sleeping quarters for the battalion. On our left, half a mile away, were Mason's farm and house, and he was a friend to the cause.

Shortly after noon the farmers began to arrive from several directions with mules and horses for our use, and these they lent to us for as long as the war might last, which they judged would be about three months. The animals were of all sizes, all colors, and all breeds. They were mainly young and frisky, and nobody in the command could stay on them long at a time, for we were town boys and ignorant of horsemanship. The creature that fell to my share was a very small mule, and yet so quick and active it could throw me without difficulty, and it did this whenever I got on it. Then it would lay—stretching its neck out, laying its ears back, and spreading its jaws till you could see down to its works. It was a disagreeable animal in every way. If I took it by the bridle and tried to lead it off the grounds, it would sit down and brace back and no one could budge it. However, I was not entirely destitute of military resources and I did presently manage to spoil this game, for I had seen many a steamboat aground in my time and knew a trick or two which even a grounded mule would be obliged to respect. There was a well by the corncrib; so I substituted thirty fathom of rope for the bridle, and fetched him home with the windlass.

I will anticipate here sufficiently to say that we did learn to ride after some days' practice, but never well. We could not learn to like our animals; they were not choice ones and most of them had annoying peculiarities of one kind or another.

Stevens' horse would carry him, when he was not noticing, under the huge excrescences which form on the trunks of oak trees, and wipe him out of the saddle; in this way Stevens got several bad hurts. Sergeant Bowers' horse was very large and tall, with slim, long legs, and looked like a railroad bridge. His size enabled him to reach all about, and as far as he wanted to, with his head; so he was always biting Bowers's legs. On the march, in the sun, Bowers slept a good deal, and as soon as the horse recognized that he was asleep he would reach around and bite him on the leg. His legs were black and blue with bites. This was the only thing that could ever make him swear but this always did; whenever his horse bit him he always swore, and of course Stevens, who laughed at everything, laughed at this and would even get into such convulsions over it as to lose his balance and fall off his horse; and then Bowers, already irritated by the pain of the horse-bite, would resent the laughter with hard language, and there would be a quarrel; so that horse made no end of trouble and bad blood in the command.

However, I will get back to where I was—our first afternoon in the sugar-camp. The sugar-troughs came very handy as horse-troughs and we had plenty of corn to fill them with. I ordered Sergeant Bowers to feed my mule,

but he said that if I reckoned he went to war to be a dry–
nurse to a mule it wouldn't take me very long to find out
my mistake. I believed that this was insubordination but I
was full of uncertainties about everything military, and so
I let the thing pass and went and ordered Smith, the blacksmith's apprentice, to feed the mule; but he merely gave
me a large, cold, sarcastic grin, such as an ostensibly
seven–year–old horse gives you when you lift his lip and
find he is fourteen, and turned his back on me. I then went
to the captain and asked him if it were not right and
proper and military for me to have an orderly. He said it
was but as there was only one orderly in the corps, it was
but right that he himself should have Bowers on his staff.
Bowers said he wouldn't serve on anybody's staff, and if
anybody thought he could make him, let him try it, So, of
course, the thing had to be dropped; there was no other
way.

Next, nobody would cook; it was considered a degradation; so we had no dinner. We lazied the rest of the
afternoon away, some dozing under the trees, some smoking cob pipes and talking sweethearts and war, some playing games. By late supper–time all hands were famished
and to meet the difficulty all hands turned to on an equal
footing, and gathered wood, and built fires, and cooked the
meal. Afterward everything was smooth for a while; then
trouble broke out between the corporal and the sergeant,
each claiming to rank the other. Nobody knew which was
the higher office; so Lyman had to settle the matter by
making the rank of both officers equal. The commander of
an ignorant crew like that has many troubles and vexations
which probably do not occur in the regular army at all.
However, with the song–singing and yarn–spinning around
the camp fire, everything presently became serene again,
and by and by we raked the corn down level in one end
of the crib and all went to bed on it, tying a horse to the
door, so that he would neigh if anyone tried to get in.*

* It was always my impression that that was what the horse was there
for, and I know that it was also the impression of at least one other of

We had some horsemanship drill every forenoon; then, afternoons, we rode off here and there in squads a few miles and visited the farmers' girls, and had a youthful good time and got an honest good dinner or supper, and then home again to camp, happy and content.

For a time life was idly delicious; it was perfect; there was nothing to mar it. Then came some farmers with an alarm one day. They said that it was rumored that the enemy were advancing in our direction from over Hyde's prairie. The result was a sharp stir among us, and general consternation.

The rumor was but a rumor—nothing definite about it; so in the confusion we did not know which way to retreat. Lyman was for not retreating at all in these uncertain circumstances, but he found that if he tried to maintain that attitude he would fare badly, for the command were in no humor to put up with insubordination. So he yielded to the point and called a council of war, to consist of himself and three other officers; but the privates made such a fuss about being left out that we had to allow them to remain, for they were already present and doing most of the talking too.

The question was, which way to retreat; but all were so flurried that nobody seemed to have even a guess to offer. Except Lyman. He explained in a few calm words that, inasmuch as the enemy were approaching from over Hyde's prairie, our course was simple: all we had to do was not to retreat *toward* him; and any other direction would answer our needs perfectly. Everybody saw in a moment how true this was, and how wise, so Lyman got a great many compliments. It was now decided that we should fall back on Mason's farm.

the command, for we talked about it at the time and admired the military ingenuity of the device; but when I was out West three years ago, I was told by Mr. A. G. Fuqua, a member of our company, that the horse was his, that the leaving him tied at the door was a matter of mere forgetfulness, and that to attribute it to intelligent invention was to give quite too much credit. In support of his position he called my attention to the suggestive fact that the artifice was not employed again. I had not thought of that before.

It was after dark by this time, and as we could not know how soon the enemy might arrive, it did not seem best to try to take the horses and things with us; so we only took the guns and ammunition, and started at once. The route was very rough and hilly and rocky, and presently the night grew very black and rain began to fall; so we had a troublesome time of it, struggling and stumbling along in the dark; and soon some person slipped and fell, and the next person behind stumbled over him and fell, and so did the rest, one after the other; and then Bowers came, with the keg of powder in his arms, while the command were all mixed together, arms and legs, on the muddy slope; and so he fell, of course, with the keg, and this started the whole detachment down the hill in a body, and they landed in the brook at the bottom in a pile, and each that was undermost pulling the hair and scratching and biting those that were on top of him; and those that were being scratched and bitten scratching and biting the rest in their turn, and all saying they would die before they would ever go to war again, if they ever got out of this brook this time, and the invader might rot for all them cared, and the country along with him—and all such talk as that, which was dismal to hear and take part in, in such smothered, low voices and such a grisly dark place and so wet, and the enemy, maybe, coming any moment.

The keg of powder was lost, and the guns too; so the growling and complaining continued straight along while the brigade pawed around the pasty hillside and slopped around in the brook hunting for these things; consequently we lost considerable time at this, and then we heard a sound and held our breath and listened, and it seemed to be the enemy coming, though it could have been a cow, for it had a cough like a cow; but we did not wait but left a couple of guns behind and struck out for Mason's again as briskly as we could scramble along in the dark. But we got lost presently among the rugged little ravines and wasted a deal of time finding the way again, so it was after nine when we reached Mason's stile at last; and then before we could open our mouths to give the countersign, several dogs came bounding over the fence with great riot and noise, and each of them took a soldier by the slack of his trousers and began to back away with him.

We could not shoot the dogs without endangering the persons they were attached to; so we had to look on helpless at what was perhaps the most mortifying spectacle of the Civil War. There was light enough and to spare, for the Masons had now run out on the porch with candles in their hands. The old man and his son came and undid the dogs without difficulty, all but Bowers'; but they couldn't undo his dog, they didn't know his combination; he was of the bull kind and seemed to be set with a Yale time lock; but they got him loose at last with some scalding water, of which Bowers got his share and returned thanks.

Peterson Dunlap afterward made up a fine name for this engagement, and also for the night march which preceded it, but both have long ago faded out of my memory.

We now went into the house, and they began to ask us a world of questions, whereby it presently came out that we did not know anything concerning who or what we were running from; so the old gentleman made himself very frank and said we were a curious breed of soldiers and guessed we could be depended on to end up the war in time, because no government could stand the expense of the shoe leather we should cost it trying to follow us around.

"Marion *Rangers!* good name, b'gosh!" said he. And wanted to know why we hadn't had a picket–guard at the place where the road entered the prairie, and why we hadn't sent out a scouting party to spy out the enemy and bring us an account of his strength, and so on, before jumping up and stampeding out of a strong position upon a mere vague rumor—and so on and so forth, till he made us all feel shabbier than the dogs had done, not half so enthusiastically welcome.

So we went to bed shamed and low–spirited, except Stevens. Soon Stevens began to devise a garment for Bowers which could be made to automatically display his battle-scars to the grateful or conceal them from the en-

vious, according to his occasions; but Bowers was in no
humor for this, so there was a fight, and when it was over
Stevens had some battle scars of his own to think about.

Then we got a little sleep. But after all we had gone
through, our activities were not over for the night, for
about two o'clock in the morning we heard a shout of
warning from down the lane, accompanied by a chorus
from all the dogs, and in a moment everybody was up and
flying around to find out what the alarm was about. The
alarmist was a horseman who gave notice that a detachment of Union soldiers was on its way from Hannibal with
orders to capture and hang any bands like ours it could
find, and said we had no time to lose. Farmer Mason was in
a flurry this time himself. He hurried us out of the house
with all haste, and sent one of his Negroes with us to show
us where to hide ourselves and our telltale guns among the
ravines half a mile away. It was raining heavily.

We struck down the lane, then across some rocky
pasture land which offered good advantages for stumbling;
consequently we were down in the mud most of the time,
and every time a man went down he blackguarded the war
and the people who started it and everybody connected
with it, and gave himself the master dose of all for being
so foolish as to go into it.

At last we reached the wooded mouth of a ravine, and
there we huddled ourselves under the streaming trees and
sent the Negro back home. It was a dismal and heart-
breaking time. We were like to be drowned with the rain,
deafened with the howling wind and the booming thunder,
and blinded by the lightning. It was indeed a wild night.
The drenching we were getting was misery enough, but a
deeper misery still was the reflection that the halter might
end us before we were a day older. A death of this shame-
ful sort had not occurred to us as being among the possibilities of war. It took the romance all out of the campaign,
and turned our dreams of glory into a repulsive nightmare.
As for doubting that so barbarous an order had been
given—not one of us did that.

The long night wore itself out at last, and then the Negro came to us with the news that the alarm had manifestly been a false one and that breakfast would soon be ready. Straightway we were lighthearted again, and the world was bright and life was full of hope and promise as ever—for we were young then. How long ago that was! Twenty–four years.

The mongrel child of philology named the night's refuge Camp Devastation, and no soul objected. The Masons gave us a Missouri country breakfast in Missourian abundance, and we needed it: hot biscuits, hot "wheat bread," prettily criss–crossed in a lattice pattern on top, hot corn-pone, fried chicken, bacon, coffee, eggs, milk, buttermilk, etc.; and the world may be confidently challenged to furnish the equal of such a breakfast as it is cooked in the South.

We stayed several days at Mason's, and after all these years the memory of the dullness and stillness and lifelessness of that slumberous farmhouse still oppresses my spirit as with a sense of the presence of death and mourning. There was nothing to do, nothing to think about; there was no interest in life. The male part of the household were away in the fields all day; the women were busy and out of our sight; there was no sound but the plaintive wailing of a spinning wheel, forever moaning out from some distant room—the most lonesome sound in nature, a sound steeped and sodden with homesickness and the emptiness of life.

The family went to bed about dark every night, and as we were not invited to intrude any new customs, we naturally followed theirs. Those nights were a hundred years long to youths accustomed to being up till twelve. We lay awake and miserable till that hour every time, and grew old and decrepit waiting through the still eternities for the clock-strikes. This was no place for town boys. So at last it was with something very like joy that we received news that the enemy were on our track again. With a new birth of the old warrior spirit, we sprang to our places in line of battle and fell back on Camp Ralls.

Captain Lyman had taken a hint from Mason's talk, and he now gave orders that our camp should be guarded against surprise by the posting of pickets. I was ordered to place a picket at the forks of the road in Hyde's prairie.

Night shut down black and threatening. I told Sergeant Bowers to go out to that place and stay till midnight and, just as I was expecting, he said he wouldn't do it. I tried to get others to go but all refused. Some excused themselves on account of weather.

This kind of thing sounds odd now, and impossible, but there was no surprise in it at the time. On the contrary, it seemed a perfectly natural thing to do. There were scores of little camps scattered over Missouri where the same thing was happening. These camps were composed of young men who had been born and reared to a sturdy independence, and who did not know what it meant to be ordered around by Tom, Dick or Harry, whom they had known familiarly all their lives in the village or on the farm. It is quite within the probabilities that this same thing was happening all over the South. James Redpath recognized the justice of this assumption and furnished the following instance in support of it.

During a short stay in East Tennessee he was in a citizen–colonel's tent one day talking, when a big private appeared at the door and, without salute or other circumlocution, said to the colonel:

"Say, Jim, I'm a goin' home for a few days."

"What for?"

"Well, I hain't b'en there for a right smart while and I'd like to see how things is comin' on."

"How long are you going to be gone?"

" 'Bout two weeks."

"Well, don't be gone longer than that, and get back sooner if you can."

That was all, and the citizen–colonel resumed his conversation where the private had broken it off. This was in the first months of the war, of course. The camps in our part of Missouri were under Brigadier-General Thomas H. Harris. He was a townsman of ours, a first-rate fellow and well liked, but we had all familiarly known him as the sole and modest-salaried operator in our telegraph office, where he had to send about one dispatch a week in ordinary times, and two when there was a rush of business; consequently, when he appeared in our midst one day on the wing, and delivered a military command of some sort in a large military fashion, nobody was surprised at the response which he got from the assembled soldiery:

"Oh, now, what'll you take to *don't,* Tom Harris?"

It was quite the natural thing. One might justly imagine that we were hopeless material for war. And so we seemed in our ignorant state, but there were those among us who afterward learned the grim trade, learned to obey like machines, became valuable soldiers; fought all through the war, and came out at the end with excellent records. One of the very boys who refused to go out on picket duty that night and called me an ass for thinking he would expose himself to danger in such a foolhardy way, had become distinguished for intrepidity before he was a year older.

I did secure my picket that night, not by authority but by diplomacy. I got Bowers to go by agreeing to exchange ranks with him for the time being, and go along and stand the watch with him as his subordinate. We stayed out there a couple of dreary hours in the pitchy darkness and the rain, with nothing to modify the dreariness but Bowers' monotonous growlings at the war and the weather; then we began to nod and presently found it next to impossible to stay in the saddle, so we gave up the tedious job and went back to the camp without waiting for the relief guard. We rode into camp without interruption or objection from anybody, and the enemy could have done the same, for there were no sentries. Everybody was asleep; at midnight there was nobody to send out another picket, so none was sent. We never tried to establish a watch at night again, as far as I remember, but we generally kept a picket out in the daytime.

In that camp the whole command slept on the corn in

the big corncrib, and there was usually a general row before morning, for the place was full of rats, and they would
scramble over the boys' bodies and faces, annoying and
irritating everybody and now and then they would bite
someone's toe, and the person who owned the toe would
start up and magnify his English and begin to throw corn
in the dark. The ears were half as heavy as bricks, and
when they struck they hurt. The persons struck would re-
spond, and inside of five minutes every man would be
locked in a death-grip with his neighbor. There was a griev-
ous deal of blood shed in the corncrib, but this was all that
was spilt while I was in the war. No, that is not quite true.
But for one circumstance it would have been all. I will
come to that now.

Our scares were frequent. Every few days rumors
would come that the enemy were approaching. In these
cases we always fell back on some other camp of ours; we
never stayed where we were. But the rumors always turned
out to be false, so at last even we began to grow indifferent
to them.

One night a Negro was sent to our corncrib with the
same old warning—the enemy was hovering in our neighborhood. We all said, let him hover. We resolved to stay
still and be comfortable. It was a fine warlike resolution,
and no doubt we all felt the stir of it in our veins—for a
moment.

We had been having a very jolly time, that was full of
horse–play and schoolboy hilarity, but that cooled down
now, and presently the fast-waning fire of forced jokes and
forced laughs died out altogether and the company became
silent. Silent and nervous. And soon uneasy—worried—ap-
prehensive. We had said we would stay and we were committed. We could have been persuaded to go, but there was
nobody brave enough to suggest it.

An almost noiseless movement presently began in the
dark by a general but unvoiced impulse. When the movement was completed, each man knew that he was not the
only person who had crept to the front wall and had his

eye at a crack between the logs. No, we were all there, all there with our hearts in our throats and staring out toward the sugar where the forest footpath came through. It was late, and there was a deep woodsy stillness everywhere. There was a veiled moonlight, which was only just strong enough to enable us to mark the general shape of objects.

Presently a muffled sound caught our ears, and we recognized it as the hoofbeats of a horse or horses. And right away a figure appeared in the forest path; it could have been made of smoke, its mass had so little sharpness of outline. It was a man on horseback, and it seemed to me that there were others behind him. I got hold of a gun in the dark, and pushed it through a crack between the logs, hardly knowing what I was doing, I was so dazed with fright. Somebody said, "Fire!" I pulled the trigger. I seemed to see a hundred flashes and hear a hundred reports; then I saw the man fall out of the saddle.

My first feeling was of surprised gratification; my first impulse was an apprentice-sportsman's impulse to run and pick up his game. Somebody said, hardly audibly, "Good—we've got him!—wait for the rest." But the rest did not come. We waited—listened—still no more came. There was not a sound, not the whisper of a leaf; just perfect stillness, an uncanny kind of stillness which was all the more uncanny on account of the damp, earthy, late–night smells now rising and pervading it. Then, wondering, we crept stealthily out and approached the man.

When we got to him, the moon revealed him distinctly. He was lying on his back with his arms abroad, his mouth was open and his chest heaving with long gasps, and his white shirt front was all splashed with blood. The thought shot through me that I was a murderer, that I had killed a man, a man who had never done me any harm.

That was the coldest sensation that ever went through my marrow. I was down by him in a moment, helplessly stroking his forehead, and I would have given anything then—my own life freely—to make him again what he had been five minutes before. And all the boys seemed to be feeling in the same way; they hung over him, full of pitying interest, and tried all they could to help him and said all sorts of regretful things. They had forgotten all about the enemy; they thought only of this one forlorn unit of the foe. Once, my imagination persuaded me that the dying man gave me a reproachful look out of his shadowy eyes, and it seemed to me I could rather he had stabbed me than done that. He muttered and mumbled like a dreamer in his sleep about his wife and his child, and I thought with a new despair, "This thing that I have done does not end with him; it falls upon *them* too, and they never did me any harm, any more than he."

In a little while the man was dead. He was killed in war, killed in fair and legitimate war, killed in battle, as you may say, and yet he was as sincerely mourned by the opposing force as if he had been their brother. The boys stood there a half–hour sorrowing over him and recalling the details of the tragedy, and wondering who he might be and if he were a spy, and saying that if it were to do over again they would not hurt him unless he attacked them first. It soon came out that mine was not the only shot fired; there were five others, a division of the guilt which was a great relief to me since it in some degree lightened and diminished the burden I was carrying. There were six shots fired at once, but I was not in my right mind at the time, and my heated imagination had magnified my one shot into a volley.

The man was not in uniform and not armed. He was a stranger in the country—that was all we ever found out about him. The thought of him got to preying upon me every night; I could not get rid of it. I could not drive it away; the taking of that unoffending life seemed such a wanton thing. And it seemed an epitome of war—that all war must be just that—the killing of strangers against whom you feel no personal animosity, strangers whom in other circumstances you would help if you found them in trouble, and who would help you if you needed it.

My campaign was spoiled. It seemed to me that I was not rightly equipped for this awful business, that war was intended for men and I for a child's nurse. I resolved to retire from this avocation of sham soldiership while I could save some remnant of my self–respect. These morbid thoughts clung to me against reason, for at the bottom I did not believe I had touched that man. The law of probabilities decreed me guiltless of his blood, for in all my small experience with guns I had never hit anything I had tried to hit, and I knew I had done my best to hit him. Yet there was no solace in the thought. Against a diseased imagination demonstration goes for nothing.

The rest of my war experience was of a piece with what I have already told of it. We kept monotonously falling back upon one camp or another and eating up the farmers and their families. They ought to have shot us; on the contrary, they were as hospitably kind and courteous to us as if we had deserved it.

In one of these camps we found Abe Grimes, an Upper Mississippi pilot who afterward became famous as a dare–devil rebel spy, whose career bristled with desperate adventures. The look and style of his comrades suggested that they had not come into the war to play, and their deeds made good the conjecture later. They were fine horsemen and good revolver shots, but their favorite arm was the lasso. Each had one at his pommel and could snatch a man out of the saddle with it every time, on a full gallop, at any reasonable distance.

In another camp the chief was a fierce and profane old blacksmith of sixty, and he had furnished his twenty recruits with gigantic home–made bowie knives, to be swung with two hands like the machetes of the Isthmus. It was a grisly spectacle to see that earnest band practising their murderous cuts and slashes under the eye of that remorseless old fanatic.

The last camp which we fell back on was in a hollow near the village of Florida where I was born, in Monroe

County. Here we were warned one day that a Union colonel
was sweeping down on us with a whole regiment at his
heel. This looked decidedly serious. Our boys went apart
and consulted; then we went back and told the other companies present that the war was a disappointment to us
and we were going to disband.

They were getting ready themselves to fall back on
some place or other, and we were only waiting for General
Tom Harris, who was expected to arrive at any moment,
so they tried to persuade us to wait a little while, but the
majority of us said no, we were accustomed to falling back
and didn't need any of Tom Harris's help; we could get
along perfectly well without him and save time, too. So
about half of our fifteen, including myself, mounted and
left on the instant; the others yielded to persuasion and
stayed—through the war.

An hour later we met General Harris on the road, with
two or three people in his company—his staff probably—but we could not tell; none of them were in uniform;
uniforms had not come into vogue among us yet. Harris
ordered us back, but we told him there was a Union colonel
coming with a whole regiment in his wake and it looked as
if there was going to be a disturbance, so we had concluded
to go home. He raged a little, but it was of no use, our
minds were made up. We had done our share, had killed
one man, had exterminated one army, such as it was; let
him go and kill the rest and that would end the war. I did
not see that brisk young general again until last year; then
he was wearing white hair and whiskers.

In time I came to know that Union colonel whose
coming frightened me out of the war and crippled the
Southern cause to that extent—General Grant. I came
within a few hours of seeing him when he was as unknown
as I was myself; at a time anyone could have said, "Grant?
—Ulysses S. Grant? I do not remember hearing the
name before." It seems difficult to realize that there was
once a time when such a remark could be rationally made

but there *was,* and I was within a few miles of the place and the occasion, too, though proceeding in the other direction.

The thoughtful will not throw this war paper of mine lightly aside as being valueless. It has this value: it is a not–unfair picture of what went on in many and many a militia camp in the first months of the rebellion, when the green recruits were without discipline, without the steadying and heartening influence of trained leaders, when all their circumstances were new and strange and charged with exaggerated terrors, and before the invaluable experience of actual collison in the field had turned them from rabbits into soldiers.

If this side of the picture of that early day has not before been put into history, then history has been to that degree incomplete, for it had and has its rightful place there. There was more Bull Run material scattered through the early camps of this country than exhibited itself at Bull Run. And yet it learned its trade presently and helped to fight the great battles later. I could have become a soldier myself if I had waited. I had got part of it learned, I knew more about retreating than the man who invented retreating. . . . [1]

4   *The Spirit Aroused*

In the fall of 1861, Hawthorne appraises the situation for an English friend.

. . . We also have gone to war, and we seem to have little, or at least a very misty idea of what we are fighting for. It depends upon the speaker; and that, again, depends upon the section of the country in which his sympathies are enlisted. The Southern man will say, "We fight for State rights, liberty, and independence." The Middle Western man will avow that he fights for the Union; while our Northern and Eastern man will swear that from the beginning his only idea was liberty to the blacks and the annihilation of slavery. All are thoroughly in earnest, and all pray for the blessing of Heaven to rest upon the enterprise.

The appeals are so numerous, fervent, and yet so contradictory, that the Great Arbiter to whom they so piously and solemnly appeal must be sorely puzzled how to decide. One thing is indisputable—the spirit of our young men is thoroughly aroused. Their enthusiasm is boundless, and the smiles of our fragile and delicate women cheer them on. When I hear their drums beating and see their colors flying and witness their steady marching, I declare, were it not for certain silvery monitors hanging by my temples, suggesting prudence, I feel as if I could catch the infection, shoulder a musket, and be off to the war myself!

Meditating on these matters, I begin to think our custom as to war is a mistake. Why draw from our young men in the bloom and heyday of their youth the soldiers who are to fight our battles? Had I my way, no man should go to war under fifty years of age, such men having already had their natural share of worldly pleasures and life's enjoyments. And I don't see how they could make a more creditable or more honorable exit from the world's stage than by becoming food for powder, and gloriously dying in defense of their home and country. Then I would add a premium in favor of recruits of threescore years and upward, as, virtually with one foot in the grave, they would not be likely to run away.

I apprehend that no people ever built up the skeleton of a warlike history as rapidly as we are doing. What a fine theme for the poet! If you were not a born Britisher, from whose country we expect no help and little sympathy, I would ask you for a martial strain—a song to be sung by our campfires, to soothe the feelings and rouse the energies of our troops, inspiring them to meet like men the great conflict that awaits them, resolved to conquer or die—if dying, still to conquer. Ten thousand poetasters have tried, and tried in vain, to give us a "Scots wha hae wi' Wallace bled." If we fight no better than we sing, may the Lord have mercy upon us and the nation.[1]

Holmes philosophizes on some of the salutary effects the war was having on life in the North.

How this war is simplifying our mode of being! We live on our emotions, as the sick man is said in the common speech to be nourished by his fever. Our ordinary mental food has become distasteful, and what would have been intellectual luxuries at other times are now absolutely repulsive.

. . . War is a new thing to all of us who are not in the last quarter of their century. We are learning many strange matters from our fresh experience. And besides, there are new conditions of existence which make war as it has been.

The first and obvious difference consists in the fact that the whole nation is now penetrated by the ramifications of a network of iron nerves which flash sensation and volition backward and forward to and from towns and provinces as if they were organs and limbs of a single living body. The second is the vast system of iron muscles, which, as it were, move the limbs of the mighty organism one upon another. What was the railroad-force which put the Sixth Regiment in Baltimore on the 19th of April, but a contraction and extension of the arm of Massachusetts with a clenched fist full of bayonets at the end of it?

This perpetual intercommunication, joined to the power of instantaneous action, keeps us alive with excitement. It is not a breathless courier who comes back with the report from an army we have lost sight of for a month, nor a single bulletin which tells us all we are to know for a week of some great engagement, but almost hourly paragraphs, laden with truth or falsehood, as the case may be, making us restless always for the last fact or rumor they are telling.

And so of the movements of our armies. Tonight the stout lumbermen of Maine are encamped under their own fragrant pines. In a score or two of hours they are among the tobacco fields and the slave pens of Virginia. The war passion burned like scattered coals of fire in the households of Revolutionary times; now it rushes all through the land like a flame over the prairie. And this instant diffusion of every fact and feeling produces another singular effect in the equalizing and steadying of public opinion. We may not be able to see a month ahead of us; but as to what has passed a week afterwards, it is as thoroughly talked out and judged as it would have been in a whole season before our national nervous system was organized.

It is at this very moment doing more to melt away the petty social distinctions which keep generous souls apart from each other than the preaching of the Beloved Disciple

himself would do. We are finding out that not only "patriotism is eloquence," but that heroism is gentility. All
ranks are wonderfully equalized under the fire of a masked
battery. The plain artisan or the tough fireman, who faces
the lead and iron like a man, is the truest representative we
can show of the heroes of Crécy and Agincourt. And if one
of our fine gentlemen puts off his straw-colored kids and
stands by the other, shoulder to shoulder, or leads him on
to the attack, he is as honorable in our eyes and in theirs
as if he were ill-dressed and his hands were soiled with
labor.

Another great fact came to the surface, and is coming
up every day in new shapes—that we are one people. It is
easy to say that a man is a man in Maine or Minnesota, but
not so easy to feel it, all through our bones and marrow.
The camp is deprovincializing us very fast. Brave Win-
throp, marching with the city *élégants,* seems to have been
a little startled to find how wonderfully human were the
hard-handed men of the Eighth Massachusetts.

It takes all the nonsense out of everybody, or ought to
do it, to see how fairly the real manhood of a country is
distributed over its surface. And then, just as we are beginning to think our own soil has a monopoly of heroes as
well as of cotton, up turns a regiment of gallant Irishmen,
like the Sixty-ninth, to show us that continual provincial-
ism is as bad as that of Coos County, New Hampshire, or
of Broadway, New York.

Here, too, side by side in the same great camp, are
half a dozen chaplains, representing half a dozen modes of
religious belief. When the masked battery opens, does the
"Baptist" Lieutenant believe in his heart that God takes
better care of him than of his "Congregationalist" Colonel? Does any man really suppose that, of a score of noble
young fellows who have just laid down their lives for their
country, the *Homoousians* are received to the mansions of
bliss, and the *Homoiousians* translated from the battle field
to the abodes of everlasting woe?

War not only teaches what man can be, but it teaches

also what he must not be: He must not be a bigot and a fool in the presence of that day of judgment proclaimed by the trumpet which calls to battle, and where a man should have but two thoughts: to do his duty, and trust his Maker. Let our brave dead come back from the fields where they have fallen for law and liberty, and if you will follow them to their graves, you will find out what the Broad Church means; the narrow church is sparing of its exclusive formulae over the coffins wrapped in the flag which the fallen heroes had defended! Very little comparatively do we hear at such times of the dogmas on which men differ; very much of the faith and trust in which all sincere Christians can agree. It is a noble lesson, and nothing less noisy than the voice of the cannon can teach it so that it shall be heard over all the angry cries of theological disputants.

Whatsoever miseries this war brings upon us, it is making us wiser, and, we trust, better. Wise, for we are learning our weakness, our narrowness, our selfishness, our ignorance, in lessons of sorrow and shame. Better, because all that is noble in men and women is defended by the time, and our people are rising to the standard the time calls for.

For this is the question the hour is putting to each of us: Are you ready, if need be, to sacrifice all that you have and hope for in this world, that the generations to follow you may inherit a whole country whose natural condition shall be peace, and not a broken province which must live under the perpetual threat, if not in the constant presence, of war and all that war brings with it? If we are all ready for this sacrifice, battles may be lost, but the campaign and its grand object must be won.

Heaven is very kind in its way of putting questions to mortals & we are not abruptly asked to give up all that we most care for, in view of the momentous issues before us. Perhaps we shall never be asked to give up all, but we have already been called upon to part with much that is dear to us, and should be ready to yield the rest as it is called for. The time may come when even the cheap public print shall be a burden our means cannot support, and we can only listen in the square that was once the market-place to the voices of those who proclaim defeat or victory. Then there will be only our daily food left. When we have nothing to read and nothing to eat, it will be a favorable moment to offer a compromise. At present we have all that nature absolutely demands—we can live on bread and the newspaper.[2]

Longfellow records in his journal Holmes's anxiety over his son (later to become a Supreme Court justice), and then tells of young Holmes having been wounded.

October 22: I walk to town and back. On the bridge meet Dr. Holmes, who is troubled about his son, Lieutenant in the Massachusetts Twentieth, which has been in an engagement on the Potomac.

October 25: Bad news. Young Putnam is killed, and Holmes wounded. I have no heart for anything. . . .[3]

Holmes himself, on November 29, writing to his friend John L. Motley, the diplomat-historian, describes in detail the circumstances surrounding his son's wound.

I know you will let me begin with my personal story, for you have heard before this time about Ball's Bluff and its disasters, and among them that my boy came in for his honorable wounds. Wendell's experience was pretty well for a youngster of twenty. He was standing in front of his men when a spent ball struck him in the stomach and knocked him flat, taking his wind out of him at the time. He made shift to crawl off a little, the colonel, at whose side he was standing, telling him to go to the rear. Presently he began to come right, and found he was not seriously injured. By the help of a sergeant he got up and went to the front again.

He had hardly been there two or three minutes when he was struck by a second ball, knocked down, and carried off. His shirt was torn from him, and he was found to be shot through the heart—it was supposed through the lungs. The ball had entered exactly over the heart on the left side and come out on the right side, where it was found—a minie ball. The surgeon thought he was mortally wounded; and he supposed so, too. Next day, better; next after that, wrote me a letter.

He had no bad symptoms, and it became evident that the ball had passed outside the cavities containing the heart and lungs. He got on to Philadelphia where he stayed a week, and a fortnight ago yesterday I brought him to Boston on a bed in the cars. He is now thriving well, able to walk, but has a considerable open wound, which, if the bone has to foliate, will keep him from camp for many weeks at the least.

A most narrow escape from instant death! Wendell is a great pet in his character of young hero with wounds in the heart, and receives visits *en grand seigneur.* I envy my white Othello, with a semicircle of young Desdemonas about him listening to the often-told story which they will have over again.

You know how well all our boys behaved. In fact, the defeat at Ball's Bluff, disgraceful as it was to the planners of the stupid sacrifice, is one as much to be remembered and to be proud of as that of Bunker Hill. They did all that men could be expected to do, and the courage and energy of some of the young captains saved a large number of men by getting them across the river a few at a time, at the imminent risk on their own part of being captured or shot while crossing.[4]

Emerson writes of the approaching Christmas and comments on the Mason and Slidell incident.

We are all knitting socks & mittens for soldiers, writing patriotic lectures, & economizing with all our mights. No Christmas boxes, no New Years' gift, this year to be offered by any honest party to any.[5]

The war begins to turn and mass to tell against activity. President Lincoln said well that the rebels "carried only the ruins of their own country as ground to invoke the aid of foreign nations." How rare are acts of will! Captain Ingraham became famous by taking away a subject of the United States from the Austrians, to whom he was a political offender. General Jackson, by "assuming the responsibility"; and now Commodore Wilkes, by taking on his own responsibility Mason and Slidell.[6]

Sidney Lanier, from July 10, 1861, was a soldier in the Confederate Army (Company D, 2nd Battalion, Georgia Infantry, C.S.A.). Stationed near Norfolk, Virginia, he tells something of his life as a soldier in a letter to his brother.

You would not think, my dear Cliff, that I was a soldier, enduring the frowns of "grim-visaged war," if you could see me with slippers and smoking-cap on, pipe in mouth, writing to you on a real pine table, surrounded by ten noisy boys, in a room with ten sleeping-bunks built against its walls, and a "great and glorious" fire blazing in the fireplace—I can hardly realize that I am in a *house,* but find myself continually asking myself if it is not some delightful dream; it is impossible for you to imagine with what delight I hail a real, bona-fide *room* as a habitation for the winter, unless you had, as I have, shivered in cold tents for the last few months, which the rains beat through and the winds blew down at every available opportunity (and oh pluvial Gods! with what astonishing frequency the said availables *did* occur!): unless you had become accustomed, 1st, to going to sleep with the expectation that your tent would blow down and the rains wet you to the skin before you could get your clothes on; and, 2nd, to having the said expectations *realized* in the most satisfactory manner; unless you had been in the habit of eating in a drenching rain which diluted your coffee (without any sugar) before you could drink it, and made mush of your biscuit before you could eat it; unless you had customarily made your ablutions in a mud puddle (which you had previously caused a swine to vacate for that purpose); unless you had, in short, been as horribly uncomfortable as it is possible for a man to be. —The room, which so excites my delight, is the one which my mess occupies in our winter-quarters, which we have been actively engaged in building for two weeks past—; and, by the way, you ought to have seen me carpentering: I have hammered, sawed, filed, planed, toted bricks and mortar in a hod (real Irish style), built partitions, bunks and gun-racks, shingled roofs, and done various and sundry feats in the house carpentering line.

We had snow night before last, which is yet on the ground; and the rest of the night was occupied with a terrible storm of wind and sleet, which had nearly blown down our winter quarters; had we been in tents we would have suffered severely.

Tell Uncle William that I took the breech-loading carbine, which he gave me, to a gunsmith in Norfolk; who hummed and hawed about it, until he made me mad, when I took the gun back to my tent and, after three days of incessant work, got the breech-chamber open! It then took me about a week to clean it out; it was the rustiest affair I have ever seen; I succeeded, however, at length, in getting it in order; and made some very good shots with it, at a quarter of a mile's distance.

It is rumored in camp that our Battalion may possibly be discharged in January, tho' I am not disposed to attach much importance to the rumor.

A steamboat came up to Norfolk from Fortress Monroe yesterday, under a flag of truce; among other items, she brought news that England has formally demanded of the Federal Government a full apology, or a fight, on account of the Mason and Slidell affair—. If the news be true, I think it extremely probable that we will have peace in the Spring.[7]

Emily Dickinson writes of Amherst's contribution to the Union Army.

Mrs. Adams had news of the death of her boy to-day, from a wound at Annapolis. Telegram signed by Frazer Stearns. You remember him. Another one died in October—from fever caught in the camp. Mrs. Adams herself has not risen from bed since then. "Happy new year" step softly over such doors as these! "Dead! Both her boys! One of them shot by the sea in the East, and one of them shot in the West by the sea." . . . Christ be merciful!

Frazer Stearns is just leaving Annapolis. His father has gone to see him to-day. I hope that ruddy face won't be brought home frozen. Poor little widow's boy, riding to-night in the mad wind, back to the village burying ground where he never dreamed of sleeping! Ah! the dreamless sleep![8]

Bryant comments on the wealth of the nation (especially the North) and how the people are using it.

The country is full of the means of subsistence—vast magazines of maize and wheat in the Western States waiting for a market, some of which has lain there for two years past. It is full of precious metals—three hundred millions of dollars in coined gold, and the richest gold mines in the world within its borders, worked by the most enterprising and active miners whom the world ever saw. All these advantages are in the hands of a sagacious, inventive, and industrious population, which knows how to obtain, from any given sources, more wealth than any other race of men.

Nor must we leave out of the account the willingness of our people to make sacrifices for the sake of sustaining the public credit and supporting the Government in the task of quelling the Southern revolt. There never was a nation more cheerfully disposed to bear the necessary burdens. The States have voluntarily taxed themselves for purposes which properly belong to the Federal Government, in the clothing, equipment, and temporary support of the troops they have furnished. Individuals all over the country, with a liberality which seems as if it could never be exhausted, have taxed themselves, and are taxing themselves every day, to supply our hospitals with comforts necessary to the sick and wounded, and to furnish our great volunteer army, composed of more than a fortieth part of the population of the free States, with articles which the Federal Government does not provide. The same spirit which has prompted the flower of our young men to volunteer for the war makes those who remain at home willing to be taxed for the purpose of paying them their wages. The general feeling is one of impatience that Congress is so slow in performing this necessary duty; the tax is as much looked for, as much called for, as the suppression of the rebellion.[9]

5   *No Hasty Peace*

Emerson introduces the new year (1862).

The first of January has found me in quite as poor a plight as the rest of the Americans. Not a penny from my books since last June, which usually yield five or six hundred a year. No dividends from the banks . . . almost all income from lectures has quite ceased. Meanwhile we are trying to be as unconsuming as candles under an extinguisher. . . . But far better that this grinding should go on, bad and worse, than we should be driven by any impatience into a hasty peace, or any peace restoring the old rottenness.

The war is a new glass to see all our old things through, how they look. Some of our trades stand the test well. Baking and butchering are good under all skies and times. Farming, haying, and woodchopping don't go out of vogue. Meat and coal and shoes we must have. But coach painting and bronze match holders we can postpone for awhile yet.

Yet the music was heard with as much appetite as ever, and our Quintettes had only to put "The Star-spangled Banner" into the programme, to gain a hurrah beside; but the concert could have prospered well without. And so if the Union were beaten, and Jeff Davis ruled Massachusetts, these flutes and fiddles would have piped and scraped all the same, and no questions asked. It only shows that those fellows have hitched on their apple–cart to a star, and so it gets dragged by might celestial. They know that few have thoughts or benefits, but all have ears; that the blood rolls to pulse-beat and tune; that the babe rhymes and the boy whistles, and they throw themselves on a want so universal; and as long as birds sing, ballad–singers will, and organ–grinders will grind out their bread.

We will not again disparage America, now that we have seen what men it will bear. What a certificate of good elements in the soil, climate, and institutions is Lowell, whose admirable verses I have just read! Such a creature more accredits the land than all the fops of Carolina discredit it.

Though practically nothing is so improbable or perhaps impossible a contingency for me, yet I do not wish to abdicate so extreme a privilege as the use of the sword or the bullet. For the peace of the man who has forsworn the use of the bullet seems to me not quite peace.

Happily we are under better guidance than of statesmen. We are drifting in currents, and the currents know the way. It is, as I said, a war of Instincts. Then I think the difference between our present and our past state is in our favour; it was war then, and is war now, but war declared is better than undeclared war.

The Southerners complained of "the electing of Lincoln by insulting majorities."

Better for us, perhaps, that we should be ruled by slow heads than by bold ones, whilst insight is withheld. Yet one conceives of a head capable of taking in all the elements of this problem, the blockade, the stone fleet, the naval landings, insurrection, English ill-will, French questionability, Texas.

And so of Slavery, we have only half a right to be so good; for Temperament cracks the whip in every Northern kitchen.

Government has no regard for men until they become property; then, it has the tenderest.

The thinking class are looked at inquisitively in these times by the actors, as if some counsel were expected from them. But the thinker seldom speaks to the actor in his time, but ever to actors in the next age.

President Lincoln said well that "the rebels carried only the ruin of their own country as ground to invoke the aid of foreign nations."

I conceive the strength of the North to lie in:

(1) its moral rectitude in this matter;
(2) its genius, manners, habits, tenure of land, and climate all of which indispose it to Slavery; its weakness to lie in its timorous literalism.[1]

Lanier writes from his Virginia camp, January 18.

I think the Montgomery folks must have forgotten me entirely; or else they cannot have received my letters—tell 'em that I'm not dead yet: "I shall live"; and still have the feelings of a soldier away from home, and mournful and lonely because his dear ones think too little of him even to bestow a passing half–hour upon a letter to him.[2]

Emerson speaks to an audience in Washington which includes President Lincoln, January 31.

At this moment in America the aspects of political society absorb attention. In every house, from Canada to the Gulf, the children ask the serious father, "What is the news of the war to–day, and when will there be better times?" The boys have no new clothes, no gifts, no journeys; the girls must go without new bonnets; boys and girls find their education this year less liberal and complete. All the little hopes that heretofore made the year pleasant are deferred. The state of the country fills me with anxiety and stern duties. We have attempted to hold together two states of civilization: a higher state where labor and the tenure of land and the right of suffrage are democratical; and a lower state, in which the old military tenure of prisoners and slaves, and of power and land in a few hands, makes an oligarchy; we have attempted to hold these two states of society under one law. But the rude and early state of society does not work well with the latter, nay, works badly, and has poisoned politics, public morals and social intercourse in the Republic, now for many years.

The times put this question: Why cannot the best civilization be extended over the whole country, since the disorder of the less civilized portion menaces the existence of the country? Is this secular progress we have described, this evolution of man to the highest powers, only to give him sensibility and not to bring duties with it? Is he not to make his knowledge practical? to stand and to withstand? Is not civilization heroic also? Is it not action? has it not a will?

"There are periods," said Niebuhr, "when something much better than happiness and security of life is attainable." We live in a new and exceptional age. America is another word for Opportunity. Our whole history appears like a last effort of the Divine Providence in behalf of the human race; and a literal, slavish following of precedents, as by a justice of the peace, is not for those who at this hour lead the destinies of this people. The evil you contend with has taken alarming proportions, and you still content yourselves with parrying the blows it aims, but, as if enchanted, abstain from striking at the cause.

If the American people hesitate, it is not for want of warning or advices. The telegraph has been swift enough to announce our disasters. The journals have not suppressed the extent of the calamity. Neither was there any want of argument or of experience. If the war brought any surprise to the North, it was not the fault of sentinels on the watchtowers, who had furnished full details of the designs, the muster and means of the enemy. Neither was anything concealed of the theory and practice of slavery. To what purpose make more big books of these statistics? There are already mountains of facts, if anyone wants them. But people do not want them. They bring their opinion into the world. If they have any comatose tendency in the brain, they are pro-slavery while they live; if of a nervous saguineous temperament, they are abolitionists. Then interests were never persuaded. Can you convince the shoe interest, or the iron interest, or the cotton interest, by reading passages from Milton or Montesquieu? You wish to satisfy people that slavery is bad economy. Why, the "Edinburgh Review" pounded on that string, and made out its case, forty years ago.

A democratic statesman said to me, long since, that, if he owned the State of Kentucky, he would manumit all the slaves, and be a gainer by the transaction. Is this new? No, everybody knows it. As a general economy it is admitted. But there is no one owner of the state, but a good many small owners. One man owns land and slaves; another owns slaves only. Here is a woman who has no other property—like a lady in Charleston I knew of, who owned fifteen sweeps and rode in her carriage.

It is clearly a vast inconvenience to each of these to make any change, and they are fretful and talkative, and all their friends are; and those less interested are inert and, from want of thought, averse to innovation. It is like free trade, certainly the interest of nations, but by no means the interest of certain towns and districts, which tariff feeds fat; and the eager interest of the few overpowers the apathetic general conviction of the many. Banknotes rob the public, but are such a daily convenience that we silence our scruples and make believe they are gold. So imposts are the cheap and right taxation; but, by the dislike of people to pay out a direct tax, governments are forced to render life costly by making them pay twice as much, hidden in the price of tea and sugar.

In this national crisis, it is not argument that we want, but that rare courage which dares commit itself to a principle, believing that Nature is its ally and will create the instruments it requires, and more than make good any petty and injurious profit which it may disturb. There never was such a combination as this of ours, and the rules to meet it are not set down in any history.

We want men of original perception and original action, who can open their eyes wider than to a nationality, namely, to considerations of benefit to the human race; can act in the interest of civilization. Government must not be a parish clerk, a justice of the peace. It has, of necessity, in any crisis of the state, the absolute powers of a Dictator. The existing Administration is entitled to the utmost candor. It is to be thanked for its angelic virtue, compared with any executive experiences with which we have been familiar. But the times will not allow us to indulge in compliment.

I wish I saw in the people that inspiration which, if Government would not obey the same, would leave the Government behind and create on the moment the means and executors it wanted. Better the war should more dangerously threaten us—should threaten fracture in what is still whole, and punish us with burned capitols and slaughtered regiments, and so exasperate the people to energy, exasperate our nationality. There are Scriptures written invisibly on men's hearts, whose letters do not come out until they are enraged. They can be read by war-fires, and by eyes in the last peril.

We cannot but remember that there have been in American history, when, if the Free States had done their duty, Slavery had been blocked by an immovable barrier, and our recent calamities forever precluded. The Free States yielded, and every compromise was surrender and invited new demands. Here again is a new occasion which Heaven offers to sense and virtue. It looks as if we held the fate of the fairest possession of mankind in our hands, to be saved by our firmness or lost by hesitation.

The one power that has legs long enough and strong enough to wade across the Potomac offers itself at this hour; the one strong enough to bring the civility up to the height of that which is best prays now at the door of Congress for leave to move. Emancipation is the demand of civilization. That is a principle; everything else is an intrigue. This is a progressive policy, puts the whole people in healthy, productive, amiable position, puts every man in the South in just and natural relations with every man in the North, laborer with laborer.

I shall not attempt to unfold the details of the project of emancipation. It has been stated with great ability by several of its leading advocates. I will only advert to some leading points of the argument, at the risk of repeating the reasons of others. The war is welcome to the Southerner; a chivalrous sport to him, like hunting, and suits his semi-civilized condition. On the climbing scale of progress he is just up to war, and has never appeared to such advantage as in the last twelve-month. It does not suit us. We are advanced some ages on the war-state—to trade, art and general cultivation. His laborer works for him at home, so that he loses no labor by the war. All our soldiers are laborers; so that the South, with its inferior numbers, is almost on a footing in effective war-population with the North.

Again, as long as we fight without any affirmative step taken by the Government, any word intimating forfeiture in the rebel states of their old privileges under the law, they and we fight on the same side, for Slavery. Again, if we conquer the enemy—what then? We shall still have to keep him under, and it will cost us as much to hold him down as it did to get him down. Then comes the summer, and the fever will drive the soldiers home; next winter we must begin at the beginning and conquer him over again. What use then to take a fort, or a privateer, or get possession of an inlet, or to capture a regiment of rebels?

But one weapon we hold which is sure. Congress can, by edict, as a part of the military defence which it is the duty of Congress to provide, abolish slavery, and pay for such slaves as we ought to pay for. Then the slaves near our armies will come to us; those in the interior will know in a week what their rights are, and will, where opportunity offers, prepare to take them. Instantly, the armies that now confront you must run home to protect their estates, and must stay there, and your enemies will disappear.

There can be no safety until this step is taken. We fancy that the endless debate, emphasized by the crime and by the cannons of this war, has brought the Free States to some conviction that it can never go well with us whilst this mischief of slavery remains in our politics, and that by concert or by might we must put an end to it. But we have too much experience of the futility of an easy reliance on the momentary good dispositions of the public. There does exist, perhaps, a popular will that the Union shall not be broken—that our trade, and therefore our laws, must have the whole breadth of the continent, and from Canada to the Gulf. But since this is the rooted belief and will of the people, so much the more are they in danger, when impatient of defeats, or impatient of taxes, to go with a rush for some peace; and what kind of peace shall at that moment be easiest attained, they will make concessions for it—will give up the slaves, and the whole torment of the past half-century will come back to be endured anew.

Neither do I doubt, if such a composition should take place, that the Southerners will come back quietly and politely, leaving their haughty dictation. It will be an era of good feelings; There will be a lull after so loud a storm; and, no doubt, there will be discreet men from that section who will earnestly strive to inaugurate more moderate and fair administration of the Government, and the North will for a time have its full share and more, in place and counsel. But this will not last;—not for want of good will in sensible Southerners, but because Slavery will again speak through them its harsh necessity. It cannot live but by injustice, and it will be unjust and violent to the end of the world.

The power of Emancipation is this, that it alters the atomic social constitution of the Southern people. Now, their interest is in keeping out white labor; then, when they must pay wages, their interest will be to let it in, to get the best labor, and, if they fear their blacks, to invite Irish,

German and American laborers. Thus, whilst Slavery makes and keeps disunion, Emancipation removes the whole objection to union. Emancipation at one stroke elevates the poor white of the South and identifies his interest with that of the Northern laborer.

Now, in the name of all that is simple and generous, why should not this great right be done? Why should not America be capable of a second stroke for the well–being of the human race, as eighty or ninety years ago she was for the first—of an affirmative step in the interests of human civility, urged on her, too, not by any romance of sentiment, but by her own extreme perils?

It is very certain that the statesman who shall break through the cobwebs of doubt, fear and petty cavil that lie in the way, will be greeted by the unanimous thanks of mankind. Men reconcile themselves very fast to a bold and good measure when once it is taken, though they condemn it in advance.

A week before the two captive commissioners were surrendered to England, every one thought it could not be done; it would divide the North. It was done, and in two days all agreed it was the right action. And this action, which costs so little (the parties injured by it being such a handful that they can very easily be indemnified), rids the world, at one stroke, of this degrading nuisance, the cause of war and ruin to nations. This measure at once puts all parties right. This is borrowing, as I said, the omnipotence of a principle. What is so foolish as the terror lest the blacks should be made furious by freedom and wages? It is denying these that is the outrage, and makes the danger from the blacks. But justice satisfies everybody—white man, red man, yellow man and black man. All like wages, and the appetite grows by feeding.

President Lincoln has proposed to Congress that the Government shall cooperate with any state that shall enact a gradual abolishment of Slavery. In the recent series of national successes [Ed. note: this paragraph was written at a later date.], this message is the best. It marks the happiest day in the political year. The American Executive ranges itself for the first time on the side of freedom. If Congress had been backward, the President has advanced. This state paper is the more interesting that it appears to be the President's individual act, done under a strong sense of duty. He speaks his own thought in his own style. All thanks and honor to the Head of the State! The Message has been received throughout the country with praise, and, we doubt not, with more pleasure than has been spoken.

If Congress accords with the President, it is not yet too late to begin the emancipation; but we think it will always be too late to make it gradual. All experience agrees that it should be immediate. More and better than the President has spoken shall the effect of his message be—but, we are sure, not more or better than he hoped in his heart, when, thoughtful of all the complexities of his position, he penned these cautious words.[3]

Bryant, in a personal letter to Lincoln, criticizes the lack of movement by the Union Army and the effect this will have on New York politics.

Allow me to say a very few words on a subject in which the friends of the administration and the country in this quarter feel a deep interest. We are distressed and alarmed at the inactivity of our armies in the work of putting down the rebellion. I have been pained to hear lately, from persons of zealous loyalty, the expression of a doubt as to whether the administration is in earnest in desiring the speedy annihilation of the rebel forces. We, who are better informed, acquit the administration of the intention to prolong the war, though we cannot relieve it from the responsibility. These inopportune pauses, this strange sluggishness in military operations, seem to us little short of absolute madness. Besides their disastrous influence on the final event of the war, they will have a most unhappy effect on the elections here, and we fear they have had in other states. The election of Seymour as Governor of the State of New York would be a public calamity, but it may happen if the army is kept idle. A victory or two would almost annihilate his party, and carry in General Wadsworth triumphantly. If what is apparently the present policy be persisted in by the generals who conduct the war, the Union, in our view, is lost, and we shall be convinced that Providence has decided the ruin of our republic.[4]

6   *Sanguine Anticipations*

Holmes has more information about the war for his friend Motley.

I got your letter of January 14th day before yester-day, Saturday. I was a little out of spirits yesterday, on account of ugly rumors as to the tone of the English press, etc., which had the effect of knocking down stocks some-what in New York, and dashing our sanguine anticipations a little for the time.

This morning the papers tell us that many of these representatives are thought to be mere secession contriv-ances, and we hear from Washington that the advices from foreign Governments were never so friendly as at this time. They begin to talk about the *entente cordiale* between this country and England as likely to be re–established —so may it prove! Not that England can ever be to us what she has been. Those sad words from John Bright's letter have expressed the feelings that have sunk deep into the hearts of all (who have hearts to be reached) among us.

"There has been shown us no generosity, such as be-comes a friendly nation, and no sympathy with us in our great calamity." Those beautiful breasts of our "mother" country, from which it seemed nothing could wean us, have shrivelled into the wolf's dugs, and there is no more milk in them for us henceforth evermore. The West end is right.

Not by aggression, but by the naked fact of existence, we are in eternal danger and an unsleeping threat to every government that founds itself on anything but the will of the governed. We begin to understand ourselves and what we represent, now that we find who are our enemies, and why, and how they would garrote us now that our hands are on these felons' throats, if they could paint a lie over so that its bones would not show through. I do believe Hell is empty of Devils for the last year, this planet has been so full of them helping the secession liars.

You don't want my rhetoric, but plain talk about what is going on. We are generally hopeful, so far as I hear talk around me. The Mason and Slidell matter has long been in the silurian strata of the past. The events that are more than six weeks old all go with pre–Adamite creations. All the world seemed to think Pilot Seward was drifting on to a lee shore, and that he would never double that terrible Cape Fear in the distance. Presently he heaves in sight, canvas all spread, and lo! it seems the wind is blowing *off* the shore, as it has been any time these fifty years.

Confidence holds good in McClellan, I feel well assured. The *Tribune* attacks him; some grumble at delays; but I believe the wisest heads are as yet reasonably patient. They know that the Virginian roads are impracticable at this particular time. They know the enlistment period of many of the rebel troops is about to expire—*before this very month is out*. It is perfectly plain from the rebel organs that the delay is telling immensely on them; that they begin to feel the pressure of the *cordon sanitaire* which is drawing its ring of fire around them.

The financial business seems now to be the immediate subject of doubts and differences of opinion. I talked with Frank Lowell this morning about it. He did not profess to be an expert in finance (though he must have a good deal of acquaintance with it). He thought the difficulty was in Chase's inexperience, not providing long enough beforehand for the inevitable want of the Treasury. About the taxation schemes, you may find out from the papers—I haven't found out what the scheme is which is likely to be adopted. I believe our people are worked up to the *paying* point, which, I take it, is to be the fighting point as boiling heat (212°) to blood heat (98°).

I have told you I am hopeful, and always have been. Hands off, and we'll lick these fellows out of their insolent adjectives. We did lick 'em at Mill Spring the other day, and at Drainsville a little before this, and, I myself entertain no matter of doubt, can whip them man for man at any time, in a fair field, picked against picked, average against average.

We are the conquerors of Nature; they of Nature's weaker children. We thrive on reverses and disappointments. I have never believed they could endure them. Like Prince Rupert's drops, the unannealed fabric of rebellion shuts an explosive element in its resisting shell that will rend it in pieces as soon as its tail, not its head, is broken fairly off. That is what I think—I, safe prophet of a private correspondence, free to be convinced by my own ignorance and presumption by events as they happen, and to prophesy again—for what else do we live for but to guess the future in small things or great, that we may help to shape it, or ourselves to it.

Your last letter was so full of interest, by the expression of your own thought and the transcripts of those of your English friends—especially the words of John Bright, one of the two foreigners that I want to see and thank—the other being Count Gasparin—that I feel entirely inadequate to make any fitting return for it. I meet a few wise persons, who for the most part know little—some who know a good deal, but are not wise.

I was at a dinner at Parker's the other day where Governor Andrew and Emerson, and various unknown dingy-linened friends of progress, met to hear Mr. Conway, the not unfamous Unitarian minister of Washington, Virginia-born, with seventeen secesh cousins, fathers, and other relatives, tell of his late experience at the seat of Government. He had talked awhile with father Abraham, who, as he thinks, is honest enough, but simply incompetent and without a plan. I don't know that his opinion is good for much. He is an out-and-out immediate emancipationist—believes that is the only way to break the strength of the South; that the black man is the life of the South; that they dread work above all things, and cling to the slave as the drudge that makes life tolerable to them. He believes that the blacks know all that is said and done with reference to them in the North; their longing for freedom is unalterable; that once assured of it under Northern protection, the institution would be doomed. . . . He talked with a good deal of spirit. I know you would have gone with him in his leading ideas. Speaking of the communication of knowledge among the slaves, he said if he stood on the upper Mississippi and proclaimed emancipation, it would be told in New Orleans before the *telegraph* would carry the news there!

My boy is here—still detailed on recruiting duty—quite well.

P. S. Our last accounts from the Burnside expedition, which had such a hard time getting to its destination, are all very encouraging.[1]

Longfellow writes in his journal for February.

Feb. 4: Newspapers take up so much of my time— too much by a great deal; but one can hardly help it now when any moment may bring the greatest tidings.

Feb. 13: The war goes on. The North is in motion at last; and great results are looked for.

Feb. 15: A week of victories all along the line, East and West. (Springfield, Fort Henry, Roanoke Island, Elizabeth City.)

Feb. 21: To-day Captain Gordon, the slaver, is to be hanged. It seems to me very illogical to hang him, and yet to protect by the Constitution all our internal slave-traders.[2]

Lanier writes again from Virginia. The letter, addressed to his father, is dated February 19.

I wrote you, a day or two ago, requesting your opinions on the re-enlistment question, especially with reference to my own action— For fear you should not receive that letter, I write again: I am particularly anxious to hear from (you) on the subject, as the question is being extensively agitated in camp now, and I do not wish to commit myself before consulting you: indeed, I do not know what to do about it, and want advice—

I was in Capt Smith's room some nights ago; he attempted then to get me to sign a re-enlistment paper which he has prepared, but I refused to do so on the ground that I had not considered the subject, and was unprepared to commit myself— He, you know, is raising a regiment, and is, of course, anxious that the Macon Volunteers should re-enlist, expecting that they will join his regiment— He gave me quite a talk: "was anxious," he said, "to *bag* me; and to provide a *good bag* for me:" all of which, of course, I understood as mere blarney, as I have neither the money nor the influence to bring men enough into his regiment to secure me a position in it— I think the Capt. will have a great deal of difficulty in raising his regiment: and Lieut. Jones, with whom I was talking, is confident that he (Capt. S) will not be able to raise it—

You have, of course, heard before this of the capture of Fort Donelson and our forces there— It is a terrible blow upon us: I have had the blues all day in consequence of it— I have very little doubt that Norfolk will shortly be attacked; how soon, of course, no one can tell— And I write so, because I think "honesty is the best policy," and you will be less anxious, knowing the exact condition of things, than when you are held in suspense by the thousand reports and rumors, which I hear of, are reaching you daily— I believe that we will whip them here: we have good fortifications, splendid batteries, plenty of ammunition, a body of the finest troops in the service, a wrath which has been nursed for ten long months, and, confidence in our ability to defeat the enemy— So *please* do not be anxious about me; if I thought you were so, I should be very unhappy— I shall keep you honestly advised of our conditions here—

I went over to Gosport Navy Yard yesterday: and went down to see the Merrimac, which was lying at one of the Navy Yard wharves, receiving her last guns— She is the ugliest–looking Monster imaginable—and will sail, certainly, in a few days—the rumor about her *failure* was a mere *hoodwink* to deceive the enemy: I laughed heartily at the article in the Telegraph on that subject! Clisby [Joseph Clisby, editor of the *Macon Daily Telegraph*] was effectually fooled by the Day-Book's hoodwinking article. . . .

Do be *very* particular to say nothing about what I have written you: either of the Merrimac, or Capt. Smith &c.[3]

On Sunday, March 16, Hawthorne writes to his daughter Una, describing his recent tour of the battle areas in and around Washington.

I have never a moment's time to write, for I move about all day, and am engaged all the evening; and if ever there is a vacant space, I want to employ it in writing my journal, which keeps terribly behindhand. But I suppose mamma and the rest of you sometimes remember there is such a person, and wish to know what I am about.

I went up yesterday to Harper's Ferry (a distance of eighty miles from Washington) by invitation of the directors of a railroad; so that I made the whole journey without expense and partook of two cold collations besides. To be sure, I paid my expenses with a speech; but it was a very short one. I shall not describe what I saw, because very likely I shall print it in the "Atlantic Monthly"; but I made acquaintance with some rebel prisoners, and liked them very much.

It rained horribly all day, and the mud was such that

nobody in New England can conceive of. I have shaken hands with Uncle Abe, and have seen various notabilities, and am infested by people who want to exhibit me as a lion. I have seen a camp, and am going in a few days to Manassas, if the mud of the Sacred Soil will permit. Tell mamma that the outcry opened against General McClellan, since the enemy's retreat from Manassas, is really terrible, and almost universal; because it is found that we might have taken their fortifications with perfect ease six months ago, they being defended chiefly by wooden guns. Unless he achieves something wonderful within a week, he will be removed from command, and perhaps shot—at least I hope so; I never did more than half believe in him.

By a message from the State Department, I have reason to think there is money enough due me from the Government to pay the expenses of my journey. I think the public buildings are as fine if not finer than anything we saw in Europe. I am very well. I have no doubt that Julian [Hawthorne's son] well supplies my place as the head of the family. . . .⁴

Emily Dickinson writes of another Amherst casualty.

You have done more for me—'tis least that I can do, to tell you of brave Frazer—"killed at Newbern," darlings. His big heart shot away by a "minie ball."

I had read of those—I didn't think that Frazer would carry one to Eden with him. Just as he fell, in his soldier's cap, with his sword at his side, Frazer rode through Amherst. Classmates to the right of him, and classmates to the left of him, to guard his narrow face! He fell by the side of Professor Clark, his superior officer—lived ten minutes in a soldier's arms, asked twice for water—murmured just, "My God!" and passed! Sanderson, his classmate, made a box of boards in the night, put the brave boy in, covered with a blanket; rowed six miles to reach the boat—so poor Frazer came. They tell that Colonel Clark cried like a little child when he missed his pet, and could hardly resume his post. They loved each other very much. Nobody here could look on Frazer—not even his father. The doctors would not allow it.

The bed on which he came was enclosed in a large casket shut entirely, and covered from head to foot with the sweetest flowers. He went to sleep from the village church. Crowds came to tell him good–night, choirs sang to him, pastors told how brave he was—early-soldier heart. And the family bowed their heads, as the reeds the wind shakes.

So our part in Frazer is done, but you must come next summer and we will mind ourselves of this young crusader—too brave that he could fear to die. We will play his tunes—maybe he can hear them; we will try to comfort his broken-hearted Ella, who, as the clergyman said, "gave him peculiar confidence." . . . Austin is stunned completely. Let us love better, children, it's most that's left to do.

Austin is chilled—by Frazer's murder—he says—his Brain keeps saying over "Frazer is killed—Frazer is killed," just as Father told it—to him. Two or three words of lead—that dropped so deep, they keep weighing—

Tell Austin—how to get over them! [5]

Longfellow's journal and letters continue through the first anniversary of the war to the middle of May.

April 9: Great battles, and great victories for Freedom.

April 20: In every country the "dangerous classes" are those who do not work; for instance, the nobility in Europe and the slaveholders here. . . . I am writing you on Easter Sunday. What an Easter this is for the Negroes in the District of Columbia! [Congress had just passed a bill emancipating the slaves of the District.] I rejoice, with you and with all true men, on this Easter of Africa.

May 8: Of the civil war I say only this. It is not a revolution but a Catalinian conspiracy. It is Slavery against Freedom; the north wind against the southern pestilence. I saw lately, at a jeweller's, a slave's collar of iron, with an iron tongue as large as a spoon, to go into the mouth. Every drop of blood in me quivered! The world forgets what Slavery really is!

May 11: News to–day of the surrender of Norfolk, and the destruction, by the Rebels, of the iron ship Merrimac.

May 17: Here is one of the best things the war has yet given us. [A newspaper paragraph containing General David Hunter's order declaring the military department of the South under martial law, and all persons held as slaves therein free.] All hail to General Hunter.[6]

Melville writes to his sea captain brother from Pittsfield, Mass., May 25.

. . . Do you want to hear about the war? —The war goes bravely on. McClellan is now within fifteen miles of the rebel capitol, Richmond. New Orleans is taken &c &c &c. You will see all no doubt in the papers at your Agents. But when the end—the wind-up—the grand pacification is coming, who knows? We beat the rascals in almost every field, and take all their ports &c, but they don't cry "Enough!" —It looks like a long lane with the turning quite out of sight. —Guert [Guert Gansevoort—Melville's first cousin] has recently been appointed to the command of a fine new sloop of war. I am rejoiced to hear it. It will do him good in more ways than one. He is brave as a lion, a good seaman, a natural-born officer, & I hope he will yet turn out the hero of a brilliant victory.[7]

Lanier writes to a friend from his new camp near Wilmington, North Carolina.

We have stopped, dear Gussie, at Wilmington, and are now encamped about two miles from the city, behind a series of batteries extending for about a mile or two near

Camp Fear River— I don't think we will stay here very long; but have no idea where we will next be ordered.

Our camp is on a hill of white sand, upon which a few scraggy pines maintain a scanty subsistence—reminding one of a bald head with two or three gray hairs on it!

As I sit here, everybody asleep *but* myself, the bare desolate hill, the wind wailing through the pines, the bleak cold rain dripping on my tent, and the murky glare of a pine torch (by which I write) : all accord well with the feelings of my desolation. . . .[8]

In a letter written after the war, Lanier outlines his movements from June, 1861, on.

. . . In June, of '61, I enlisted as a private in the 2nd Georgia Battalion of Infantry, then stationed amongst the marshes of Sewall's Point, Va., immediately opposite Fort Monroe. Here we played "Marsh-Divers" or "Meadow-Crakes" for six months, our principal duties being to picket the beach : and our pleasures and sweet rewards-of-toil consisting in Agues that played dice with our bones, and blue mass pills that played the deuce with our livers. Unless you've had a real James River chill and fever, you'll utterly fail to appreciate the beauties of the situation.

We were next ordered to Wilmington, N.C., where we experienced a pleasant change in the style of fever; indulging for two or three months in what are called "the dry shakes of the sand-hills," a sort of brilliant tremolo movement brilliantly executed upon "that pan–pipe, man," by an invisible but very powerful performer.

We were then sent to Drury's Bluff; and, from there, to the Chickahominy, participating in the famous Seven Days battles around Richmond— Shortly afterward, my regiment went upon a special expedition down the south bank of the James, and, after a little gunboat fight or two, was sent to Petersburg to rest.[9]

Lowell writes on June 5.

They say the news is good last evening, but it does not put me in spirits. I fear we shall go to trying our old fire-and-gunpowder-cement over again, and then what waste of blood and treasure and hope! [10]

Emerson's letter is dated June 11.

Our town is still searched for troops. Captain Bowers has a commission & Mr. Shepherd is his lieutenant & Galen Hoar is one of his men. I have just shaken hands with Cyrus Hosmer, who has grown fat in prison. (in New Orleans). His comrades are not expected in town until tomorrow.[11]

Bryant defends the Evening Post's *criticism of the administration.*

You anticipate a bad effect upon the recruiting service from such criticism on the conduct of the Government as the *Evening Post* had thought it necessary to make. The mischief was done before the *Evening Post* began to criticize. A gloomy and discouraged feeling prevailed, throughout this city and this State at least, which seemed to make the raising of the necessary number of volunteers hopeless. The only remedy that the case seemed to admit was the adoption by the press and by public speakers of a more vigorous style of animadversion on the conduct of the war, and the representations of disinterested persons made personally to the President. . . . They have all regarded the cause of the Union as drifting to ruin if instant and powerful means were not applied to give things a new direction.

I believe their representations, and the language held in public meetings, and to some degree also the comments of the press, have had a certain effect. I hear this morning that it was Pope who recommended Halleck to the President as a fit person to force McClellan into action, and to push on the war with vigor. Other proceedings of the administration within a few days give token that it is waking to a sense of the danger we are in from causes very much like those of which you speak.[12]

7 Hawthorne Tours Battle Areas

Hawthorne observes and philosophizes during his tour of the battle areas near Washington, March, 1862, and concludes his account with a description of life in the lobby of the Willard, Washington's finest hotel.

On our way we heard many rumors of the war, but saw few signs of it. The people were staid and decorous, according to their ordinary fashion; and business seemed about as brisk as usual—though I suppose it was considerably diverted from its customary channels into war–like ones. In the cities, especially in New York, there was a rather prominent display of military goods at the shop windows—such as swords with gilded scabbards and trappings, epaulets, carabines, revolvers, and sometimes a great iron cannon at the edge of the pavement, as if Mars had dropped one of his pocket pistols there, while hurrying to the field.

As railway companions, we had now and then a volunteer in his French-gray greatcoat, returning from furlough, or a new-made officer travelling to join his regiment, in his new-made uniform, which was perhaps all of the military character that he had about him—but proud of his eagle buttons, and likely enough to do them honor before the gilt should be wholly dimmed.

The country, in short, so far as bustle and movement went, was more quiet than in ordinary times, because so large a proportion of its restless elements had been drawn towards the seat of the conflict. But the air was full of a vague disturbance.

Beyond Philadelphia there was a much greater abundance of military people. Between Baltimore and Washington a guard seemed to hold every station along the railroad; and frequently, on the hillsides, we saw a collection of weather-beaten tents, the peaks of which, blackened with smoke, indicated that they had been made comfortable by stove heat throughout the winter. At several commanding positions we saw fortifications, with the muzzles of cannon protruding from the ramparts, the slopes of which were made of the yellow earth of that region.

Our stopping-places were thronged with soldiers, some of whom came through the cars asking for newspapers that contained accounts of the battle between the Merrimac and Monitor, which had been fought the day before. A railway train met us, conveying a regiment out of Washington to some unknown point; and reaching the capitol, we filed out of the station between lines of soldiers, with shouldered muskets, putting us in mind of similar spectacles at the gates of European cities. It was not without sorrow that we saw the free circulation of the nation's lifeblood (at the very heart, moreover) clogged with such strictures as these, which have caused chronic diseases in almost all countries save our own.

Among other excursions to camps and places of interest in the neighborhood of Washington, we went, one day, to Alexandria. In peaceful times it no doubt bore an aspect of decorous quietude and dullness; but it was now thronged with the Northern soldiery, whose stir and bustle contrasted strikingly with the many closed warehouses, the absence of citizens from their customary haunts, and the lack of any symptom of healthy activity, while army wagons trundled heavily over the pavements, and sentinels paced the sidewalks, and mounted dragoons dashed to and fro on military errands.

I tried to imagine how very disagreeable the presence of a Southern army would be in a sober town of Massachusetts; and the thought considerably lessened my wonder at the cold and shy rewards that are cast upon our troops, the gloom, the sullen demeanor, the declared or scarcely hidden sympathy with rebellion, which are so frequent here. It is a strange thing in human life that the greatest errors both of men and women often spring from their sweetest and most generous qualities; and so, undoubtedly thousands of warm-hearted, sympathetic, and impulsive persons have joined the Rebels, not from any real zeal for the cause, but because, between two conflicting loyalties, they chose that which necessarily lay nearest the heart.

There never existed any other government against which treason was so easy, and could defend itself by such plausible arguments, as against that of the United States. The anomaly of two allegiances (of which that of the State comes nearest home to a man's feelings, and includes the altar and the hearth, while the General Government claims his devotion only to an airy mode of law, and has no symbol but a flag) is exceedingly mischievous in this point of view; for it has converted crowds of honest people into traitors, who seem to themselves not merely innocent, but patriotic, and who die for a bad cause with as quiet a conscience as if it were the best.

Driving out of Alexandria, we stopped on the edge of the city to inspect an old slave pen, which is one of the lions of the place, but a very poor one. Reaching the open country, we saw forts and camps on all sides, some of the tents being placed immediately on the ground, while others were raised over a basement of logs, laid lengthwise, like those of a circle—thus forming a solid wall, the chinks closed up with Virginia mud, and above it the pyramidal shelter of the tent.

Here were in progress all the occupations, and all the

idleness, of the soldier in the tented field; some were cooking the company rations in pits hung over fires in the open air; some played at ball, or developed their muscular power by gymnastic exercise; some read newspapers; some smoked cigars or pipes; and many were cleaning their arms and accoutrements—the more carefully, perhaps, because their division was to be reviewed by the Commander-in-Chief that afternoon; others sat on the ground while their comrades cut their hair—it being a soldierly fashion (and for excellent reasons) to crop it within an inch of the skull; others, finally, lay asleep in breast-high tents, with their legs protruding into the open air.

We paid a visit to Fort Ellsworth, and from its ramparts (which have been heaped up out of the muddy soil within the last few months, and will require still a year or two to make them verdant) we had a beautiful view of the Potomac, a truly majestic river, and the surrounding country. The fortifications, so numerous in all this region, and now so unsightly with their bare, precipitous sides, will remain as historic monuments, grass-grown and picturesque memorials of an epoch of terror and suffering.

Even in an aesthetic point of view, however, the war has done a great deal of enduring mischief, by causing the devastation of great tracts of woodland scenery, in which this part of Virginia would appear to have been very rich. Around all the encampments and everywhere along the road, we saw the bare sites of what had evidently been tracts of hardwood forest, indicated by the unsightly stumps of well-grown trees, not smoothly felled by regular ax-men, but hacked, haggled, and unevenly amputated, as by a sword or other miserable tool, in an unskillful hand. Fifty years will not repair this desolation.

The carcasses of horses were scattered along the wayside.

One very pregnant token of a social system thoroughly disturbed was presented by a party of contrabands, escaping out of the mysterious depths of Secessia; and its strangeness consisted in the leisurely delay with which they trudged forward as dreading no pursuer, and encountering nobody to turn them back.

They were unlike the specimens of their race whom we are accustomed to see at the North, and, in my judgment were far more agreeable.

So rudely were they attired—as if their garb had grown upon them spontaneously; so picturesquely natural in manners; and wearing such a crust of primeval simplicity (which is quite polished away from the Northern black man), that they seemed a kind of creature by themselves, not altogether human, but quite as good, and akin to the fauns and rustic deities of olden times. I wonder whether I shall excite anybody's wrath by saying this. It is no great matter.

At all events, I felt most kindly towards these poor fugitives, but knew not precisely what to wish in their behalf, nor in the least how to help them. For the sake of the manhood which is latent in them, I would not have turned them back; but I should have felt almost as reluctant, on their own account, to hasten them forward to the stranger's land; and I think my prevalent idea was, that, whoever may be benefited by the results of this war, it will not be the present generation of Negroes, the childhood of whose race is now gone forever, and who must henceforth fight a hard battle with the world, on very unequal terms. On behalf of my own race, I am glad and can only hope that an inscrutable Providence means good to both parties.

While we drove onward, a young officer on horseback looked earnestly into the carriage, and recognized some faces that he had seen before; so he rode along by our side. . . . It seems to me that the war had brought good fortune to the youth of this epoch, if to none beside; since they now make it their daily business to ride a horse and handle a sword, instead of lounging listlessly through the duties, occupations, pleasures—all tedious alike—to which the artificial (nature of) society limits a peaceful generation. The atmosphere of the camp and the smoke of the battlefield are morally invigorating; the hardy virtues flourish in them, the nonsense dies like a wilted weed. The enervating effects of centuries of civilization vanish at once, and leave these young men to enjoy a life of hardship, and the exhilarating sense of danger—to kill men blamelessly, or to be killed gloriously—and to be happy in following out their native instincts of destruction, precisely in the spirit of Homer's heroes, only with some considerable change of mode.

Another of our excursions was to Harper's Ferry. . . . Immediately on the shore of the Potomac, and extending back towards the town, lay the dismal ruins of the United States arsenal and armory, consisting of piles of broken bricks and a waste of shapeless demolition, amid which we saw gun barrels in heaps of hundreds together. They were relics of the conflagration, bent with the heat of the fire and rusted with the wintry rain to which they had since been exposed. The brightest sunshine could not have made the scene cheerful, nor taken away the gloom from the dilapidated town; for, besides the natural shabbiness, and decayed, unthrifty look of a Virginian village, it has an inexpressible forlornness resulting from the devastation of war and its occupation by both armies alternately.

There was a small shop, which appeared to have nothing for sale. A single man and one or two boys were all the inhabitants in view, except the Yankee sentinels and soldiers, belonging to Massachusetts regiments, and who were scattered about pretty numerously. A guard house stood on the slope of the hill; and in the level street at its base were the offices of the Provost Marshall and other military authorities, to whom we forthwith reported ourselves.

The Provost Marshall kindly sent a corporal to guide us to the little building which John Brown seized upon as his fortress, and which, after it was stormed by the United States Marines, became his temporary prison. It is an old engine house, rusty and shabby, like every other work of man's hands in the God-forsaken town, and stands fronting upon the river, only a short distance from the bank, nearly at the point where the pontoon bridge touches the

Virginia shore. In its front wall, on each side of the door, are two or three ragged loopholes, which John Brown perforated for his defense, knocking out merely a brick or two, so as to give himself and his garrison a sight over their rifles. Through these orifices the sturdy old man dealt a good deal of deadly mischief among his assailants, until they broke down the door by thrusting against it with a ladder, and tumbled headlong in upon him.

From these and various excursions, and a good many others (including one to Manassas), we gained a pretty lively idea of what was going on; but, after all, if compelled to pass a rainy day in the hall and parlors of Willard's Hotel, it proved about as profitably spent as if we had floundered through miles of Virginia mud, in quest of interesting matter. This hotel, in fact, may be much more justly called the centre of Washington and the Union than either the Capitol, the White House, or the State Department. Everybody may be seen there.

It is the meeting place of the true representatives of the country—not such as are chosen blindly and amiss by electors who take a folded ballot from the hand of a local politician, and thrust it into the ballot box unread, but men who gravitate or are attracted hither by real business, or a native impulse to breathe the intensest atmosphere of the nation's life, or a genuine anxiety to see how this life-and-death struggle is going to deal with us. Nor these only, but all manner of loafers. Never, in any other spot, was there such a miscellany of people. You exchange nods with governors of sovereign States; you elbow illustrious men, and tread on the toes of generals; you hear statesmen and orators speaking in their familiar tones. You are mixed up with office–seekers, wire–pullers, inventors, artists, poets, prosers (including editors, army correspondents, attachés of foreign journals, and long-winded talkers), clerks, diplomatists, mail contractors, railway directors, until your own identity is lost among them.

We saw at Willard's many who had thus found out for themselves that, when Nature gives a young man no other utilizable faculty, she must be understood as intending him for a soldier. The bulk of the army had moved out of Washington before we reached the city; yet it seemed to us that at least two thirds of the guests and idlers at the hotel wore one or another token of the military profession. Many of them, no doubt, were self-commissioned officers, and put on the buttons and the shoulder straps, and booted themselves to the knees, merely because captain, in these days, is so good a travelling name. The majority, however, had been duly appointed by the President, but might be none the better warriors for that. It was pleasant, occasionally, to distinguish a grizzly veteran among this crowd of carpet-knights—the trained soldier of a lifetime, long ago from West Point, who had spent his prime upon the frontier, and very likely could show an Indian bullet-mark on his breast—if such decorations, won in an obscure warfare, were worth the showing now.

The question often occurred to me—and, to say the truth, it added an indefinable piquancy to the scene—what proportion of all these people, whether soldiers or civilians, were true at heart to the Union; and what part were tainted, more or less, with treasonable sympathies and wishes, even if such had never blossomed into purpose. Traitors there were among them—no doubt of that—civil servants of the public, very reputable persons, who yet deserved to dangle from a cord; or men who buttoned military coats over their breasts, hiding perilous secrets there, which might bring the gallant officer to stand pale-faced before a file of musketeers, with his open grave behind him.

But, without insisting upon such picturesque criminality and punishment as this, an observer, who kept both his eyes and heart open, would find it by no means difficult to discern that many residents and visitors of Washington so far sided with the South as to desire nothing more nor better than to see everything re-established a little worse than its former basis. If the cabinet of Richmond were transferred to the Federal city, and the North awfully snubbed, at least, and driven back within its old political limits, they would deem it a happy day.

It is no wonder, and, if we look at the matter generously, no unpardonable crime. Very excellent people hereabouts remember the many dynasties in which the Southern character has been predominant, and contrast the genial courtesy, the warm and graceful freedom of that region, with what they call (though I utterly disagree with them) the frigidity of our Northern manners, and the Western plainness of the President. They have a conscientious, though mistaken, belief that the South was driven out of the Union by intolerable wrong on our part, and that we are responsible for having compelled true patriots to love only half their country instead of the whole, and brave soldiers to draw their swords against the Constitution which they once would have died for;—to draw them, too, with a bitterness of animosity which is the only symptom of brotherhood (since brothers hate each other best) that any longer exists. They whisper these things with tears in their eyes, and shake their heads, and stoop their poor old shoulders, at the tidings of another and another Northern victory, which, in their opinion, puts farther off the remote, the already impossible, chance of a reunion.

I am sorry for them, though it is by no means a sorrow without hope. Since the matter has gone so far, there seems to be no way but to go on winning victories, and establishing peace and a truer union, in another generation, at the expense, probably, of greater trouble in the present one than any other people ever voluntarily suffered. We woo the South "as the lion woos his bride"; it is a rough courtship, but perhaps love and a quiet household may come of it at last.[1]

8　The Test of Men

Emerson deliberates on some of the more profound aspects of the war.

War, the searcher of character, the test of men, has tried already so many reputations, has pricked so many bladders. 'Tis like the financial crises which, once in ten or twenty years, come to try the men and institutions of trade; using, like them, no ceremony, but plain laws of gravity and force, to try tension and resistance. Scott, McDowell, McClellan, Fremont, Banks, Butler, and I know not how many more, are brought up, each in turn, dragged up irresistibly to the anthropometer, measured and weighed, and the result proclaimed to the universe.

With this dynamometer, and not so much that as *rack*, to try the tension of your muscles and bones standing close at hand, everybody takes the hint, drops much of brag and pretension, and shortens his speeches. The fop in the street, the beau at the ball, feels the war in the air—the examiner, the insatiate demand for reality—and becomes modest and serious. The writer is less florid, the wit is less fantastical. The epicure and the man of pleasure put some check or cover on their amusements. Everybody studies entrenchment and economy. Everybody bethinks himself how he shall behave, if worst should come to worst. It will not always serve, or may not, to stand aloof and contribute money. Should we carry on a war by subscription and politely? They will conquer who take up the bayonet, or leave their other business and apply themselves to the business of the war; the war searches character, and acquits those whom I acquit, whom life acquits, those whose reality and spontaneous honesty and singleness appear. Force it requires. 'Tis not so much that you are moral as that you are genuine, sincere, frank and bold. I do not approve those who give money or give their voices for liberty from long habit and the feminine predominance of sentiment, but the rough Democrat who hates Garrison, but detests those Southern traitors. The first class will go in the right way, but they are devoured by sentiments, like premature fruit ripened by the worm.

Much mischief from the Negro race. We pretend to christianize them, but they heathenize us.

The Supreme Court under Southern dictation pronounced that, "The Negro had no rights which the white man was bound to respect." To-day, by the rebellion, the same rule holds and is worked against the Southerner: "The rebel has no rights which Negro or white man is bound to respect." The world is upside down when this dictum comes from the Chief Justice of the Supreme Court of the United States of America.

The man McClellan ebbed like a sea.

I read a good sentence of General Scott's in the newspaper, that "resentment is a bad basis for a campaign."

The points that glowed a little in yesterday's conversation were that the North must succeed. That is sure; was sure for thirty or sixty years back; was in the education, culture, and climate of our people; they are bound to put through their undertakings. . . . Our success is sure. Its roots are in our poverty, our Calvinism, our schools, our thrifty habitual industry, in our snow, east wind, and farm life, and sea life. These able and generous merchants are the sons and grandsons of farmers and mechanics and sailors.

In the caprice and credulity of people, all these rumours and opinions take their rise, to which Whigs and statesmen and cities attach great weight, shaking their heads and looking grave. "But Kentucky, but Baltimore, but Wall Street, and State Street." "Aye, be sure we had not thought of that." The rumours, the opinions are allowed to have importance, and therefore we must wait, and Congress is justified and the President is right in caution, and in suspending his purpose. But by listening thus in here, and out there, to each new report, one is left in a chronic puzzle, and incapacity to move.

By and by, a strong wind of a battle or of one energetic mind appears, and the whole drift and scud, with all its forms of bears, mountains, and dragons, vanishes out of sight, and the plain way of reason and right reappears once and forever. Why did we not obey it? This, only this, persists to be, and is forever wisdom and power.

Now how many foreign or domestic opinions on our war shall I suffer from not knowing? I do not know that Lord Palmerston's or Lord Russell's opinion or existence is of the least importance.

You men who have come back have not lost your time. Certain truths have been imprinted on you. You have seen the world. You have learned somewhat of your country. Without dishonour you have seen Virginia and Carolina. It has been true, though people have tried to disguise it for years, that a man of the Free States could not travel on his necessary business in that country without seeing or hearing something on which it was necessary he should shut his eyes and his ears. If he said what he thought, he was certain of injury or insult; if he did not speak, he lost his own respect. You have been able to hear and see much disagreeable truth, without loss of your own honour. No one will hereafter be able to persuade you that no society is sweet and happy and enlightened unless it is founded on stealing.

You can teach us, and I know that your votes, your charities, your plans of life, and courses of action will draw incessantly on this painful experience of the last year. You have earned the freedom of this town and this State. We welcome you home to the houses and lands that are dear to you, to your old companions and to new friends. We shall never see you without respect and gratitude.

—These are they who bore our sins on their shoulders, and by their suffering we are at peace. Sweet are the uses of adversity, and I am sure that many a time in these weary weeks by night and by day, our quiet landscape, the silent river and the inland ponds and the plain house have loomed up in your fancy; and Fairhaven and Walden Pond, and Nine Acre Corner, and the East Quarter School-house, you would have given a month's wages to look upon.

I suppose the war does not recommend Slavery to anybody. If it cost ten years of war, and ten to recover the general prosperity, the destruction of Slavery is worth so much. But it does not cost so much time to get well again. How many times France has been a warfield! Every one of her towns has been sacked; the harvest has been a hundred times trampled down by armies. And yet, when you suppose, as after the first Napoleon's time, that the country must be desolate, a year's labour, a new harvest, almost the hours of one perfect summer day create prodigious wealth, and repair the damage of ten years of war.

Why are the people so sensitive about the reputation of General McClellan? There is always something rotten about a sensitive reputation. Besides, is not General McClellan an American citizen? And is not the attribute and distinction of an American to be abused and slandered as long as he is heard of?

Yesterday in town talked with George Sennott, Esq., who hoped the rumour true that Sigel had shot McDowell, for he liked that any man should shoot any other, as that showed character, whilst most men would do nothing, either good or bad, but only compromise and neutralize. He railed at Sumner, and thought the war had brought out only new New England men, Butler and Banks.

I grieve to see that the Government is governed by the hurrahs of the soldiers or the citizens. It does not lead opinion, but follows it.

Several urgent motives point to the Emancipation:

1. The eternal right of it.

2. The military necessity of creating an army in the rear of the enemy, and throughout his country, and even plantation, compelling him to disband his army, and rush home to protect his family and estate.

3. The danger of the adoption by the South of the policy of Emancipation.

France and England may peaceably recognize the Southern Confederacy, on the condition of Emancipation. Instantly we are thrown into falsest position. All Europe will back France and England in the act, because the cause of the South will then be the cause of Freedom, the cause of the North will be that of Slavery.

See the effect of recognition. It breaks at once the blockade. The South at once will acquire a navy, buying ships of France and England, and buying sailors and officers, too, if needed, of them, and will face us on the sea, and, at last protect themselves. Then our war is fruitless. Our enormous debt remains real. The Border States sympathize with the South, and, not wishing to pay this debt, join the South. Neither will California, Wisconsin, Minnesota care to pay the debt, but will secede. Utah combines with California, being always hostile to the States. The Mississippi Valley north and south combines to save the river. And an eastern tier of States is left to bear the load, and the load is too great, and the debt is repudiated.

Emancipation makes all this impossible. European governments dare not interfere for Slavery, as soon as the Union is pronounced for Liberty.

France says, I know very well the avoirdupois of the North, but it will not succeed, because it will not take this step (for Emancipation) to make its weight tell.[1]

Lowell writes a letter dated August 2.

But what shall one say? Who feels like asking more recruits to go down into McClellan's beautiful trap, from

which seventy thousand men can't get away? Hasn't he
pinned his army there like a bug in a cabinet? —Only you
don't have to *feed* your bug! I feel "blue as the blue
forget-me-not," and don't see how we are to be saved but
by a miracle, and miracles aren't wrought for folks without heads, at least since the time of St. Denys.[2]

*Hawthorne, while traveling in Maine, makes an entry in
his journal for August 15.*

It is a week ago, Saturday, since Julian and I reached
this place. . . .
At Hallowell, and subsequently all along our route, the
country was astir with volunteers, and the war is all that
seems to be alive—and even that doubtfully so. Nevertheless, the country certainly shows a good spirit, the towns
offering everywhere most liberal bounties, and every able-
bodied man feels an immense pull and pressure upon him
to go to the wars. I doubt whether any people were ever
actuated by more genuine and disinterested public spirit;
though, of course, it is not unalloyed with baser motives
and tendencies. We met a train of cars with a regiment or
two just starting for the war and apparently in high
spirits.
Everywhere some insignia of soldiership were to be
seen—buttons, a red stripe down the trousers, a military
cap; and sometimes, a round-shouldered bumpkin in the
entire uniform. They require a great deal to give them the
aspect of soldiers; indeed, it seems as if they needed a
good deal taken away and added, like the rough clay of a
sculptor as it grows to be a model. The whole talk of the
bar-rooms and every other place of intercourse was about
enlisting and the war—this being the very crisis of trial,
when the voluntary system is drawing to an end, and the
draft almost immediately to commence.[3]

*Emerson deals mainly with personal matters in a series of
letters dating from July 8 through August 5.*

The war drags on & drags us all into it, in some sort, by ourselves, our children, or our friends. Thus far I do not think it will have harmed you, and I hope it will not make more craving claims. But the adult generation seems to have for the most part yielded the point that the juniors must on this matter take their own course.

Mr. J. R. Lowell told me on Monday, that the message which came to Mrs. Lowell that her son was alive on Wednesday evening came from Nelson's Landing, & without a name, but from a rebel source. He was struck on Monday, by a shell, & sent his father word, then, that "he was dressing his company at the moment" (by way of signifying to his father that he was perfectly cool). The assurance that he was alive on Wednesday evening gives Dr. Wyman much hope of life.

You will have seen I suppose Army news, & learned that Capt. James Lowell was mortally wounded. He was left with the rebels & his fate is unknown here though Mrs. Lowell received a message from some unknown rebel source that he was alive on Wednesday night, after the Monday when he was struck by the shell. This leaves a little hope. In Concord we are to raise 22 men for the new forces, and I believe 8 have enlisted. At a town meeting we have agreed to pay $100. as a bounty to each recruit. . . .

I think we have no domestic news for you. Haven is a medical cadet, & at present in the "Euterpe," a hospital ship or boat in the James River. Charles writes from the Seventh Regiment, in Baltimore, in good spirits.

I read in a N. Y. paper that every road from Oregon to Washington Territory is filled with a solid column of emigrants going to the Salmon River mines—600 to 1000 passing daily from Lewistown to Florence . . . all forgetting us & our war.[4]

Holmes again pours out his feelings in a letter to Motley.

. . . There is a class of men one meets with who seem to consider it due to their antecedents to make the worst of everything. I suppose —— —— may be one of these. I met him a day or two since, and lost ten minutes in talk with him on the sidewalk; lost them, because I do not wish to talk with any man who looks at this matter empirically as an unlucky accident, which a little prudence might have avoided, and not a theoretical necessity. However, he said to me that the wisest man he knew . . . said to him long ago that this war would outlast him, an old man, and his companion also, very probably.

You meet another man, and he begins cursing the Government as the most tyrannical one that ever existed. "That is not the question," I answer. "How much money have you given for this war? How many of your boys have gone to it? How much of your own body and soul have you given to it?" I think Mr.—— ——is the most forlorn of all the Jeremiahs I meet with. *Faith,* faith is the only thing that keeps a man up in times like these; and those persons who, by temperament or under-feeding of the soul, are in a state of spiritual anaemia are the persons I like least to meet, and try hardest not to talk with.

For myself, I do not profess to have any political wisdom. I read, I listen, I judge to the best of my ability. The best talk I have heard from any of our home politicians was that of Banks, more than a year and a half ago. In a conversation I had with him, he foreshadowed more clearly the plans and prospects, and estimated more truly the resources, of the South than anyone else with whom I had met. But prophets in America and Europe have been at a very heavy discount of late. . . . If we could be sure of no intermeddling, I should have no anxiety except for individuals and for temporary interests. If we have grown unmanly and degenerate in the north wind, I am willing that the sirocco should sweep us off from the soil. If the course of nature must be reversed for us, and the Southern Goths must march to the "beggarly land of ice" to overrun and recolonize us, I have nothing to object. But I have a most solid and robust faith in the sterling manhood of the North, in its endurance, its capacity for a military training, its plasticity for every need, in education, in political equality, in respect for man as man in peaceful development, which is our law, in distinction from aggressive colonization; in human qualities as against bestial and diabolical ones; in the Lord as against the Devil.

If I never see peace and freedom in this land, I have faith that my children will see it. If they do not live long enough to see it, I believe their children will. The revelations we have had from the Old World have shed a new light for us on feudal barbarism. We know now where we are not to look for sympathy. But oh! it would have done your heart good to have seen the processions of day before yesterday and to-day, the air all aflame with flags, the streets shaking with the tramp of long-stretched lines, and only one feeling showing itself, the passion of the first great uprising, only the full flower of which that was the opening bud.

There is a defence of blubber about the arctic creatures through which the harpoon must be driven before the vital parts are touched. Perhaps the Northern sensibility is protected by some such encasing shield. The harpoon is, I think, at last through the blubber. In the meanwhile I feel no doubt in my own mind that the spirit of hostility to slavery as the cause of this war is speedily and certainly increasing. They were talking in the cars to-day of Fremont's speech at the Tremont Temple last evening. His allusions to slavery—you know what they must have been—were received with an applause which they never would have gained a little while ago. Nay, I think a miscellaneous Boston audience would be more like to cheer any denunciation of slavery now than almost any other sentiment.[5]

Bryant criticizes those Northerners who believed that only Richmond had to be captured to defeat the Confederacy.

They think, if this purpose can be accomplished, they will have disposed effectively of the rebellion, so that our distracted people may give themselves no further trouble about traitors or treason. Jefferson Davis and his Cabinet, when they see our armies approaching their stronghold, and likely to possess it, will, of course, remain in the place and surrender. They are too chivalric to run away out of the back door, and they will propose, as one of the terms of capitulation, to come into the Union again on the old terms. The whole bubble of revolt will then go out like a snuffed candle. The rebel armies will be dispersed, the rebel congress incontinently declared an abortion, or never to have come to birth, the rebel constitution be burnt at the four crossroads. . . .

An expectation of this sort alone accounts for the singular pertinacity with which the plan of the capture of Richmond has been pursued. General Scott first laid the egg, and incubated it all the time he was in command. It was the object of McDowell when he marched into the fatal snares of Bull Run; it was the sublime study of McClellan for eighteen months, when he undertook the campaign of the Peninsula, to carry it out—with what results we know. Pope was sent to the Rapidan to help him in the process; Burnside flung himself upon the sharp spikes back of Fredericksburg to attain it; and Hooker was enveloped in the wild destruction of Chancellorsville.

For the same end we have tried it in front, we have tried it from behind, we have tried it from the sides, and, though always in vain, though we have been repulsed a dozen times, and sacrificed five armies in the effort, the official mind at Washington still clings to it as the one thing needful. It will give up everything else, but Richmond it will not give up; it will allow Pennsylvania to be ravaged, but Richmond must be watched; it will call our young men from their shops and harvest-fields to defend the frontiers, but the veterans must keep their eyes on Richmond; it will even allow the political metropolis to be threatened by a hostile army, to be visited by a hostile cavalry, but it will not recall the troops who might defend the frontier and the capital, because they are squinting at the distance of forty or a hundred miles toward the in-trenchments of Richmond. It is our fixed idea, our enchant-ment, our pleasant illusion, our fatuity. . . .

But supposing us to get into Richmond—what then? We have no idea that the rebel cabinet keep a large amount of supplies in that city, or any which they would not carry off in the event of an assault. Their government itself is a migratory one, and would be just as valid and effective at Knoxville, or Petersburg, or Montgomery, as it is in the present location.

By the capture of Richmond, therefore, we should drive Jefferson Davis and his followers somewhere else, and possess one more Virginian town, difficult to hold and of little use to us, ever so well held. It is the centre, it is true, of an important railroad system, but not of an indis-pensable railroad system. The same communications can be made elsewhere, if not with the same facility, at least with certainty.

But, if Richmond were of ten times the importance that it is, the capture of it would not compensate us for the loss of Washington, which would carry with it certainly the loss of Baltimore, and perhaps that of Philadelphia. Not a solitary man should be spared to the former object so long as a single doubt exists of the perfect security of our seat of Government.

Suppose that Lee should overcome Meade and march upon Washington: what satisfaction would it be to be told that General Dix had invested Richmond? Suppose Meade defeated: would the people of the country ever forgive the administration? Does it imagine that the awful failure to re-inforce Hooker, at the critical moment, on the Rap-pahannock, can be repeated? It knows better; it knows that it will be handled with a severity that has as yet no parallel in our annals if it commits that mistake a second time; and hence we infer that it is absolutely sure of success on the Potomac, or it would not authorize enterprises on the Pamunkey. . . .[6]

9 Search for a Wounded Captain

Holmes tells of his search for his wounded son, Oliver Wendell Jr., and at the same time describes the effects of the war on parts of southern Pennsylvania and northern Maryland.

In the dead of the night which closed upon the bloody field of Antietam, my household was startled from its slumbers by the loud summons of a telegraphic messenger. The air had been heavy all day with rumors of battle, and thousands and tens of thousands had walked the streets with throbbing hearts, in dread anticipation of the tidings any hour might bring.

We rose hastily, and presently the messenger was admitted. I took the envelope from his hand, opened it, and read:

Hagerstown 17th

To —— H——
Capt H —— was wounded shot through the neck thought not mortal at Keedysville

WILLIAM G LEDUC

Through the neck—no bullet left in wound. Windpipe, foodpipe, carotid, jugular, half a dozen smaller, but still formidable, vessels, a great braid of nerves, each as big as a lamp-wick, spinal cord—ought to kill at once, if at all. *Thought not* mortal, or *not thought* mortal—which was it? The first; that is better than the second would be; —"Keedysville, a post office, Washington Co, Maryland." Leduc? Leduc? Don't remember that name. The boy is waiting for his money. A dollar and thirteen cents. Has nobody got thirteen cents? Don't keep that boy waiting—how do we know what messages he has got to carry?

The boy *had* another message to carry. It was to the father of Lieutenant Colonel Wilder Dwight, informing him that his son was grievously wounded in the same battle, and was lying at Boonesborough, a town a few miles this side of Keedysville. This I learned the next morning from the civil and attentive officials at the Central Telegraph Office.

Calling upon this gentleman, I found that he meant to leave in the quarter past two o'clock train, taking with him Dr. George H. Gray, an accomplished and energetic surgeon, equal to any difficult question or pressing emergency. I agreed to accompany them, and we met in the cars. I felt myself peculiarly fortunate in having companions whose society would be a pleasure, whose feelings would harmonize with my own, and whose assistance I might, in case of need, be glad to claim.

I set out with a full and heavy heart, though many times chilled with what were perhaps needless and unwise fears, though I broke through all my habits without thinking about them, which is almost as hard in certain circumstances as for one of our young fellows to leave his sweetheart and go into a Peninsular campaign.

Not long after leaving Philadelphia, we passed a solitary sentry keeping guard over a short railroad bridge. It was the first evidence that we were approaching the perilous borders, the marshes where the North and the South mingle their angry hosts, where the extremes of our so-called civilization meet in conflict, and the fierce slave-driver of the Lower Mississippi stares into the stern eyes of the forest–feller from the banks of the Aroostook. All the way along, the bridges were guarded more or less strongly. In a vast country like ours, communications play a far more complex part than in Europe, where the whole territory available for strategic purposes is so comparatively limited.

There was nothing worthy of special note in the trip to Frederick, except our passing a squad of Rebel prisoners, whom I missed seeing as they flashed by, but who were said to be a most forlorn-looking crowd of scarecrows. Arrived at the Monacacy River, about three miles this side of Frederick, we came to a halt, for the railroad bridge had been blown up by the Rebels, and its iron pillars and arches were lying in the bed of the river. The unfortunate wretch who fired the train was killed by the explosion, and lay buried hard by, his hands sticking out of the shallow grave into which he had been huddled.

There was a great confusion of carriages and wagons at the stopping place of the train, so that it was a long time before I could get anything that would carry us. At last I was lucky enough to light on a sturdy wagon, drawn by a pair of serviceable bays, and driven by James Grayden with whom I was destined to have a somewhat continued acquaintance. We took up a little girl who had been in Baltimore during the late Rebel inroad. It made me think of the time when my own mother, at that time six years old, was hurried off from Boston, then occupied by the British soldiers, to Newburyport, and heard the people saying that "the redcoats were coming, killing and murdering everybody as they went along."

Frederick looked cheerful for a place that had so recently been in an enemy's hands. There and there a house or shop was shut up, but the national colors were waving in all directions, and the general aspect was peaceful and contented. I saw no bullet marks or other signs of the fighting which had gone on in the streets. The Colonel's lady was taken in charge by a daughter of that hospitable family to which we had been commended, and I proceeded to inquire for wounded officers at the various temporary hospitals.

At the United States Hotel, where many were lying, I heard mention of an officer in an upper chamber, and, going there, found Lieutenant Abbot, of the Twentieth Massachusetts Volunteers, lying ill with what looked like typhoid fever. While there, who should come in but the almost ubiquitous Lieutenant Wilkins, of the same Twentieth, whom I had met repeatedly before on errands of kindness or duty, and who was just from the battle ground. He was going to Boston in charge of the body of the lamented Dr. Revere, the Assistant Surgeon of the regiment, killed on the field.

From his lips, I learned something of the mishaps of the regiment. My Captain's wound he spoke of as less grave than at first thought; but he mentioned incidentally having heard a story recently that he was *killed*—a fiction, doubtless—a mistake—a palpable absurdity—not to be remembered or made any account of. Oh, no! but what dull ache is this where the nervous centre called the *semilunar ganglion* lies unconscious of itself until a great grief or a mastering anxiety reaches it through all the non-conductors which isolate it from ordinary impressions?

I talked awhile with Lieutenant Abbot, who lay prostrate, feeble, but soldier–like and uncomplaining, carefully waited upon by a most excellent lady, a captain's wife, New England born, loyal as the Liberty on a golden ten-dollar piece, and of lofty bearing enough to have sat for that Goddess's portrait. She had stayed in Frederick through the Rebel inroad, and kept the star-spangled banner where it would be safe, to unroll it as the last Rebel hoofs clattered off from the pavement of the town.

And now, as we emerged from Frederick, we struck at once upon the trail from the great battle-field. The road was filled with straggling and wounded soldiers. All who could travel on foot—multitudes with slight wounds of the upper limbs, the head, or face—were told to take up their beds—a light burden or none at all—and walk. Just as the

battlefield sucks everything into its red vortex for the conflict, so does it drive everything off in long, diverging rays
after the fierce centripetal forces have met and neutralized
each other.

For more than a week there had been sharp fighting
all along this road. Through the streets of Frederick,
through Crampton's Gap, over South Mountain, sweeping
at last the hills and the woods that skirt the windings of
the Antietam, the long battle had travelled, like one of
those tornadoes which tear their path through our fields
and villages. The slain of higher condition, "embalmed"
and iron-cased, were sliding off on the railways to their far
homes; the dead of the rank and file were being gathered up
and committed hastily to the earth; the gravely wounded
were cared for hard by the scene of conflict, or pushed a
little way along to the neighboring villages; while those
who could walk were meeting us, as I have said, at every
step in the road.

It was a pitiable sight, truly pitiable, yet so vast, so
far beyond the possibility of relief, that many single sor-
rows of small dimensions have wrought upon my feelings
more than the sight of this great caravan of maimed pil-
grims. The companionship of so many seemed to make a
joint stock of their suffering; it was next to impossible to
individualize it, and so bring it home, as one can do with a
single broken limb or aching wound. Then they were all of
the male sex, and in the freshness or the prime of their
strength. Though they tramped so wearily along, yet there
was rest and kind nursing in store for them. These wounds
they bore would be the medals they would show children
and grandchildren by and by. Who would not rather wear
his decorations beneath his uniform than on it?

Yet among them were figures which arrested our attention and sympathy. Delicate boys, with more spirit than
strength, flushed with fever or pale with exhaustion or
haggard with suffering, dragged their weary limbs along
as if each step would exhaust their slender store of
strength. At the roadside sat or lay others, quite spent

with their journey. Here and there was a house at which the wayfarers could stop, in the hope, I fear often vain, of getting refreshment; and in one place was a clear, cool spring, where the little hands of the long procession halted for a few moments, as the trains that traverse the desert rest by its fountains.

My companions had brought a few peaches with them, which the Philanthropist bestowed upon the tired and thirsty soldiers with a satisfaction which we all shared. I had with me a small flask of strong waters, to be used as a medicine in case of inward grief. From this, also, he dispensed relief, without hesitation, to a poor fellow who looked as if he needed it. I rather admired the simplicity with which he applied my limited means of solace to the first-comer who wanted it more than I; a genuine benevolent impulse does not stand on ceremony, and had I perished of colic for want of a stimulus that night, I should not have reproached my friend the Philanthropist, any more than I grudged my other ardent friend the two dollars and more which it cost me to send the charitable message he left in my hands.

At intervals, a dead horse lay by the roadside, or in the fields unburied, not grateful to gods or men; I saw no bird of prey, no ill-omened fowl, on my way to the carnival of death, or at the place where it had been held . . . no black wing was spread over these animal ruins, and no call to the banquet pierced through the heavy-laden and sickening air.

Full in the middle of the road, caring little for whom or what they met, came long strings of army wagons, returning empty from the front after supplies. I liked the looks of these equipages and their drivers; they meant business. Drawn by mules mostly, six, I think, to a wagon, powdered well with dust—wagon, beast, and driver, they came jogging along the road, turning neither to right nor left—some driven by bearded, solemn white men, some by careless, saucy-looking Negroes, of a blackness like that of anthracite or obsidian. . . . Sometimes a mule would give out on the road; then he was left where he lay, until by and by he would think better of it, and get up, when the first public wagon that came along would hitch him on and restore him to the sphere of duty.

On Sunday morning, the twenty–first, having engaged James Grayden and his team, I set out with the Chaplain and the Philanthropist for Keedysville. Our track lay through the South Mountain Gap, and led us first to the town of Boonesborough, where, it will be remembered Colonel Dwight had been brought after the battle. We saw the positions occupied in the battle of South Mountain, and many traces of the conflict. In one situation a group of young trees was marked with shot, hardly one having escaped.

As we walked by the side of the wagon, the Philanthropist left us for a while and climbed a hill, where, along the line of a fence, he found traces of the most desperate fighting.

A ride of some three hours brought us to Boonesborough, where I roused the unfortunate army surgeon who had charge of the hospitals, and who was trying to get a little sleep after his fatigues and watchings. He bore his cross very creditably, and helped me to explore all places where my soldier might be lying among the crowds of wounded. After the useless search, I resumed my journey, fortified with a note of introduction to Dr. Letterman; also with a bale of oakum which I was to carry to that Gentleman, this substance being employed as a substitute for lint. We were obliged also to procure a pass to Keedysville from the Provost Marshal of Boonesborough. As we came near the place, we learned that General McClellan's headquarters had been removed from this village some miles farther to the front.

On entering the small settlement of Keedysville, there were some thousands of wounded in the place, he told me, scattered about everywhere. It would be a long job to hunt up my Captain; the only way would be to go to every house and ask for him. Just then a medical officer came up.

"Do you know anything of Captain H. of the Massachusetts Twentieth?"

"Oh yes; he is staying in that house. I saw him there, doing very well."

A chorus of hallelujahs arose in my soul, but I kept them to myself. Now, then, for our twice-wounded volunteer, our young centurion whose double-barred shoulder straps we have never yet looked upon. Let us observe the proprieties, however; no swelling upward of the mother— no *hysterica passio*—we do not like scenes. A calm salutation—then swallow and hold hard. That is about the programme.

A cottage of squared logs, filled in with plaster, and white-washed. A little yard before it, with a gate swinging. The door of the cottage ajar—no one visible as yet. I push open the door and enter. An old woman, Margaret Kitxmuller her name proves to be, is the first person I see.

"Captain H. here?"

"Oh no, sir—he left yesterday morning for Hagerstown—in a milk-cart."

But there was the great battle-field only about three miles from Keedysville.

We followed the road through the village for a space, then turned off to the right, and wandered somewhat vaguely, for want of precise directions, over the hills. Inguiring as we went, we forded a wide creek in which soldiers were washing their clothes, the name of which we did not then know, but which must have been the Antietam. At one point we met a party, women among them, bringing off various trophies they had picked up on the battlefield. Still wandering along, we were at last pointed to a hill in the distance, a part of the summit of which was covered with Indian corn. There, we were told, some of the fiercest fighting of the day had been done. The fences were taken down so as to make a passage across the fields, and the tracks worn within the last few days looked like old roads. We passed a fresh grave under a tree near the road. A board was nailed to the tree, bearing the name, as well as I could make it out, of Gardiner, of a New Hampshire regiment.

On coming near the brow of the hill, we met a party carrying picks and spades. "How many?" "Only one." The dead were nearly all buried, then, in this region of the field of strife. We stopped the wagon, and, getting out, began to look around us. Hard by was a large pile of muskets, scores, if not hundreds, which had been picked up, and were guarded for the Government. A long ridge of fresh gravel rose before us. A board stuck up in front of it bore this inscription, the first part of which was, I believe, not correct: "The Rebel General Anderson and 80 Rebels are buried in this hole."

Other smaller ridges were marked with the number of dead lying under them. The whole ground was strewn with fragments of clothing, haversacks, canteens, cap boxes, bullets, cartridges, scraps of paper, portions of bread and meat. I saw two soldiers' caps that looked as though their owners had been shot through the head. In several places I noticed dark red patches where a pool of blood had curdled and caked, as some poor fellow poured his life out on the sod. I then wandered about in the cornfield. It surprised me to notice, that, though there was every mark of hard fighting having taken place here, the Indian corn was not generally trodden down.

One of our cornfields is a kind of forest, and even when fighting, men avoid the tall stalks as if they were trees. At the edge of this cornfield lay a gray horse, said to have belonged to a Rebel colonel, who was killed near the same place. Not far off were two dead artillery horses in their harness. Another had been attended to by a burying-party, who had thrown some earth over him; but his last bedclothes were too short, and his legs stuck out stark and stiff from beneath the gravel coverlet.

It was a great pity that we had no intelligent guide to explain to us the position of that portion of the two armies which fought over this ground. There was a shallow trench before we came to the cornfield, too narrow for a road, as I should think, too elevated for a watercourse, and which seemed to have been used as a rifle pit. At any rate, there had been hard fighting in and about it. This and the corn-field may serve to identify the part of the ground we visited, if any who fought there should ever look over this paper. The opposing tides of battle must have blended their waves at this point, for portions of gray uniform were mingled with the "garments rolled in blood" torn from our own dead and wounded soldiers.

I picked up a Rebel canteen, and one of our own—but there was something repulsive about the trodden and stained relics of the stale battlefield. It was like the table of some hideous orgy left uncleared, and one turned away dis-gusted from its broken fragments and muddy heeltaps. A bullet or two, a button, a brass plate from a soldier's belt served well enough for mementos of my visit, with a letter which I picked up, directed to Richmond, Virginia, its seal unbroken. "N. C., Cleveland County, E. Wright to J. Wright." On the other side, "A few lines from W. L. Vaughn," who has just been writing for the wife to her husband and continues on his own account. The postscript, "tell John that nancy's folks are all well and has a very good little Crop of corn a growing."

I wonder, if, by one of those strange chances of which I have seen so many, this number or leaf of the "Atlantic" will not sooner or later find its way to Cleveland County, North Carolina, and E. Wright, widow of James Wright, and Nancy's folks, get from these sentences the last glimpse of husband and friend as he threw up his arms and fell in the bloody cornfield of Antietam? I will keep this stained letter for them until peace comes back, if it comes in my time.

Lieutenant P——, of the Pennsylvania——th, was a very fresh, bright-looking young man, lying in bed from the effects of a recent injury received in action. A grape-shot, after passing through a post and a board, had struck him in the hip, bruising, but not penetrating or breaking. He had good news for me.

That very afternoon, a party of wounded officers had

passed through Harrisburg, going East. He had conversed
in the bar–room of this hotel with one of them, who was
wounded about the shoulder (it might be the lower part of
the neck), and had his arm in a sling. He belonged to the
Twentieth Massachusetts; the Lieutenant saw that he was
a Captain, by the two bars on his shoulder strap. His name
was my family name; he was tall and youthful, like my
Captain. At four o'clock he had left in the train for Philadelphia. . . .

What more could I ask to assure me of the Captain's
safety? As soon as the telegraph office opens to-morrow
morning we will send a message to our friends in Philadelphia, and get a reply, doubtless, which will settle the whole
matter.

The hopeful morrow dawned at last, and the following
reply was received:

> "Phil sept 24 I think the report you have heard
> that W has gone East must be an error we have not
> seen or heard of him here MLH"

He *could* not have passed through Philadelphia without visiting the house called Beautiful, where he had been
so tenderly cared for after his wound at Ball's Bluff, and
where those whom he loved were lying in grave peril of life
or limb. Yet *did* he pass through Harrisburg, going East,
going to Philadelphia, on his way home? Ah, this is it! He
must have taken the late night train from Philadelphia for
New York, in his impatience to reach home. There is such a
train, not down in the guide book, but we are assured of
the fact at the Harrisburg depot.

By and by came the reply from Dr. Wilson's tele-
graphic message: nothing had been heard of the Captain at
Chambersburg. Still later, another message came from our
Philadelphia friend, saying he was last seen at the house of
Mrs. K, a well–known Union lady in Hagerstown. . . . A
telegram was at once sent to Mrs. K.—asking information.
But when the answer would be received was uncertain, as
the Government almost monopolized the line. . . .

Ten o'clock in the evening was approaching. The telegraph office would presently close, and as yet there were no tidings from Hagerstown. Let us step over and see for ourselves. A message! A message!

"Captain H. still here leaves tomorrow for Harrisburg Penna Is doing well

Mrs H K

A note from Dr. Cuyler to the same effect came soon afterwards to the hotel. . . . We shall sleep well to-night. . . .

The time approached for the train to arrive from Hagerstown, and we went to the station.

The expected train came in so quietly that I was almost startled to see it on the track. Let us walk calmly through the cars, and look around us.

In the first car, on the fourth seat to the right, I saw my Captain; there saw I him, even my first-born, whom I had sought through many cities.

"How are you, Boy?"

"How are you, Dad?"

Such are the proprieties of life, as they are observed among us Anglo-Saxons of the nineteen century, decently disguising those natural impulses that made Joseph, the Prime Minister of Egypt, weep aloud so that the Egyptians and the house of Pharaoh heard—nay which had once overcome his shaggy old uncle Esau so entirely that he fell on his brother's neck and cried like a baby, in the presence of all the women. But the hidden cisterns of the soul may be filling fast with sweet tears, while the windows through which it looks are undimmed by a drop or a film of moisture.

These are times in which we cannot live solely for selfish joys or griefs. I had not let fall the hand I held, when a sad, calm voice addressed me by name. I fear that at the moment I was too much absorbed in my own feelings; for certainly at any other time I should have yielded myself without stint to the sympathy which this meeting might well call forth.

"You remember my son, Cortland Saunders, whom I brought to see you once in Boston?"

"I do remember him well."

"He was killed on Monday, at Shepherdstown. I am carrying his body back with me on this train. He was my only child. If you could come to my house—I can hardly call it my home now—it would be a pleasure to me."

This young man, belonging in Philadelphia, was the author of a *New System of Latin Paradigms,* a work showing extraordinary scholarship and capacity. It was this book which first made me acquainted with him, and I kept him in my memory, for there was genius in the youth. . . .

He was a dark, still, slender person, always with a trance-like remoteness, a mystic dreaminess of manner, such as I never saw in any other youth. . . . For such a young man, seemingly destined for the inner life of contemplation, to be a soldier seemed almost unnatural. Yet he spoke to me of his intention to offer himself to his country, and his blood must now be reckoned among the precious sacrifices which will make her soil sacred forever. Had he lived, I doubt not that he would have redeemed the rare promise of his earlier year. He has done better, for he has died that unborn generations may attain the hopes held out to our nation and to mankind. . . .

The source of my repeated disappointments was soon made clear enough. The Captain had gone to Hagerstown, intending to take the cars at once for Philadelphia, as his three friends actually did, and as I took it for granted he certainly would. But as he walked languidly along, some ladies saw him across the street, and seeing, were moved with pity, and pitying, spoke such soft words that he was tempted to accept their invitation and rest awhile beneath their hospitable roof. The mansion was old, as the dwellings of gentlefolks should be; the ladies were some of them young, and all were full of kindness; there were gentle cares, and unasked luxuries, and pleasant talk, and music–

sprinklings from the piano, with a sweet voice to keep them company—and all this after the swamps of the Chickahominy, the mud and flies of Harrison's Landing, the dragging marches, the desperate battles, the fretting wound, the jolting ambulance, the log-house and the ricketty milk cart! Thanks, uncounted thanks to the angelic ladies whose charming attentions detained him from Saturday to Thursday, to his great advantage and my infinite bewilderment! As for his wound, how could it do otherwise than well under such hands? The bullet had gone smoothly through, dodging everything but a few nervous branches, which would come right in time and leave him as well as ever.[1]

10   *Emerson's Emancipation Proclamation*

Emerson comments on the Proclamation of Emancipation when it was first promulgated by President Lincoln, in September, 1862.

The Proclamation has defined every man's position. In reading every speech, or any sentence of any speech, but a few words show at once the animus of the men, show them friends of Slavery; show us that the battleground is fast changing from Richmond to Boston. They unmask themselves, and though we tried to think them free men, they are not. Look where they rage at Sumner. They find not Lincoln, for they do not think him really anti–slavery, but the abolitionist they find in Sumner, and him they hate. If Sumner were pro–slavery, there would be no chemical analysis and magnifying glass to exhibit his foibles.

It seems to promise an extension of the war. For there can be no durable peace, no sound Constitution, until we have fought this battle, and the rights of man are vindicated. It were to patch a peace to cry Peace whilst this vital difference exists.

In so many arid forms which States incrust themselves with, once in a century, if so often, a poetic act and record occur. These are the jets of thought into affairs, when, roused by danger or inspired by genius, the political leaders of the day break the else insurmountable routine of class and local legislation, and take a step forward in the direction of catholic and universal interests. Every step in the history of political liberty is a sally of the human mind into the untried Future, and has the interest of genius, and is fruitful in heroic anecdotes. Liberty is a slow fruit. It comes, like religion, for short periods, and in rare conditions, as if awaiting a culture of the race which shall make it organic and permanent.[1]

The extreme moderation with which the President advanced his design—his long-avowed expectant policy, as if he chose to be strictly the executive of the best public sentiment of the country, waiting only till it should be unmistakenly pronounced—so fair a mind that none ever listened so patiently to such extreme varieties of opinion—so reticent that his decision has taken all parties by surprise, whilst yet it is just the sequel of his prior acts—the firm tone in which he announces it, without inflation or surplusage—all these have bespoken such favor to the act, that, great as the popularity of the President has been, we are beginning to think that we have underestimated the capacity and virtue which the Divine Providence has made an instrument of benefit so vast. He has been permitted to do more for America than any other American man. He is well entitled to the most indulgent construction. Forget all that we thought shortcomings, every mistake, every delay. In the extreme embarrassments of his part, call these endurance, wisdom, magnanimity; illuminated, as they now are, by this dazzling success.

When we consider the immense opposition that has been neutralized or converted by the progress of the war (for it is not long since the President anticipated the resignation of a large number of officers in the army, and the secession of three States, on the promulgation of this policy)—when we see how the great stake which foreign nations hold in our affairs has recently brought every European power as a client into this court, and it became every day more apparent what gigantic and what remote interests were to be affected by the decision of the President—one can hardly say the deliberation was too long. Against all timorous counsels he had the courage to seize the moment; and such was his position, and such the felicity attending the action, that he has replaced Government in the good graces of mankind.

"Better is virtue in the sovereign than plenty in the season," say the Chinese. 'Tis wonderful what power is, and how ill it is used, and how its ill use makes life mean, and the sunshine dark. Life in America had lost much of its attraction in the later years. The virtues of a good magistrate undo a world of mischief, and, because Nature works with rectitude, seem vastly more potent than the acts of bad governors, which are ever tempered by the good nature in the people, and the incessant resistance which fraud and violence encounter. The acts of good governors work a geometrical ratio, as one midsummer day seems to repair the damage of a year of war.

A day which most of us dared not hope to see, an event worth the dreadful war, worth its cost and uncertainties, seems now to be close before us. October, November, December will have passed over beating hearts and plotting brains; then the hour will strike, and all men of African descent who have faculty enough to find their way to our lines are assured of the protection of American law.

It is by no means necessary that this measure should be suddenly marked by any signal results on the Negroes or on the Rebel masters. The force of the act is that it commits the country to this justice—that it compels the innumerable officers, civil, military, naval, of the Republic to range themselves on the line of this equity. It draws the fashion to this side. It is not a measure that admits of being taken back. Done, it cannot be undone by a new Administration.

For slavery overpowers the disgust of the moral sentiment only through immemorial usage. It cannot be introduced as an improvement of the nineteenth century. This act makes that the lives of our heroes have not been sacri-

ficed in vain. It makes a victory of our defeats. Our hurts
are healed; the health of the nation is repaired. With a victory like this, we can stand many disasters. It does not
promise the redemption of the black race; that lies not
with us: but it relieves it of our opposition.

The President by this act has paroled all the slaves in
America; they will not more fight against us; and it relieves our race once for all of its crime and false position.
The first condition of success is secured in putting ourselves right. We have recovered ourselves from our false
position, and placed ourselves on a law of Nature. . . .
The Government has assured itself of the best constituency
in the world: every spark of intellect, every virtuous feeling, every religious heart, every man of honor, every poet,
every philosopher, the generosity of the cities, the health
of the country, the strong arms of the mechanic, the endurance of the farmers, the passionate conscience of
women, the sympathy of distant nations—all rally to its
support.

Of course, we are assuming the firmness of the policy
thus declared. It must not be a paper proclamation. We
confide that Mr. Lincoln is in earnest, and, as he has been
slow in making up his mind, has resisted the importunacy
of parties and of events to the latest moment, he will be as
absolute in his adhesion. Not only will he repeat and follow
up his stroke, but the nation will add its irresistible
strength. If the ruler has duties, so has the citizen. In times
like these, when the nation is imperilled, what man can,
without shame, receive good news from day to day without
giving good news of himself? What right has anyone to
read in the journals tidings of victories, if he has not
bought them by his own valor, treasure, personal sacrifice,
or by service as good in his own department? With this
blot removed from our national honor, this heavy load
lifted off the national heart, we shall not fear hencefor-
ward to show our faces among mankind. We shall cease to
be hypocrites and pretenders, but what we have styled our
free institutions will be such.

In the light of this event the public distress begins to be removed. What if the brokers' quotations show our stocks discredited, and the gold dollar costs one hundred and twenty–seven cents? These tables are fallacious. Every acre in the Free States gained substantial value on the twenty–second of September. The cause of disunion and war has been reached and begun to be removed. Every man's house–lot and garden are relieved of the malaria which the purest winds and strongest sunshine could not penetrate and purge. The territory of the Union shines to–day with a lustre which every European emigrant can discern from far; a sign of inmost security and permanence.

Whilst we have pointed out the opportuneness of the Proclamation, it remains to be said that the President had no choice. He might look wistfully for what variety of courses lay open to him; every line but one was closed up with fire. This one, too, bristled with danger, but through it was the sole safety. The measure he has adopted was imperative. It is wonderful to see the unseasonable senility of what is called the Peace Party, through all its masks, blinding their eyes to the main feature of the war, namely, its inevitableness. The war existed long before the cannonade of Sumter, and could not be postponed. It might have begun otherwise or elsewhere, but war was in the minds and bones of the combatants; it was written on the iron leaf; and you might as easily dodge gravitation.

If we had consented to a peaceable secession of the Rebels, the divided sentiment of the Border States made peaceable secession impossible, the insatiable temper of the South made it impossible, and the slaves on the border, wherever the border might be, were an incessant fuel to rekindle the fire. Give the Confederacy New Orleans, Charleston, and Richmond, and they would have demanded St. Louis and Baltimore. Give them these, and they would have insisted on Washington. Give them Washington, and they would have assumed the army and navy, and, through these, Philadelphia, New York, and Boston.

It looks as if the battlefield would have been at least as large in that event as it is now. The war was formidable, but could not be avoided. The war was and is an immense mischief, but brought with it the immense benefit of drawing a line and rallying the Free States to fix it impassably—preventing the whole force of Southern connection and influence throughout the North from distracting every city with endless confusion, detaching that force and reducing it to handfuls, and, in the progress of hostilities, disinfecting us of our habitual proclivity, through the affection of trade and the traditions of the Democratic party, to following Southern leading.

These necessities which have dictated the conduct of the Federal Government are overlooked especially by our foreign critics. The popular statement of the opponents of the war abroad is the impossibility of our success. "If you could add," they say, "to your strength the whole army of England, of France and of Austria, you could not coerce eight millions of people to come under this Government and against their will."

This is an odd thing for an Englishman, a Frenchman, or an Austrian to say, who remembers Europe of the last seventy years—the condition of Italy, until 1859;—of Poland, since 1793;—of France, of French Algiers;—of British Ireland, and British India.

But granting the truth, rightly read, of the historical aphorism, that "the people always conquer," it is to be noted that, in the Southern States, the tenure of land and the local laws, with slavery, give the social system not a democratic but an aristocratic complexion; and those states have shown every year a more hostile and aggressive temper, until the instinct of self–preservation forced us into the war. And the aim of the war on our part is indicated by the aim of the President's Proclamation, namely, to break up the false combination of Southern society, to destroy the piratic feature in which it makes our enemy only as it is the enemy of the human race, and so allow its reconstruction on a just and healthful basis. Then new affinities will act, the old repulsions will cease, and, the cause of war being removed, Nature and trade may be trusted to establish a lasting peace.

We think we cannot overstate the wisdom and benefit of this act of Government. The malignant cry of the Secession press within the Free States, and the recent action of the Confederate Congress, are decisive as to its efficiency and correctness of aim. Not less so is the silent joy which has greeted it in all generous hearts, and the new hope it has breathed into the world.

It was well to delay the steamers at the wharves until this edict could be put on board. It will be an insurance to the ship as it goes plunging through the sea with glad tidings to all people. Happy are the young, who find the pestilence cleansed out of the earth, leaving to them an honest career. Happy the old, who see Nature purified before they depart. Do not let the dying die: hold them back to this world, until you have charged their ear and heart with the message to other spiritual societies, announcing the melioration of our planet. . . .

Meantime that ill–fated, much–injured race which the Proclamation respects will lose somewhat of the dejection sculptured for ages in their bronze countenance, uttered in the wailing of their plaintive music—a race naturally benevolent, docile, industrious, and whose very miseries sprang from their great talent for usefulness, which, in a more moral age, will not only defend their independence, but will give them a rank among nations.[2]

11 Digging Down to the Pan

Lanier writes from his camp at Petersburg, Va., September 10, 1862.

Events have followed each other in such rapid succession, here, that I am dazzled, and, under the influence of exultant feelings, can hardly form a sober opinion in regard to the future—Jackson, Longstreet, A. P. Hill, and D. H. Hill, with their respective corps, are across the Potomac, and are reported, in this morning's papers, at the Relay House— In the same report, Lee is said to occupy Arlington Heights— These are only well–founded rumors; but our brave fellows have accomplished such astonishing things lately, that unbounded credulity in regard to their rumored exploits seems to be, on the whole, about as safe a policy as the most captious skepticism— If the two reports which I have just mentioned be true, the fall of Washington is inevitable— And after the fall of Washington—? Perhaps Peace! I somehow feel a presentiment of great events: at any rate, I had as lief utter, nowadays, the wildest and most visionary prophecy, as the most guarded speculation: for the former has at least the charm of *daring,* and is as likely of fulfillment as the latter— [1]

Whitman gives an account of the fighting that took place at a bridge over the Antietam Creek, September 17.

This was a stone bridge over Antietam Creek, in a position naturally almost impregnable and fortified by the rebels. Orders were given to carry this point at all hazards, and the work was deputed to the 51st New York and the 51st Pennsylvania. At 1 o'clock these regiments made a charge with the bayonet, carrying this through with a determination and courage never surpassed. They cleared the bridge, gained the opposite side and held it, in the contest losing a large number of officers and men, the 51st going on picket on the hill in advance.[2]

Lanier reports to his father on the purchase of uniforms for himself and his brother.

We have engaged a uniform suit of the Corps, consisting of gray double–breasted frock coat, vest and pants, for Thirty Dollars a piece: also a pair of shoes for Ten Dollars— The Suit is by far the cheapest one we could procure: we are confident it will be a good investment, as it is made of very thick gray cloth, which was purchased by one of our Lieutenants for the Corps, in the mountains of Virginia—and is at least thirty Dollars cheaper than any other suit that could be obtained— The shoes are less than half of what we would have to pay for them in Petersburg: they are to be made by one of the Corps who was at our station, and got detached to go to his home at Salem (above Lynchburg) for the purpose of making shoes for the Corps. So that, in the course of ten days we shall need at least Forty Dollars apiece—

You cannot imagine, My dear Pa, with how much reluctance we call upon you for so much money— You would doubtless be amused if I could record for you the proceedings of the innumerable councils of War which Cliff and I have held on the subject: the investigations we have instituted as to prices, and the calculations we have made: with the thousand wild projects, successively named and abandoned, for *making* the money ourselves— We had to give it up, at last, however, in despair: and write you for the money— The only consoling reflection is, that after we are fitted out with winter clothes we will have no further occasion to call on you for a long time— We have been as economical in our selection as possible: as it is I do not know what we shall do this winter, without overcoats: but Forty Dollars, which is the lowest price for which one can be obtained here, is out of the question— [3]

Emerson's main concern is the freedom of the slaves.

This country seems to be ruined not so much by the malignity as by the levity of people. A vast force of voters allow themselves, by mere compliments and solicitations of a few well-dressed intriguers, to promise their support to a party whose wish is to drag back Slavery into the government of the Union.

Great is the virtue of the Proclamation. It works when men are sleeping, when the army goes into winter headquarters, when generals are treacherous or imbecile.

The bankers believe that the moment peace shall allow a return of trade, we shall have better times than were ever known. The rotten firms broken up, the markets all cleaned out, the old stocks got rid of, all is hungry for supply. Well, I think also it will be a better time in Church and State. This detestable Slavery being killed out, the lips of the churchman will no longer be padlocked on that and other public sins. It will be easy to stretch moral rules to their universal extent.

Ergo, the Christian religion will triumph and Slavery will go to the wall.

I look on the Southern victories as I look on those of the Mussulman over Christendom, due to fanaticism, to the petulance and valour of a people who had nothing else and must make a brilliant onset and raid here and there. But ideas and their slow massive might are irresistible at last. The few lessons which the first had to teach are learned by the last in one or two campaigns, but the last vegetates eternally. The other reaches its short acme and decomposes in a day; violence and cunning are no match for wisdom. For they may find dogma that are not ridiculous, that none can travesty, but that still return immortal like the sky, how long soever you have hid yourself in cellars.

It is said Mr. Lincoln has a policy and adheres to it. He thinks Emancipation almost morally wrong and resorts to it only as a desperate measure, and means never to put radicals into power. When he puts one into office, as Fremont, or Phelps, or Lane, he takes care to neutralize him by a Democrat or a Kentuckian who will thwart him. And prudent people say, ''Quite right, for these hot heads have no administrative talent.'' Perhaps not; but they cannot have less than the ruling party, which has shown none whatever. Perhaps, also, they have a great deal. They respect principles, which, it may still be believed, have a certain force, if not in the Whig Club, yet in the Universe of Man.

Besides, those defeats are incidents and not crises to a well-principled man, not affecting the general result (which he contemplates as a foregone conclusion) any more than headwinds or calms to a good sailor, who uses them also to make his port.

I must think that the immense advantage of power of resistance on a foot of solid land outweighs all advantages of motion in the attack by ships. After Ericsson has built his ironclad, if the problem is how to resist it and destroy it from a battery in New York or Boston Harbour, I must think Ericsson, or any other man in his senses, if you offer him the sea attack or the land defence, would choose the last as the most feasible. For it is the choice between an anvil afloat and an anvil on shore. There is a speedy limit to the weight of metal a ship can carry, and then to the explosive force its decks and timbers can resist; but there is no limit to the resistance of the planet; it is used to earthquakes and volcanoes and lightnings, and minds them no more than seas. Why not, then, to a gun which throws four hundred or eight hundred pounds of iron ball?

There never was a nation great except through trial. A

religious revolution cuts sharpest, and tests the faith and endurance. A civil war sweeps away all the false issues on which it began, and arrives presently at real and lasting questions.

A movement in an aristocratic state does not argue a deep cause. A dozen good fellows may have had a supper and warmed each other's blood to some act of spite or arrogance, which they talk up and carry out the next month; or one man, Calhoun, or Rhett, may have grown bilious, and his grumble and fury are making themselves felt at the legislature. But in a Democracy, every movement has a deep–seated cause.

George Francis Train said in a public speech in New York, "Slavery is a divine Institution." "So is hell," exclaimed an old man in the crowd.

When we build, our first care is to find good foundation. If the surface be loose, or sandy, or springy, we clear it away, and dig down to the hard pan, or, better, to the living rock, and bed our courses in that. So will we do with the State. The war is serving many good purposes. It is no respecter of respectable persons or of worn–out party platforms. War is a realist, shatters everything flimsy and shifty, sets aside all false issues, and breaks through all that is not real as itself; comes to organize opinions and parties, resting on necessities of man; like its own cannonade, comes crushing in through party walls that have stood fifty or sixty years as if they were solid. The screaming leaders, the votes by acclamation, conventions, are all idle wind. They cry for mercy, but they cry to one who never knew the word. He is the arm of the Fates, and, as has been said, "Nothing prevails against God but God." Everything must perish except that which must live.

Well, this is the task before us, to accept the benefit of the War; it has not created our false relations, they have created it. It simply demonstrates the rottenness it found. We watch its course as we did the cholera, which goes where predisposition already existed, took only the susceptible, set its seal on every putrid spot, and on none other; followed the limestone, and left the granite. So the War. Anxious statesmen try to rule it, to slacken it here and let it rage there, to not exasperate, to keep the black man out of it; to keep it well in hand, nor let it ride over old party lines, nor much molest trade, and to confine it to the frontier of the two sections. Why need Cape Cod, why need Casco Bay, why need Lake Superior, know anything of it? But the Indians have been bought, and they came down on Lake Superior; Boston and Portland are threatened by the pirate; Secession unexpectedly shows teeth in Boston; our parties have just shown you that the War is already in Massachusetts, as in Richmond.

Let it search, let it grind, let it overturn, and, like the fire when it finds no more fuel, it burns out. The War will show, as all wars do, what is wrong is intolerable, what wrong makes and breeds all this bad blood. I suppose that it shows two incompatible states of society, Freedom and Slavery. If a part of this country is civilized up to a clean insight of Freedom, and of its necessity, and another part is not so far civilized, then I suppose that the same difficulties will continue; the War will not be extinguished; no treaties, no peace, no constitution can paper over the lips of that red crater. Only when, at last, so many parts of the country as can combine on an equal and moral contract— not to protect each other in polygamy, or in kidnapping, or in eating men, but in humane and just activities—only so many can combine firmly and durably.

I speak the speech of an idealist. I say let the rule be right. If the theory is right, it is not so much a matter about the facts. If the plan of your fort is right, it is not so much matter that you have got a rotten beam or a cracked gun somewhere; they can by and by be replaced by better without tearing your fort to pieces. But if the plan is wrong, then all is rotten, and every step adds to the ruin; every screw is loose, and all the machine crazy.

The question stands thus. Reconstruction is no longer matter of doubt. All our action now is new and unconstitutional, and necessarily so. To bargain or treat at all with the rebels, to make arrangements with them about exchange of prisoners, or hospitals, or truces to bury the dead, all unconstitutional and enough to drive a strict constructionist out of his wits. Much more in our future action touching peace, any and every arrangement short of forcible subjugation of the rebel country, will be flat disloyalty, on our part.

Then how to reconstruct. I say, this time, go to work right, go down to the pan. See how that works on a jewel. Do not make an impossible mixture. Do not lay your cornerstone on a shaking morass that will let down the superstructure into a bottomless pit again.

Leave Slavery out, since (unfortunately as some may think) God is God, and nothing gratifies all men but justice. Let us have that, and let us stifle our prejudices against common sense and humanity, and agree that every man shall have what he honestly earns, and, if he is a sane and innocent man, have an equal vote in the state, and a fair chance in society.

And I, speaking in the interest of no man and no party, but simply as a geometer of his forces, say that the smallest beginning, so that it is just, is better and stronger than the largest that is not quite just. This time, no compromises, no concealments, no crimes that cannot be called by name shall be tucked in under another name, like "persons held to labour," meaning persons stolen, and "held," meaning held by handcuffs, when they are not under whips, Now the smallest state so formed will and must be strong, the interest and the affection of every man will make it strong by his entire strength, and it will mightily persuade every other man, and every neighboring territory to make it larger, and it will not reach its limits until it comes to people who think that they are a little cunninger than the Maker of this world and of the consciences of men.

Plainly we must have a worthy cause for such soldiers as we send to battle, or they shall not go. Do you think that such lives as this State has yielded up already, the children of this famed city, the children of our public schools, the

children of Harvard College, the best blood of our educated counties, objects of the most romantic hope and love,
poets and romancers themselves—I attended the funeral of
one of them and heard with hearty assent the voice that
said that the whole State of South Carolina was not worth
that one life—Lander, Lowell, Putnam, Dwight, Willard
—well, that these precious young men—the voice will
choke to name them—are given up to bring back into the
Capitol of Washington the reckless politicians who had
reeled out of it with threats to destroy it, or come back
into it to rule again?

Never; better put gunpowder under its foundations and
plough up the ground where its streets stand than that
they die for the disgraceful dynasty which had brought our
Freedom to be a lie, and our civilization and wealth to dishonour as a partnership of thieves.

No, they died for the largest and noblest sentiment,
the largest interpretation that could be put on the meaning
and action of the North; died for what an American might
die for;—and the Governor of the Commonwealth nobly
spoke the sense of his people when he said, We will enlist if
you send us out for Freedom, and not if you send us out to
return slaves. Whatever mean carpers and the owls and
jackals who squeak and gibber to the contrary will say, he
spoke the voice of patriot fathers and mothers who offered
their sons, and of the patriot youths who offered up themselves, when he said, See that the cause is clear and great,
and you shall have them and us; but we go not to restore
those falsehearted usurpers of the power of Union, or the
like of them, to their places—God in his mercy forbid! but
to restore the spirit of the American Constitution, and not
its forced and falsely construed letter. . . .

In every crisis people look for the master of the situation, who is usually slow to appear. We have found none in
America. But in England, which our politics immensely
concern, they have found none. The one foreign interest of
England is to assure herself in all times of the alliance of
America, as bound by blood, language, trade, power, and
equal civilization.[4]

12 Dark Sky

On the eve of Fredericksburg, Emerson brings Carlyle up to date.

I would wait perhaps for happier days, as our President Lincoln will not even emancipate slaves, until on the heels of a victory, or the semblance of such. But he waited in vain for his triumph.

Here we read no books. The war is our sole and doleful instructor. All our bright young men go into it, to be misused and sacrificed hitherto by incapable leaders. One lesson they all learn—to hate slavery, *teterrima causa.* But the issue does not yet appear. We must get ourselves morally right. Nobody can help us. 'Tis of no account what England or France may do. Unless backed by our profligate parties, their action would be nugatory, and, if so backed, the worst.

But even the war is better than the degrading and descending politics that preceded it for decades of years, and our legislation has made great strides, and if we can stave off that fury of trade which rushes to peace at the cost of replacing the South in the *status ante bellum,* we can, with something more of courage, leave the problem to another score of years—free labor to fight with the Beast, and see if bales and barrels and baskets cannot find out that they pass more commodiously and surely to their ports through free hands, than through barbarians.[1]

*Bierce describes the ordeal of a single artillery crew in the
midst of battle.*

Within that defile, barely broad enough for a single
gun, were piled the wrecks of no fewer than four. . . . The
debris lay on both sides of the road; the men had managed
to keep an open way between, through which the fifth piece
was now firing. The men?—they looked like demons of the
pit! All were hatless, all stripped to the waist, their reek-
ing skins black with blotches of powder and spattered with
gouts of blood. They worked like madmen, with rammer
and cartridge, lever and lanyard. They set their swollen
shoulders and bleeding hands against the wheels at each
recoil and heaved the heavy gun back to its place.

There were no commands; in that awful environment
of whooping shot, exploding shells, shrieking fragments of
iron and flying splinters of wood, none could have been
heard. Officers, if officers there were, were indistinguish-
able; all worked together—each while he lasted—governed
by the eye. When the gun was sponged, it was loaded; when
loaded, aimed and fired. . . . The gun was bleeding at the
mouth! In temporary default of water, the man sponging
had dipped his sponge into a pool of comrade's blood.

In all this work there was no clashing; the duty of the
instant was obvious. When one fell, another, looking a
trifle cleaner, seemed to rise from the earth in the dead
man's tracks, to fall in his turn.

With the ruined guns lay the ruined men—alongside
the wreckage, under it and atop of it; and back down the
road—a ghastly procession!—crept on hands and knees
such of the wounded as were able to move. "One Officer,
One Man."

An army in line–of–battle awaiting attack, or prepared to deliver it, presents strange contrasts. At the front
are precision, formality, fixity, and silence. Toward the
rear these characteristics are less and less conspicuous,
and finally, in point of space, are lost altogether in confusion, motion and noise. The homogeneous becomes hetero-

geneous. Definition is lacking; repose is replaced by an apparently purposeless activity; harmony vanishes in hub-bub, form in disorder. Commotion everywhere and cease-less unrest. The men who do not fight are never ready.[2]

Holmes is depressed over the news of Burnside's defeat.

I could have wished that my letter and the mail had gone yesterday. We get to-day the news that Burnside has withdrawn all his troops over to this side of the Rap-pahannock, and taken up his pontoon bridges. He failed in his repeated attempts to storm the rebel works, and found it such a desperate undertaking that he seems to have given up for the present.

There is no question that this news has exercised a most depressing effect on all but the secession sympathiz-ers, who, grudging every success to the Cabinet and its new general, are secretly comforted, as I guess by certain signs, that the "Onward to Richmond" has again met with a check.

It looks to me now as if the movement were a precau-tion against a possible necessity rather than an immediate necessity. The river was fast rising with the rain which was falling. It would never do to be cut off from supplies and reinforcements by a swollen stream, and so Burnside, quietly, and as it seems without loss, without the enemy's being aware of what he was about, last night sent over his artillery, and then followed it by all his infantry.

We have become so used to disappointments that we have learned to bear them with a good deal of equanimity. We hope this is only temporary, but it has dashed our spirits, and begun to knock stocks about a little. . . .

You will think, I know, of my firstborn in the midst of the scenes his regiment has been going through. He is suffering from dysentery, I am afraid pretty sick, but we are impatiently waiting to hear from him. A note of two or

three lines written to a friend in Philadelphia on the 10th
was the first news we had of his being ill, and is the last
thing we have heard from him to the present moment. He
cannot have been in the fights, and therefore must have
been really "down," as he says in his note. The experience
has no doubt brought on with aggravated symptoms the
trouble from which he suffered so severely on the Chickahominy, but which did not keep him from being on duty
until the last of the battles—Malvern Hill—had been
fought.

Let us keep up our courage for our country and ourselves. It is harder for you, I have no doubt, than for me,
at home and getting the news two or three times daily.
Many things that sound ill do not worry me long, for I am
a man of large faith, and though the Devil is a personage
of remarkable talents, I think the presiding wisdom is sure
to be too much for him in the end. We are nervous just
now, and easily put down, but if we are to have a second
national birth, it must be purchased by throes and agonies,
harder, perhaps, than we have yet endured.[3]

Bryant editorializes on Fredericksburg. .

How long is such intolerable and wicked blundering to
continue? What does the President wait for? We hear that
a great, a horrible crime has been committed; we do not
hear that those guilty of it are under arrest; we do not
hear even that they are to be removed from their places of
trust which they have shown themselves so incapable to
fill.

The President has required too little from his agents;
his good nature has led him to be less strict toward them
than he ought to be, while at the same time his confidence
in himself and his advisers has led him, unfortunately, to
deny himself that general counsel of the nation by which he
might have benefited had he kept up confidential relations
between himself and the people.[4]

Longfellow opens on a cheerful note as the new year begins.

January 1, 1863: A great day. The President's Proclamation for Emancipation of Slaves in the rebel States, goes into effect. A beautiful day, full of sunshine, ending in a tranquil moonlight night. May it be symbolical of the Emancipation! There was a grand meeting in Boston, at which Emerson recited a poem.[5]

Emerson watches the casting of a cannon at Pittsburgh.

Yesterday with Mr. Gilman, a purser of the Navy, with whom I came here, I visited the Arsenal & afterwards the forge [during his lecture tour while in Pittsburgh] of Knapp, Rudd, & Cox, to see the casting of a 15-inch cannon, which is the sublime in mechanics. The look into the furnace is like looking at the sun, and, after the eye is a little used to it, you begin to see the white iron thawing into drops & rivulets, like thawing glaciers, until presently you see floating islands, all white, in the white sea.

We stayed a couple of hours; at last the ore was ready in the two great furnaces; the great clay spouts, one from each, were heated by burning chips, &c. and the rosy iron brooks rushed out along these channels, say 40 feet long each, into the mould, which is sunk into a perpendicular pit 18 or 20 ft deep. 'Tis a wonderful spectacle, & one comes to look at every one in the crowd of workmen with vast respect.[6]

Emily Dickinson writes to her friend Colonel Higginson.

I did not deem that planetary forces annulled—but suffered an Exchange of Territory, or World—

I should have liked to see you, before you became improbable. War feels to me an oblique place—Should there be other Summers, would you perhaps come?

I found you were gone by accident, as I find Systems are, or Seasons of the year, and obtain no cause—but suppose it is a treason of Progress—that dissolves as it goes. Carlo [her dog]—still remained—and I told him—

Best Gains—must have the Losses' Test—
To constitute them—Gains—

My Shaggy Ally assented—
Perhaps Death—gave me awe for friends—striking sharp and early, for I held them since—in a brittle love —of more alarm, than peace. I trust you may pass the limit of War, and though not reared to prayer—when service is had in Church, for Our Arms, I include myself—
But I fear I detain you—
Should you, before this reaches you, experience immortality, who will inform me of the Exchange? Could you, with honor, avoid Death, I entreat you—Sir—It would bereave

Your Gnome—

I trust the "Procession of Flowers" was not a premonition—[7]

Emerson justifies the war on two accounts.

Our sky is very dark but the feeling is very general in the Union that bad as the war is, it is far safer & better than the foregoing peace. Our best ground of hope now is in the healthy sentiment which appears in reasonable people all over the country, accepting sacrifices, but meaning riddance from slavery, & from Southern domination.[8]

13   Forty Ambulances from Fredericksburg

Whitman's brother George was wounded in the battle of Fredericksburg on December 13, and Whitman journeyed down to Virginia to find him. He tells us something of the battle and of its grim aftermath.

Sunday, 14th December, 1862, the day after the engagement. —The general engagement was Saturday 13th. Sunday was comparatively quiet, with occasional picket firing. On Sunday night, the 51st was ordered on a picket in force, to relieve the men holding a hill in advance of our line, south of Fredericksburg, perhaps two miles beyond the river. The 51st men went on this duty about 9 o'clock Sunday night. Any member of the regiment will recollect till his dying day the circumstances of this night and the following day—up to 12 o'clock Monday night—the regiment being on continuous duty in a most dangerous position about twenty-seven hours.

During the whole of that time, everyone, from the Colonel down, was compelled to lie at full length on his back or belly in the mud, which was deep and tenacious. The surface of the ground, slightly elevated just south of them, served as a natural bulwark and protection against the Rebel batteries and sharpshooters, as long as the men lay in this manner. But the moment the men raised their heads or a limb, even if only a few inches—snap and o-s-st went the weapons of Secesh! In this manner, the 51st remained spread out in the mud all Sunday night, all Monday, and Monday night till after midnight. Although the troops could plainly hear the Rebels whistling, etc., the latter did not dare advance upon them.

. . . Soon after midnight, the 51st (as a blind) took up their march (the relief soon followed) through Fredericksburg, over the pontoon bridge to Falmouth, where they halted and took their old camping ground. The 51st was relieved Tuesday morning, 16th, about 3 o'clock, after four days' absence.

Taking the army as a whole, it is almost certain that never did mortal man in an aggregate fight better than our troops at Fredericksburg. In the highest sense, it was no failure. The main body troops descending the hills on the Falmouth side to cross the pontoon bridge could plainly see, over back of Fredericksburg, the Secesh batteries rising in tremendous force and plenty on the terrace required to our men's crossing exposed stretches on land—which were fearfully commanded by their batteries—and also the flats thick with their rifle pits. Yet all the brigade went forward unflinchingly.

Nearer view on Saturday, the day of the fight, made everything still more ominous to our side. But still the men advance with unsurpassed gallantry—and would have gone further, if ordered.

The results of the late battle are exhibited everywhere about here in thousands of cases (hundreds die every day) in the camp, brigade, and division hospitals. These are merely tents—and sometimes very poor ones—the wounded lying on the ground, lucky if their blankets are spread on layers of pine or hemlock twigs or small leaves. No cots; seldom even a mattress. It is pretty cold. The ground is frozen hard, and there is occasional snow. . . .

. . . Spend a good part of the day in a large brick mansion on the banks of the Rappahannock, used as a hospital since the battle; seems to have received only the worst cases . . . Outdoors, at the front of the tree, within ten yards of the front of the house, I noticed a heap of amputated feet, legs, arms, hands, etc.—a full load for a one–horse cart. Several dead bodies lie near, each covered with its brown woolen blanket. In the dooryard, towards the river, are fresh graves, mostly of officers, their names on pieces of barrel staves or broken boards stuck in the dirt. . . .

The large mansion is quite crowded upstairs and down—everything impromptu, no system, all bad enough—but I have no doubt the best that can be done; all the wounds pretty bad, some frightful; the men in their old clothes, unclean and bloody.

Some of the wounded are rebel soldiers and officers, prisoners. . . . I went through the rooms downstairs and up. Some of the men were dying. I had nothing to give at that visit (December 21) but wrote a few letters to folks home, mothers, etc. Also talked to three or four who seemed most susceptible to it and needing it. . . .[1]

Louisa May Alcott narrates the experience of her fourth day in the Washington hospital to which she had just been appointed as a nurse.

"They've come! they've come! hurry up, ladies—you're wanted."

"Who have come? the rebels?"

This sudden summons in the gray dawn was somewhat startling to a three days' nurse like myself, and as the thundering knock came at our door, I sprang up in my bed . . .

"Bless you, no, child; it's the wounded from Fredericksburg; forty ambulances are at the door, and we shall have our hands full in fifteen minutes."

"What shall we have to do?"

"Wash, dress, feed, warm and nurse them for the next three months, I dare say. Eighty beds are ready, and we were getting impatient for the men to come. Now you will

begin to see hospital life in earnest, for you won't probably find time to sit down all day, and may think yourself
fortunate if you get to bed by midnight. Come to me in the
ballroom when you are ready; the worst cases are always
carried there, and I shall need your help.''

So saying, the energetic little woman twirled her hair
into a button at the back of her head, in a ''clear for action'' sort of style, and vanished, wrestling her way into a
feminine kind of peajacket as she went.

I am free to confess that I had a realizing sense of the
fact that my hospital bed was not a bed of roses. . . . My
three days' experiences had begun with a death, and, owing
to the defalcation of another nurse, a somewhat abrupt
plunge into the superintendence of a ward containing forty
beds, where I spent my shining hours washing faces, serving rations, giving medicine, and sitting in a very hard
chair, with pneumonia on one side, diphtheria on the other,
five typhoids on the opposite, and a dozen dilapidated patriots, hopping, lying, and lounging about, all staring more
or less at the new ''nuss,'' who suffered untold agonies, but
concealed them under as matronly an aspect as a spinster
could assume, and blundered through her trying labors
with a Spartan firmness . . . I had rather longed for the
wounded to arrive, for rheumatism wasn't heroic, neither
was liver complaint . . . but when I peeped into the dusky
street lined with what I at first had innocently called market cars, now unloading their sad freight at our door. . . .
I indulged in a most unpatriotic wish that I was safe at
home again. . . . A second bang at the door sent this rec-
reant desire to the right about, as a little woolly head
popped in, and Joey (a six years' old contraband), announced—

''Miss Blank is jes' wild fer ye, and says fly round
right away, They's comin' in, I tell yer, heaps on 'em—one
was took out dead, and I see him—ky! warn't he a goner!''

With which cheerful intelligence the imp scuttled
away, singing like a blackbird, and I followed. . . .

The first thing I met was a regiment of the vilest

odors that ever assaulted the human nose . . . and the worst of this affliction was everyone assured me that it was a chronic weakness of all hospitals, and I must bear it. I did, armed with lavendar water, with which I so besprinkled myself and premises, that . . . I was soon known among my patients as "the nurse with the bottle."

Having been run over by three excited surgeons, bumped against by migratory coal hods, water pails, and small boys; nearly scalded by an avalanche of newly–filled teapots, and hopelessly entangled in a knot of colored sisters coming to wash, I progressed by slow stages up stairs and down, till the main hall was reached, and I paused to take breath and a survey.

There they were! "our brave boys," as the papers justly call them, for cowards could hardly have been so riddled with shot and shell, so torn and shattered, nor have borne suffering for which we have no name, with an uncomplaining fortitude, which made one glad to cherish each as a brother. In they came, some on stretchers, some in men's arms, some feebly staggering along propped on rude crutches; and one lay stark and still with covered face, as a comrade gave his name to be recorded before they carried him away to the dead house. All was hurry and confusion; the hall was full of these wrecks of humanity, for the most exhausted could not reach a bed till duly ticketed and registered; the walls were lined with rows of such as could sit, the floor covered with the more disabled, the steps and doorways filled with helpers and lookers on; the sound of many feet and voices made that usually quiet hour as noisy as noon, and, in the midst of it all, the matron's motherly face brought more comfort to many a poor soul than the cordial draughts she administered or the cheery words that welcomed all, making of the hospital a home. . . .

The house had been a hotel before hospitals were needed, and many of the doors still bore their old names; some not so inappropriate as might be imagined, for my ward was in truth a *ball-room,* if gunshot wounds could christen it. Forty beds were prepared, many already tenanted by tired men who fell down anywhere, and drowsed till the smell of food roused them. Round the great stove was gathered the dreariest group I ever saw—ragged, gaunt and pale, mud to the knees, with bloody bandages untouched since put on days before; many bundled up in blankets, coats being lost or useless; and all wearing that disheartened look which proclaimed defeat, more plainly than any telegram of the Burnside blunder. I pitied them so much, I dared not speak to them, though, remembering all they had been through since the route at Fredericksburg, I yearned to serve the dreariest of them all.

Presently, Miss Blank tore me from my refuge behind piles of one–sleeved shirts, odd socks, bandages and lint; put basin, sponge, towels and a block of brown soap into my hands, with these appalling directions:

"Come, my dear, begin to wash as fast as you can. Tell them to take off socks, coats and shirts, scrub them well, put on clean shirts, and the attendants will finish them off, and lay them in bed."

. . . And, having resolved when I came, to do everything I was bid, I drowned my scruples in my washbowl, clutched my soap manfully, and, assuming a businesslike air, made a dab at the first dirty specimen I saw. . . . I chanced to light on a withered old Irishman, wounded in the head. . . . He was so overpowered by the honor of having a lady wash him, as he expressed it, that he did nothing but roll up his eyes, and, bless me, in an irresistible style which was too much for my sense of the ludicrous; so we laughed together, and when I knelt down to take off his shoes, he "flopped" also and wouldn't hear of my touching "them dirty craters" . . . trousers, socks, shoes and legs were a mass of mud. . . . Some of them took the performance like sleepy children, leaning their tired heads against me as I worked, others looked grimly scandalized, and several of the roughest colored like bashful girls. . . .

The next scrubbee was a nice looking lad with a curly brown mane and a budding trace of gingerbread over the lip, which he defended stoutly when the barber jocosely suggested its immolation. He lay on a bed, with one leg gone, and the right arm so shattered that it must evidently follow; yet the little Sergeant was as merry as if his afflictions were not worth lamenting over, and when a drop or two of salt water mingled with my suds at the sight of this strong young body, so marred and maimed, the boy looked up, with a brave smile, though there was a little quiver of his lips, as he said,

"Now don't you fret yourself about me, miss; I'm first–rate here, for it's nuts to lie still on this bed, after knocking about in those confounded ambulances, that shake what there is left of a fellow to jelly. I never was in one of those places before, and think this cleaning up is a jolly thing for us, though I'm afraid it isn't for you ladies."

"Is this your first battle, Sergeant?"

"No, Miss; I've been in six scrimmages, and never got a scratch till this last one; but it's done the business pretty thoroughly for me, I should say. Lord! what a scramble there'll be for arms and legs, when we old boys come out of our graves, on the Judgment Day: wonder if we shall get our own again. If we do, my leg will have to tramp from Fredericksburg, my arm from here, I suppose, and meet my body, wherever it may be. . . ."

The fancy seemed to tickle him mightily, for he laughed blithely, and so did I; which, no doubt, caused the new nurse to be regarded as a light–minded sinner by the Chaplain, who roamed vaguely about, informing the men that they were all worms, corrupt of heart, with perishable bodies, and souls only to be saved by a diligent perusal of certain tracts, and other equally cheering bits of spiritual consolation, when spirituous ditto would have been preferred.

"I say, Mrs.!" called a voice behind me; and, turning, I saw a rough Michigander, with an arm blown off at the shoulder, and two or three bullets still in him—as he afterwards mentioned, as carelessly as if gentlemen were in the habit of carrying such trifles about with them. I went to him, and, while administering a dose of soap and water, he whispered, irefully:

"That red-headed devil, over yonder, is a reb, damn him! You'll agree to that, I'll bet? He's got shet of a foot, or he'd a cut like the rest of the lot. Don't you wash him, nor feed him, but jest let him holler till he's tired. It's a blasted shame to fetch them fellers in here, along side of us; and so I'll tell the chap that bosses this concern; cuss me if I don't."

I regret to say that I did not deliver a moral sermon upon the duty of forgiving our enemies, and the sin of profanity, then and there; but, being a red–hot Abolitionist, stared fixedly at the tall rebel, who was a copperhead, in every sense of the word, and privately resolved to put soap in his eyes, rub his nose the wrong way, and excoriate his cuticle generally, if I had the washing of him.

My amiable intentions, however, were frustrated; for, when I approached, with as Christian an expression as my principles would allow, and asked the question—"Shall I try to make you more comfortable, sir?" all I got for my pains was a gruff—

"No; I'll do it myself."

"Here's your Southern chivalry, with a witness," thought I, dumping the basin down before him, thereby quenching a strong desire to give him a summary baptism, in return for his ungraciousness; for my angry passions rose at this rebuff, in a way that would have scandalized good Dr. Watts. He was a disappointment in all respects, . . . for he was neither fiendish, romantic, pathetic, or anything interesting; but a long, fat man, with a head like a burning bush, and a perfectly expressionless face; so I could hate him without the slightest drawback, and ignored his existence from that day forth. . . .

Having done up our human wash, and laid it out to dry . . . , great trays of bread, meat, soup and coffee appeared; and both nurses and attendants turned waiters, serving bountiful rations to all who could eat. . . . It was a lively scene; the long room lined with rows of beds, each filled by an occupant, whom water, shears, and clean raiment, had transformed from a dismal ragamuffin into a recumbent hero, with a cropped head. To and fro rushed matrons, maids, and convalescent "boys," skirmishing with knives and forks; retreating with empty plates . . . while the clash of busy spoons made most inspiring music. . . .

Very welcome seemed the generous meal, after a week of suffering, exposure, and short commons; soon the brown faces began to smile, as food, warmth, and rest, did their pleasant work; and the grateful "Thankee's" were followed by more graphic accounts of the battle and retreat, than any paid reporter could have given us.

Curious contrasts of the tragic and comic met one everywhere; and some touching as well as ludicrous episodes, might have been recorded that day. A six foot New Hampshire man, with a leg broken and perforated by a piece of shell, so large that, had I not seen the wound, I should have regarded the story as a Munchhausenism, beckoned me to come and help him, as he could not sit up, and both his bed and beard were getting plentifully anointed with soup. As I fed my big nestling with corresponding mouthfuls, I asked him how he felt during the battle.

"Well, 'twas my fust, you see, so I aint ashamed to say I was a trifle flustered in the beginnin', there was such an all–fired racket; for ef there's anything I do spleen agin, it's noise. But when my mate, Elph Sylvester, caved with a bullet through his head, I got mad, and pitched in, licketty cut. Our part of the fight didn't last long; so a lot of us larked around Fredericksburg, and give some of them houses a pretty cons'able of rummage, till we was ordered out of the mess. Some of our fellows cut like time, but I warn't a–goin to run for nobody; and, fust thing I knew, a shell bust, right in front of us, and I keeled over, feelin' as if I was blowed higher'n a kite. I sung out, and the boys come back for me, double quick; but the way they chucked me over them fences was a caution, I tell you. Next day I was most as black as that darkey yonder, lickin' plates on the sly. This is bully coffee, ain't it? Give us another pull at it, and I'll be obleeged to you.''

I did; and as the last gulp subsided, he said, with a rub of his old handerchief over eyes as well as mouth:

''Look a here; I've got a pair of earbobs and a hand-kerchief that I'm going to give you . . . they'll do to memorize the rebs by.''

Observing that the man next him had left his meal un-touched, I offered the same service I had performed for his neighbor, but he shook his head.

''Thank you, ma'am; I don't think I'll ever eat again, for I'm shot in the stomach. But I'd like a drink of water, if you aint too busy.''

I rushed away, but the water pails were gone to be re-filled, and it was some time before they reappeared. I did not forget my patient, meanwhile, and with the first mug-ful, hurried back to him. He seemed asleep; but something in the tired white face caused me to listen at his lips for a breath. None came. I touched his forehead; it was cold; and then I knew that, while he waited, a better nurse than I had given him a cooler draught, and healed him with a touch. I laid the sheet over the quiet sleeper, whom no noise could now disturb; and, half an hour later, the bed was empty. It seemed a poor requital for all he had sacri-ficed and suffered—that hospital bed, lonely even in a crowd, for there was no familiar face for him to look his last upon . . . no friendly voice to say, Goodbye . . . and he vanished, like a drop in that red sea upon whose shores so many women stand lamenting. . . .

All having eaten, drunk, and rested, the surgeons began their rounds; and I took my first lesson in the art of dressing wounds. It wasn't a festive scene, by any means; for Dr. P., whose Aid I constituted myself, fell to work with a vigor which soon convinced me that I was a weaker vessel, though nothing would have induced me to confess it then. He had served in the Crimea, and seemed to regard a dilapidated body very much as I should have regarded a damaged garment! and, turning up his cuffs, whipped out a very unpleasant–looking housewife, cutting, sawing, patching and piecing, with the enthusiasm of an accomplished surgical seamstress; explaining the process, in scientific terms, to the patient, meantime; which, of course, was immensely cheering and comfortable. There was an uncanny sort of fascination in watching him, as he peered and probed into the mechanism of those wonderful bodies, whose mysteries he understood so well. The more intricate the wound, the better he liked it. A poor private, with both legs shot off, and shot through the lungs, possessed more attractions for him than a dozen generals, slightly scratched in some "masterly retreat"; and had any one appeared in small pieces, requesting to be put together again, he would have considered it a special dispensation.

The amputations were reserved till the morrow, and the merciful magic of ether was not thought necessary that day, so the pour souls had to bear their pains as best they might. It is all very well to talk of the patience of woman, and far be it from me to pluck that feather from her cap, for heaven knows, she isn't allowed to wear many; but the patient endurance of these men, under trials of the flesh, was truly wonderful; their fortitude seemed contagious, and scarcely a cry escaped them, though I often longed to groan for them, when pride kept their white lips shut, while great drops stood upon their foreheads, and the bed shook with the irrepressible tremor of their tortured bodies. One or two Irishmen anathematized the doctors with the frankness of their nation . . . but, as a general thing, the work went on in silence, broken only by some quiet request for roller, instruments, or plaster, a sigh from the patient, or a sympathetic murmur from the nurse.

It was long past noon before these repairs were even partially made; and, having got the bodies of my boys into something like order, the next task was to minister to their minds, by writing letters to the anxious souls at home; answering questions, reading papers, taking possession of money and valuables; for the eighth commandment was reduced to a very fragmentary condition, both by the blacks and whites. . . . Pocket books, purses, miniatures, and watches, were sealed up, labelled, and handed over to the matron, till such times as the owners thereof were ready to depart homeward or campward again. The letters dictated to me, and revised by me, that afternoon, would have made an excellent chapter for some future history of the war; for, like that which Thackeray's "Ensign Spooney" wrote his mother just before Waterloo, they were "full of affection, pluck, and bad spelling"; nearly all giving lively accounts of the battle, and ending with a somewhat sudden plunge from patriotism to provender, desiring, "Marm," "Mary Ann," or "Aunt Peters," to send along some pies, pickles, sweet stuff, and apples, "to yours in haste" Jo, Sam, or Ned, as the case might be.

My little Sergeant insisted on trying to scribble something with his left hand, and patiently accomplished some half dozen lines of hieroglyphics, which he gave me to fold and direct, with a boyish blush, that rendered a glimpse of "My Dearest Jane," . . . though no further confidences were made that day, for Sergeant fell asleep, and judging from his tranquil face, visited his absent sweetheart in the pleasant land of dreams.

At five o'clock a great bell rang, and the attendants flew . . . to their trays, to bring up supper, when a second uproar announced that it was ready. The new comers woke at the sound; and I presently discovered that it took a very bad wound to incapacitate the defenders of the faith for the consumption of their rations; the amount that some of them sequestered was amazing; but when I suggested the probability of a famine hereafter, to the matron, that motherly lady cried out: "Bless their hearts, why shouldn't they eat? It's their only amusement; so fill every one, and, if there's not enough ready to-night, I'll lend my share to the Lord by giving it to the boys." And, whipping up her coffee-pot and plate of toast, she gladdened the eyes and stomachs of two or three dissatisfied heroes, by serving them with a liberal hand. . . .

Then came the doctor's evening visit; the administration of medicines; washing feverish faces; smoothing tumbled beds; wetting wounds; singing lullabies; and preparations for the night. By eleven, the last labor of love was done; the last "good night" spoken; and, if any needed a reward for that day's work, they surely received it, in the silent eloquence of those long lines of faces, showing pale and peaceful in the shaded rooms, as we quitted them, followed by grateful glances that lighted us to bed, where rest, the sweetest, made our pillows soft, while Night and Nature took our places, filling that great house of pain with the healing miracles of Sleep, and his diviner brother, Death.[2]

14 The Hospitals

Whitman describes the military hospitals.

The military hospitals, convalescent camps, etc. in Washington and its neighborhood sometimes contain over fifty thousand sick and wounded men. Every form of wound . . . every kind of malady—like a long procession, with typhoid, and diarrhoea at the head as leaders—are here in steady motion. The soldiers' hospital! How many sleepless nights, how many women's tears, how many long and waking hours and days of suspense from every one of the Middle, Eastern, and Western states have concentrated here! Our own New York, in the form of hundreds and thousands of her young men, may consider herself here; Pennsylvania, Ohio, Indiana, and all the West and Northwest the same, and all the New England states the same!

 . . . These are not like other hospitals. By far the greatest proportion (I should say five-sixths) of the patients are American young men, intelligent, of independent spirit, tender feelings, used to a hardy and healthy life; largely the farmers are represented by their sons—largely the mechanics and workingmen of the cities. Then they are soldiers. All these points must be borne in mind.

People through our Northern cities have little or no idea of the great and prominent feature which these military hospitals and convalescent camps make in and around Washington. There are not merely two or three or a dozen, but some fifty of them of different degrees of capacity. Some have a thousand or more patients. The newspapers here find it necessary to print every day a directory of the hospitals—a long list something like what a directory of the churches would be in New York, Philadelphia, or Boston.

The government (which really tries, I think, to do the best and quickest it can for these sad necessities) is gradually settling to adopt the plan of placing the hospitals in clusters of one-story wooden barracks, with their accompanying tents and sheds for cooking and all needed purposes. Taking all things into consideration, no doubt these are best adapted to the purpose, better than using churches and large public buildings like the Patent Office. These sheds now adopted are long, one-story edifices, sometimes ranged along in a row with their heads to the street, and numbered either alphabetically—Wards A or B, C, D, and so on; or Wards 1, 2, 3, etc. The middle one will be marked by a flagstaff, and is the office of the establishment, with rooms for the ward surgeons, etc. One of these sheds or wards will contain sixty cots; sometimes, on an emergency, they move them closer together and crowd in more. Some of the barracks are larger, with, of course, more inmates. Frequently there are tents—more comfortable here than one might think—whatever they may be down in the army.

Each ward has a ward master and generally a nurse for every ten or twelve men. A ward surgeon has, generally, two wards—although this varies. Some of the wards have a woman nurse. . . .

. . . One of the government hospitals here is a city in itself. . . .

Imagine a long, one-story wooden shed, like a short, wide rope-walk, well whitewashed; then cluster ten or a dozen of these together with several smaller sheds and tents. . . . There is a regular staff and a substaff of big and little officials. Military etiquette is observed, and it is getting to become very stiff.[1]

Miss Alcott takes us behind the scenes of the Union Hotel Hospital in Georgetown, Washington, D.C.

I never began the year in a stranger place than this: five hundred miles from home, alone, among strangers, doing painful duties all day long, and leading a life of constant excitement in this great house, surrounded by three or four hundred men in all stages of suffering, disease, and death. Though often homesick, heartsick, and worn out, I like it, find real pleasure in comforting, tending, and cheering these poor souls who seem to love me, to feel my sympathy though unspoken, and acknowledge my hearty good-will, in spite of the ignorance, awkwardness, and bashfulness which I cannot help showing in so new and trying a situation. . . . The men are docile, respectful and affectionate, with but few exceptions; truly lovable and manly, many of them.

I shall record the events of a day as a sample of the days I spend:—

Up at six, dress by gaslight, run through my ward and throw up the windows, though the men grumble and shiver; but the air is bad enough to breed a pestilence; and as no notice is taken of our frequent appeals for better ventilation, I must do what I can. Poke up the fire, add blankets, joke, coax, and command; but continue to open doors and windows as if life depended upon it. Mine does, and doubtless many another, for a more perfect pestilence-box than this house I never saw—cold, damp, dirty, full of vile odors from wounds, kitchens, wash-rooms, and stables. No competent head, male or female, to right matters, and a jumble of good, bad, and indifferent nurses, surgeons, and attendants, to complicate the chaos still more.

After this unwelcome progress through my stifling ward, I go to breakfast with what appetite I may; find the uninvitable fried beef, salt butter, husky bread, and washy coffee; listen to the clack of eight women and a dozen men;—the first silly, stupid, or possessed of one idea; the last absorbed with their breakfast and themselves to a degree that is both ludicrous and provoking, for all the dishes are ordered down the table *full* and returned *empty;* the conversation is entirely among themselves, and each announces his opinion with an air of importance that frequently causes me to choke in my cup, or bolt my meals with undignified speed lest a laugh betray to the famous beings that a "chiel's amang them takin' notes."

'Till noon I trot, trot giving out rations, cutting up food for helpless "boys," washing faces, teaching my attendants how beds are made or floors are swept, dressing wounds, taking Dr. F. P.'s orders (privately wishing all the time that he would be more gentle with my big babies), dusting tables, sewing bandages, keeping my tray tidy, rushing up and down after pillows, bed linen, sponges, books, and directions, till it seems as if I would joyfully pay down all I possess for fifteen minutes' rest. At twelve the big bell rings, and up comes dinner for the boys, who are always ready for it and never entirely satisfied. Soup, meat, potatoes, and bread is the bill of fare.

Charley Thayer, the attendant, travels up and down the room serving out the rations, saving little for himself, yet always thoughtful of his mates, and patient as a woman with their helplessness. When dinner is over, some sleep, many read, and others want letters written. This I like to do, for they put in such odd things, and express their ideas so comically, I have great fun interiorly, while as grave as possible exteriorally. A few of the men word their paragraphs well and make excellent letters. John's was the best of all I wrote. The answering of letters from friends after someone had died is the saddest and hardest duty a nurse has to do.

Supper at five sets every one to running that can run; and when that flurry is over, all settle down for the evening amusements, which consist of newspapers, gossip, the doctor's last round, and, for such as need them, the final doses for the night. At nine the bell rings, gas is turned down, and day nurses go to bed. Night nurses go on duty, and sleep and death have the house to themselves.[2]

Wandering up and down these lower halls, I often heard cries from above, steps hurrying to and fro, saw surgeons passing up, or men coming down carrying a stretcher, where lay a long white figure, whose face was shrouded and whose fight was done.

My ward was now divided into three rooms; and, under favor of the matron, I had managed to sort out the patients in such a way that I had what I called, "my duty room," "my pleasure room," and my "pathetic room," and worked for each in a different way. One I visited, armed with a dressing tray, full of rollers, plasters, and pins; another, with books, flowers, games, and gossip; a third, with teapots, lullabies, consolation, and, sometimes, a shroud.

I would have given much to have possessed the art of sketching, for many of the faces became wonderfully interesting when unconscious. Some grew stern and grim, the men evidently dreaming of war, as they gave orders, groaned over their wounds, or damned the rebels vigorously; some grew sad and infinitely pathetic, as if the pain borne silently all day revenged itself by now betraying what the man's pride had concealed so well.

Often the roughest grew young and pleasant when sleep smoothed the hard lines away, letting the real nature assert itself; many almost seemed to speak, and I learned to know these men better by night than through any intercourse by day. Sometimes they disappointed me, for faces that looked merry and good in the light, grew bad and sly when the shadows came; and though they made no confidences in words, I read their lives, leaving them to wonder at the change of manner this midnight magic wrought in their nurse. A few talked busily; one drummer boy sang sweetly, though no persuasions could win a note from him by day, and several depended on being told what they had talked of in the morning.

My headquarters were beside the bed of a New Jersey boy, crazed by the horrors of that dreadful Saturday. A slight wound in the knee brought him there; but his mind

had suffered more than his body; some string of that delicate machine was overstrained, and, for days, he had been
reliving, in imagination, the scenes he could not forget, till
his distress broke out in incoherent ravings, pitiful to hear.
As I sat by him, endeavoring to soothe his poor distracted
brain by the constant touch of wet hands over his hot forehead, he lay cheering his comrades on, hurrying them back,
then counting them as they fell around him, often clutching
my arm, to drag me from the vicinity of a bursting shell,
or covering up his head to screen himself from a shower of
shot; his face brilliant with fever; his eyes restless; his
head never still; every muscle strained and rigid; while an
incessant stream of defiant shouts, whispered warnings,
and broken laments, poured from his lips with that force-
ful bewilderment which makes such wanderings so hard to
overhear.

It was past eleven, and my patient was slowly weary-
ing himself into fitful intervals of quietude, when, in one of
these muses, a curious sound arrested my attention. Looking over my shoulder, I saw a one-legged phantom hopping
numbly down the room; and, going to meet it, recognized a
certain Pennsylvania gentleman, whose wound-fever had
taken a turn for the worse, and, depriving him of the few
wits a drunken campaign had left him, set him literally
tripping on the light, fantastic toe "toward home," as he
blandly informed me, touching the military cap which
formed a striking contrast to the severe simplicity of the
rest of his decidedly *undress* uniform. When sane, the least
movement produced a roar of pain or a volley of oaths;
but the departure of reason seemed to have wrought an
agreeable change, both in the man and his manners; for,
balancing himself on one leg, like a meditative stork, he
plunged into an animated discussion of the war, the President, lager beer, and Enfield rifles, regardless of any suggestions of mine as to the propriety of returning to bed,
lest he be courtmartialed for desertion.

Anything more supremely ridiculous can hardly be
imagined than this figure, scantily draped in white, its one

foot covered with a big blue sock, a dingy cap set rakingly askew on its shaven head, and placid satisfaction beaming in its broad red face, as it flourished a mug in one hand, an old boot in the other, calling them canteen and knapsack, while it skipped and fluttered in the most unearthly fashion. What to do with the creature I didn't know; Dan was absent, and if I went to find him, the perambulator might festoon himself out of the window, set his toga on fire, or do some of his neighbors a mischief. The attendant of the room was sleeping like a near relative of the celebrated Seven, and nothing short of pins would rouse him; for he had been out that day, and whiskey asserted its supremacy in balmy whiffs. Still declaiming in a fine flow of eloquence, the demented gentleman hopped on, blind and deaf to my graspings and entreaties; and I was about to slam the door in his face, and run for help, when a second and saner phantom, "all in white," came to the rescue, in the likeness of a big Prussian, who spoke no English, but divined the crisis, and put an end to it, by bundling the lively monoped into his bed, like a baby, with an authoritative command to "stay put," which received added weight from being delivered in an odd conglomeration of French and German, accompanied by warning wags of a head decorated with a yellow cotton night cap, rendered most imposing by a tassel like a bellpull.

Rather exhausted by his excursion, the member from Pennsylvania subsided; and, after an irrepressible laugh together, my Prussian ally and myself were returning to our places, when the echo of a sob caused us to glance along the beds. It came from one in the corner—such a little bed!—and such a tearful little face looked up at us, as we stopped beside it! The twelve year old drummer boy was not singing now, but sobbing, with a manly effort all the while to stifle the distressful sounds that would break out.

"What is it, Teddy?" I asked, as he rubbed the tears away, and checked himself in the middle of a great sob to answer plaintively:

"I've got a chill, ma'am, but I ain't cryin' for that, 'cause I'm used to it. I dreamed Kit was here, and when I waked up he wan't and I couldn't help it, then.''

The boy came in with the rest, and the man who was taken dead from the ambulance was the Kit he mourned. Well he might; for when the wounded were brought from Fredericksburg, the child lay in one of the camps thereabout, and this good friend, though sorely hurt himself, would not leave him to the exposure and neglect of such a time and place; but, wrapping him in his own blanket, carried him in his arms to the transport, tended him during the passage, and only yielded up his charge when Death met him at the door of the hospital which promised care and comfort for the boy. For ten days, Teddy had shivered or burned with fever and ague, pining the while for Kit, and refusing to be comforted, because he had not been able to thank him for the generous protection, which, perhaps, had cost the giver's life. The vivid dream had wronged the childish heart with a fresh pang, and when I tried the solace fitted for his years, the remorseful fear that haunted him found vent in a fresh burst of tears, as he looked at the wasted hands I was endeavoring to warm:

"Oh! if I'd only been as thin when Kit carried me as I am now, maybe he wouldn't have died; but I was heavy, he was hurt worser than we knew, and so it killed him; and I didn't see him, to say good bye.''

This thought had troubled him in secret; and all my assurances that his friend would probably have died at all events, hardly assuaged the bitterness of his regretful grief.

At this juncture, the delirious man began to shout; the one–legged rose up in his bed, as if preparing for another dart; Teddy bewailed himself more piteously than before: and if ever a woman was at her wit's end, that distracted female was Nurse Periwinkle, during the space of two or three minutes, as she vibrated between the three beds, like an agitated pendulum. Like a most opportune reinforcement, Dan, the bandy, appeared, and devoted himself to the

lively party, leaving me free to return to my post; for the
Prussian, with a nod and a smile took the lad away to his
own bed, and lulled him to sleep with a soothing murmur,
like a mammoth bumble bee. . . .

Hardly was I settled again, when the inevitable bowl
appeared, and its bearer delivered a message I had expected, yet dreaded to receive:

"John is going, ma'am, and wants to see you, if you
can come."

"The moment this boy is asleep; tell him so, and let
me know if I am in danger of being too late." [3]

*Although a doctor by profession, Holmes' visits to the
hospitals were unofficial.*

. . . We visited the schoolhouse hospital. A fine young
fellow, whose arm had been shattered, was just falling into
the spasms of lockjaw. The beads of sweat stood large and
round on his flushed and contracted features. He was under
the effect of opiates—why not (if his case was desperate as
it seemed to be considered) stop his sufferings with chloro-
form? It was suggested that it might *shorten life.* "What
then?" I said, "Are a dozen additional spasms worth living for?"

The same morning we visited several of the temporary
hospitals, churches and schoolhouses, where the wounded
were lying. In one of these, after looking around as usual, I
asked aloud, "Any Massachusetts men here?" Two bright
faces lifted themselves from their pillows and welcomed me
by name. . . . I learned then and since . . . that they and
their comrades were completely overwhelmed by the attentions of the good people of Harrisburg—that the ladies
brought them fruits and flowers, and smiles, better than
either—and that the little boys of the place were almost
fighting for the privilege of doing their errands. [4]

15　Old Abe Vis-a-Vis

It was in March, 1861, not long after the Inauguration and a month before Sumter was fired upon, that Melville shook hands with the President.

. . . I was on the second levee at the White House. There was a great crowd & a brilliant scene. Ladies in full dress by the hundred. A steady stream of two-&-two's wound thru' the apartments shaking hands with "Old Abe" and immediately passing on. This continued without cessation for an hour & a half. Of course I was one of the shakers. Old Abe is much better-looking than I expected & younger-looking. He shook hands like a good fellow—working hard at it like a man sawing wood at so much per cord. Mrs. Lincoln is rather good-looking I thought. The scene was very fine altogether. Superb furniture—flood of light—magnificent flowers—full band of music &c.[1]

Hawthorne relates his impressions of Lincoln a year later.

Of course, there was one other personage, in the class of statesmen, whom I should have been truly mortified to leave Washington without seeing, since (temporarily, at least, and by force of circumstances), he was the man of men. But a private grief had built up a barrier about him, impeding the customary free intercourse of Americans with their chief magistrate; so that I might have come away without a glimpse of his very remarkable physiognomy, save for a semi-official opportunity of which I was glad to take advantage. The fact is, we were invited to annex ourselves, as supernumeraries, to a deputation that was about to wait upon the President, from a Massachusetts whip factory, with a present of a splendid whip.

Our immediate party consisted only of four or five (including Major Ben Perley Poore, with his notebook and pencil), but we were joined by several other persons, who seemed to have been lounging about the precincts of the White House, under the spacious porch, or within the hall, and who swarmed in with us to take the chances of a presentation.

Nine o'clock had been appointed as the time for receiving the deputation, and we were punctual to the moment; but not so the President, who sent us word that he was eating his breakfast, and would come as soon as he could.

His appetite we are glad to think must have been a pretty fair one; for we waited about half an hour in one of the antechambers, and then were ushered into a reception room, in one corner of which sat the Secretaries of War and of the Treasury, expecting, like ourselves, the termination of the Presidential breakfast. During this interval there were several new additions to our group, one or two of whom were in a working-garb, so that we formed a very miscellaneous collection of people, mostly unknown to each other, and without any common sponsor, but all with an equal right to look our head servant in the face.

By and by there was a little stir on the staircase and in the passageway, and in lounged a tall, loose-jointed figure of an exaggerated Yankee port and demeanor, whom (as being about the homeliest man I ever saw, yet by no means repulsive or disagreeable) it was impossible not to recognize as Uncle Abe.

Unquestionably, Western man though he be, and Kentuckian by birth, President Lincoln is the essential representative of all Yankees, and the veritable specimen, physically, of what the world seems determined to regard as our characteristic qualities. It is the strangest and yet the fittest thing in the jumble of human vicissitudes, that he, out of so many millions, unlooked for, unselected by any intelligible process that could be based upon his genuine qualities, unknown to those who chose him, and unsuspected of what endowments may adapt him for his tremendous responsibility, should have found this way open for him to fling his lank personality into the chair of state— where, I presume, it was his first impulse to throw his legs on the council-table, and tell the Cabinet Ministers a story.

There is no describing his lanky awkwardness nor the uncouthness of his movement; and yet it seemed as if I had been in the habit of seeing him daily, and had shaken hands with him a thousand times in some village street; so true was he to the aspect of the pattern American, though with a certain extravagance, which, possibly, I exaggerated still further by the delighted eagerness with which I took it in. If put to guess his calling and livelihood, I should have taken him for a country schoolmaster as soon as anything else. He was dressed in a rusty black frock coat and pantaloons, unbrushed, and worn so faithfully that the suit had adapted itself to the curves and angularities of his figure, and had grown to be an outer skin of the man. He had shabby slippers on his feet. His hair was black, still unmixed with gray, stiff, somewhat bushy, and had apparently been acquainted with neither brush nor comb that morning, after the disarrangement of the pillow; and as to a nightcap, Uncle Abe probably knows nothing of such effeminacies. His complexion is dark and sallow, betokening, I fear, an insalubrious atmosphere around the White House. He has thick black eyebrows and an impending brow; his nose is large, and the lines about his mouth are very strongly defined.

The whole physiognomy is as coarse a one as you would meet anywhere in the length and breadth of the States; but, withal, it is redeemed, illuminated, softened, and brightened by a kindly though serious look out of his eyes, and an expression of homely sagacity, that seems weighted with rich results of village experience. A great deal of native sense; no bookish cultivation, no refinement; honest at heart, and thoroughly so, and yet, in some sort, sly—at least, endowed with a sort of tact and wisdom that are akin to craft, and would impel him, I think, to take an antagonist in flank, rather than to make a bull-run at him right in front.

But, on the whole, I like this sallow, queer, sagacious visage, with the homely human sympathies that warmed it; and, for my small share in the matter, would as lief have Uncle Abe for a ruler as any man whom it would have been practicable to put in his place.

Immediately, on his entrance, the President accosted our member of Congress, who had us in charge, and, with a comical twist of his face, made some jocular remark about the length of his breakfast. He then greeted us all round, not waiting for an introduction, but shaking and squeezing everybody's hand with the utmost cordiality, whether the individual's name was announced to him or not. His manner towards us was wholly without pretence, but yet had a kind of natural dignity, quite sufficient to keep the forwardest of us from clapping him on the shoulder and asking him for a story.

A mutual acquaintance being established, our leader took the whip out of its case, and began to read the address of presentation. The whip was an exceedingly long one, its handle wrought in ivory (by some artist in the Massachusetts State Prison, I believe), and ornamented with a medallion of the President, and other equally beautiful devices; and along its whole length there was a succession of golden bands and ferrules. The address was shorter than the whip, but equally well made, consisting chiefly of an explanatory description of these artistic designs, and closing with a hint that the gift was a suggestion and an emblematic one, and that the President would recognize the use to which such an instrument should be put.

This suggestion gave Uncle Abe rather a delicate task in his reply, because, slight as the matter seemed, it appar-

ently called for some declaration, or intimation, or faint
foreshadowing of policy in reference to the conduct of the
war, and the final treatment of the Rebels. But the President's Yankee aptness and not-to-be-caughtness stood him
in good stead, and he jerked or wiggled himself out of the
dilemma with an uncouth dexterity that was entirely in
character; although, without his gesticulation of eye and
mouth—and especially the flourish of the whip with which
he imagined himself touching up a pair of fat horses—I
doubt whether his words would be worth recording, even if
I could remember them.

The gist of the reply was, that he accepted the whip as
an emblem of peace, not punishment; and, this great affair
over, we retired out of the presence in high good humor,
only regretting that we could not have seen the President
sit down and fold up his legs (which is said to be an extraordinary spectacle) or have heard him tell one of those
delectable stories for which he is so celebrated. A good
many of them are afloat upon the common talk of Washington, and are certainly the aptest, pithiest, and funniest
little things imaginable; though, to be sure, they smack of
the frontier freedom, and would not always bear repetition
in a drawing-room, or on the immaculate pages of the
Atlantic.*

Good Heavens! What liberties have I been taking with
one of the potentates of the earth, and the man on whose
conduct more important consequences depend than on that

---

* [*Hawthorne's note:*] The above passage relating to President Lincoln
was one of those omitted from the article as originally published, and
the following was appended:

> We are compelled to omit two or three pages in which the author
> describes the interview, and gives his idea of the personal appearance
> and deportment of the President. The sketch appears to have been
> written in a benign spirit, and perhaps conveys a not inaccurate im-
> pression of its august subject; but it lacks *reverence,* and it pains us
> to see a gentleman of ripe age, and who has spent years under the
> corrective influence of foreign institutions, falling into the character-
> istic and most ominous fault of Young America.

of any other historical personage of the century! But with whom is an American citizen entitled to take a liberty, if not with his own chief magistrate? However, lest the above allusions to President Lincoln's little peculiarities (already well known to the country and to the world) should be misinterpreted, I deem it proper to say a word or two in regard to him of unfeigned respect and measurable confidence.

He is evidently a man of keen faculties, and, what is still more to the purpose, of powerful character. As to his integrity, the people have that intuition of it which is never deceived. Before he actually entered upon his great office, and for a considerable time afterwards, there is no reason to suppose that he adequately estimated the gigantic task about to be imposed on him, or, at least, had any distinct idea how it was to be managed; and I presume there may have been more than one veteran politician who proposed to himself to take the power out of President Lincoln's hands into his own, leaving our honest friend only the public responsibility for the good or ill success of the career. The extremely imperfect development of his statesmanship qualities, at that period, may have justified such designs. But the President is teachable by events, and has now spent a year in a very arduous course of education; he has a flexible mind, capable of much expansion, and convertible towards far loftier studies and activities than those of his early life; and if he came to Washington a backwoods humorist, he has already transformed himself into as good a statesman (to speak moderately) as his prime minister.[2]

Whitman's comments are based on personal observation, although he was never formally presented to Lincoln.

I see the President almost every day, as I happen to live where he passes to and from his lodgings out of town. He never sleeps at the White House during the hot season, but has quarters at a health location some three miles north of the city—the Soldiers' Home—a United States military establishment.

I saw him this morning about 8:30 coming in to business, riding on Vermont Avenue, near L Street. He always has a company of twenty-five or thirty cavalry, with sabers drawn and held upright over their shoulders. They say the guard was against his personal wish, but he let his counselors have their way.

The party makes no great show in uniform or horses. Mr. Lincoln on the saddle generally rides a good-sized, easy-going, gray horse; is dressed in plain black, somewhat rusty and dusty; wears a stiff black hat; and looks about as ordinary in attire, etc. as the commonest man. A lieutenant with yellow straps rides at his left; and, following behind, two by two, come the cavalry men in their yellow-striped jackets. They are generally going at a slow trot, as that is the pace set them by the one they wait upon. The sabers and accoutrements clank, and the entirely unornamental cortege as it trots toward Lafayette Square arouses no sensation; only some curious stranger stops and gazes.

I see very plainly Abraham Lincoln's dark brown face, with the deep-cut lines, the eyes always, to me, with a deep latent sadness in the expression. We have got so we exchange bows, and very cordial ones.

Sometimes the President goes and comes in an open barouche. The cavalry always accompanies him, with drawn sabers. Often I notice, as he goes out evenings and sometimes in the mornings when he returns early, he turns off and halts at the large and handsome residence of the Secretary of War on K Street and holds conference there. If in his barouche, I can see from my window he does not alight, but sits in his vehicle, and Mr. Stanton comes out to attend him. Sometimes one of his sons, a boy of ten or twelve, accompanies him, riding at his right on a pony.

Earlier in the summer I occasionally saw the President and his wife toward the latter part of the afternoon, out in a barouche on a pleasure ride through the city. Mrs. Lincoln was dressed in complete black, with a long crepe veil. The equipage is of the plainest kind—only two horses and they nothing extra.

They passed me very close, and I saw the President in the face fully, as they were moving slowly; and his look, though abstracted, happened to be directed steadily in my eye. He bowed and smiled, but far beneath the smile I noticed well the expression I have alluded to. None of the artists or pictures have caught the deep though subtle and indirect expression of this man's face. There is something else there; one of the great portrait painters of two or three centuries ago is needed.

. . . Lincoln's face . . . of technical beauty it had nothing—but to the eye of a great artist it furnished a rare study, a feast, and fascination. The current portraits are all failures—most of them caricatures.

. . . It . . . had . . . wonderful reserve, restraint of expression, fine nobility staring at you out of that ruggedness. . . .[3]

Emerson adds to Whitman's portrait.

You cannot refine Mr. Lincoln's taste, extend his horizon, or clear his judgment; he will not walk dignifiedly through the traditional part of the President of America, but will pop out his head at each railroad station and make a little speech, and get into an argument with Squire A and Judge B. He will write letters to Horace Greeley, and any editor or reporter or saucy party committee that writes to him, and cheapen himself.

But this we might be ready for, and let the clown appear, and hug ourselves that we are well off, if we have got good nature, honest meaning, and fidelity to public interest, with bad manners—instead of an elegant roué and malignant self-seeker.

At Washington. . . . Saw . . . President Lincoln. The President impressed me more favorably than I had hoped. A frank, sincere, well–meaning man, with a lawyer's habit of mind, good clear statement of his fact; correct enough, not vulgar, as described, but with a sort of boyish cheerfulness, or that kind of sincerity and jolly good meaning that our class meetings on Commencement days show, in telling our old stories over. When he has made his remark, he looks up at you with great satisfaction, and shows all his white teeth and laughs. He argued to Sumner the whole case of Gordon, the slave trader, point by point, and added that he was not quite satisfied yet, and meant to refresh his memory by looking again at the evidence. All this showed a fidelity and conscientiousness very honorable to him.

When I was introduced to him, he said, "Oh, Mr. Emerson, I once heard you say in a lecture that a Kentuckian seems to say by his air and manners, 'Here am I; if you don't like me, the worse for you.' "[4]

Bryant visits Lincoln in Washington in an effort to urge him to more decisive action.

. . . Some of our best and most eminent men have visited Washington to remonstrate with him, but only with partial effect. The influence of Seward is always at work, and counteracts the good impressions made in the interviews with men of a different class. I was strongly pressed to go to Washington myself, and went somewhat reluctantly, not having any confidence in my powers of persuasion. I saw Mr. Lincoln, and had a long conversation with him on the affairs of the country, in which I expressed myself plainly and without reserve, though courteously.

He bore it well, and I must say that I left him with a perfect conviction of the excellence of his intentions and the singleness of his purposes, though with sorrow for his indecision. A movement is now afoot to bring the influence of our best men to bear upon him in a more concentrated manner, by a wider concert among them. Meetings have been held for that purpose and a committee raised.[5]

16 General McClellan on Trial

Hawthorne comes face to face with General McClellan.

We now approached General McClellan's headquarters, which, at that time, were established at Fairfield Seminary. The edifice was situated on a gentle elevation, amid very agreeable scenery, and, at a distance looked like a gentleman's seat. Preparations were going forward for reviewing a division of ten or twelve thousand men, the various regiments composing which had begun to array themselves on an extensive plain, where, methought, there was a more convenient place for a battle than is usually found on this broken and difficult country. Two thousand cavalry made a portion of the troops to be reviewed.

By and by we saw a pretty numerous troop of mounted officers, who were congregated on a distant part of the plain, and whom we finally ascertained to be the Commander-in-Chief's staff, with McClellan himself at their head. Our party managed to establish itself in a position conveniently close to the General, to whom, moreover, we had the honor of an introduction; and he bowed, on his horse-back, with a good deal of dignity and martial courtesy, but no airs nor fuss nor pretension beyond what his character and rank inevitably gave him.

Now, at that juncture, and, in fact, up to the present

moment, there was, and is, a most fierce and bitter outcry, and detraction loud and low, against General McClellan, accusing him of sloth, imbecility, cowardice, treasonable purposes, and, in short, utterly denying his ability as a soldier, and questioning his integrity as a man. Nor, was this to be wondered at; for when before, in all history, do we find a general in command of half a million of men, and in presence of an enemy inferior in numbers, and no better disciplined than his own troops, leaving it still debatable, after the better part of a year, whether he is a soldier or no?

The question would seem to answer itself in the very asking. Nevertheless, being most profoundly ignorant of the art of war, like the majority of the General's critics, and, on the other hand, having some considerable impressibility by men's characters, I was glad of the opportunity to look him in the face, and to feel whatever influence might reach me from his sphere. So I stared at him, as the phrase goes, with all the eyes I had.

The General was dressed in a simple, dark blue uniform, without epaulets, booted to the knee, and with a cloth cap upon his head; and, at first sight, you might have taken him for a corporal of dragoons, of particularly neat and soldier–like aspect, and in the prime of his age and strength. He is only of middling stature, but his build is very compact and sturdy, with broad shoulders, and a look of great physical vigor, which, in fact, he is said to possess—he and Beauregard having been rivals in that particular, and both distinguished above other men.

His complexion is dark and sanguine, with dark hair. He has a strong, bold, soldierly face, full of decision; a Roman nose, by no means a thin prominence, but very thick and firm; and if he follows it (which I should think likely), it may be pretty confidently trusted to guide him aright. His profile would make a more effective likeness than the full face, which, however, is much better in the real man than in any photograph that I have seen.

His forehead is not remarkably large, but comes for-

ward at the eyebrows; it is not the brow nor countenance
of a prominently intellectual man (not a natural student, I
mean, or abstract thinker) but of one whose office it is to
handle things practically and to bring about tangible results. His face looked capable of being very stern, but
wore, in its repose, when I saw it, an aspect pleasant and
dignified; it is not, in its character, an American face nor
an English one. The man on whom he fixed his eye is conscious of him. In his natural disposition he seems calm and
self–possessed, sustaining his great responsibilities cheerfully, without shrinking, or weariness, or spasmodic effort,
or damage to his health, but all with quiet, deep–drawn
breaths; just as his broad shoulders would bear up a heavy
burden without aching beneath it.

After we had had sufficient time to peruse the man (so
far as it could be done with one pair of very attentive
eyes), the General rode off, followed by his cavalcade, and
was lost to sight among the troops. They received him with
loud shouts, by the eager uproar of which—now near, now
in the centre, now on the outskirts of the division, and now
sweeping back towards us in a great volume of sound—we
could trace his progress through the ranks. If he is a
coward, or a traitor, or a humbug, or anything less than a
brave, true, and able man, that mass of intelligent soldiers,
whose lives and honor he had in charge, were utterly deceived, and so was this present writer; for they believed in
him, and so did I; and had I stood in the ranks, I should
have shouted with the lustiest of them.

Of course I may be mistaken; my opinion on such a
point is worth nothing, although my impression may be
worth a little more; neither do I consider the General's
antecedents as bearing very decided testimony to his practical soldiership. A thorough knowledge of the science of
war seems to be conceded to him; he is allowed to be a
good military critic; but all this is possible without his
possessing any positive qualities of a great general, just as
a literary critic may show his profoundest acquaintance
with the principles of epic poetry without being able to

produce a single stanza of an epic poem. Nevertheless, I shall not give up my faith in General McClellan's soldier-ship until he is defeated, nor in his courage and integrity even then.[1]

Whitman takes a backward look at McClellan.

. . . Poor McClellan! Poor McClellan! how they laid it on him! Yet I don't doubt but it is just—that he deserved it. . . .

. . . It would take a great deal to persuade me from my conviction, my old conviction, born at the time and never by any later developments shaken—my old conviction that McClellan straddled. I was on the spot at the time—in the midst of all the controversy, the suspicion, the tension, and the patriotism; and from it all, fairly and sternly, I drew my estimate of McClellan.

He thought: the time will come when these sections will be united again (he saw it; we all saw it; knew it was sure to be); then the lucky man, he thought, the man with the most power, will be the man who dealt most gently with the malcontents. . . .

I do not believe he (Lincoln) would have taken the position he did towards McClellan except for some reason the logic of which could not be denied—some last reason of all reasons which the most conservative man would find he must obey.

. . . As between Lincoln and McClellan, there is an obvious distinction to be made—their natures were related as higher to lower. Lincoln had a point to make—the Union; McClellan contemplated the prospect of an early end of the war—felt that the man who dealt the softest blows all around would be the great man, the general idol, the savior. So he kept one foot on each side, waiting for the certain sure turn of events which was to give him his immortality.

But events did not turn out the way he expected —McClellan expected. In all that went along with this

clash of policies, Lincoln's benignity shone resplendent;
the personalism of McClellan was always discouraging,
perilous, injurious; Lincoln always stood aside—kept his
individual motives in rein—loved, hated, for the common
good.

Somebody . . . says somewhere that the best saints
are those who have been the worst sinners. I consider
McClellan as in some respects a seamed man: he paltered
with the army. Yet at Antietam, when pushed to it, he displayed undoubted qualities. They all said, and say now, the
battle was well managed to begin with; the fault seems to
have been in neglecting to follow out an opportunity—in
the loaferly after-hours; in McClellan's "no—no—the
army must be rested." [2]

*Lowell uses General McClellan's published defense of him-
self as the basis for a discussion of the General's qualities.*

. . . No commander ever had more of . . . paid–up
capital of fortune . . . fame in advance . . . success before succeeding, than General McClellan. That dear old
domestic bird, the Public, which lays the golden eggs out of
which greenbacks are hatched, was sure she had brooded
out an eagle chick at last. How we all waited to see him
stoop on the dovecote of Richmond!

Never did nation give such an example of faith and
patience as while the Army of the Potomac lay during all
those weary months before Washington. Every excuse was
invented, every palliation suggested, except the true one,
that our chicken was no eagle, after all. He was hardening
his seres, he was waiting for his wings to grow, he was
whetting his beak; we should see him soar at last and
shake the thunder from his wings. But do what we could,
hope what we might, it became daily clearer that, whatever
other excellent qualities he might have, this of being aqui-
line was wanting.

. . . . General McClellan puts himself upon the country, and, after taking so much time to make up his mind as

when he wearied and imperilled the nation in his camp on the Potomac, endeavors to win back from public opinion the victory which nothing but his own overcaution enabled the Rebels to snatch from him before Richmond. He cannot give us back our lost time or our squandered legions; but how nice it would be if we would give him back his reputation, which has never been of any great use to us, and yet would be so convenient for him! It was made for him, and accordingly fits him better than it would any one else. But it is altogether too late. There is no argument for the soldier but success, no wisdom for the man but to acknowledge defeat and be silent under it.

. . . We believe him to be honest in his opinions, and patriotic so far as those opinions will allow him to be; we know him to be capable of attaching those about him in a warm personal friendship, and we reject with the contempt they deserve the imputations on his courage and his military honor; but at the same time we consider him a man like other men, with a head liable to be turned by a fame too easily won. His great misfortune was that he began his first important campaign with a reputation to save instead of to earn, so that he was hampered by the crowning disadvantage of age in a general without the experience which might neutralize it. Nay, what was still worse, he had two reputations to keep from damage, the one as soldier, the other as politician.

. . . He appears to have thought it within the sphere of his duty to take charge of the statesmanship of the President no less than of the movements of the army, nor was it long before there were unmistakable symptoms that he began to consider himself quite as much the chief of an opposition who could dictate terms as the military subordinate who was to buy orders.

Whatever might have been his capacity as a soldier, his divided allegiance could not fail of disastrous consequences to the public service, for no mistress exacts so jealously the entire devotion of her servants as war. A mind distracted with calculations of future political contingencies was not to be relied on in the conduct of move-

ments which above all others demand the constant presence, undivided energy, of all the faculties, and the concentration of every personal interest on the object of immediate success.

A general who is conscious that he has an army of one
hundred and fifty thousand voters at his back will always
be weakened by those personal considerations which are
the worst consequence of the elective system. General
McClellan's motions were encumbered in every direction
by the huge train of political baggage. This misconception
of his own position, or rather his confounding the two
characters of possible candidate and actual general, forced
the growth of whatever egotism was latent in his nature.

He began ere long to look at everything from a personal point of view, to judge men and measures by their
presumed relation to his own interests, and at length fairly
persuaded himself that the inevitable results of his own
want of initiative were due to the hostile combination
against him of Mr. Lincoln, Mr. Stanton, and General
Halleck. Regarding himself too much in considering the
advantages of success, he regards others too little in re-
warding the responsibility of failure.

. . . From the time of his taking command till his removal, he was constantly asking for more men, constantly
receiving them, and constantly unable to begin anything
with them after he got them. He could not move without
one hundred and fifty thousand pairs of legs, and when his
force had long reached that number, the President was
obliged by overtaxed impatience of the country to pry him
up from his encampment on the Potomac with a special
order.

What the army really needed was an addition of one
man, and that at the head of it; for a general, like an
orator, must be moved himself before he can move others.
The larger his army, the more helpless was General
McClellan . . . he was swamped in his own supplies. With
every reinforcement sent him on the Peninsula, his estimate of the numbers opposed to him increased. His own
imagination faced him in superior numbers at every turn.

Since Don Quixote's enumeration of the armies of the Emperor Alifanfaron and King Pentapolin of the Naked Arm, there has been nothing like our General's vision of the Rebel forces, with their ever-lengthening list of leaders, gathered for the defence of Richmond. His anxiety swells their muster roll at least to two hundred thousand.

. . . He can compose a good campaign beforehand, but he cannot improvise one out of events of the moment, as is the wont of great generals. Occasion seldom offers her forelock twice to the grasp of the same man, and yet General McClellan by the admission of the Rebels themselves, had Richmond at his mercy more than once.

. . . The stiffness rather than the firmness of mind, the surrender of all spontaneous action in the strait-waistcoat of a preconceived plan . . . unfitted him for the rapid change of combinations on the great chess-board of battle. . . .

If General McClellan had been as prompt in attacking the enemy as he showed himself in this assault on his superiors, we think his campaign in the Peninsula would have ended more satisfactorily. We have no doubt that he would conduct a siege or a defence with all the science and all the proprieties of warfare, but we think he has proved himself singularly wanting in the qualities which distinguish the natural leaders of men. . . . He never knew how to find opportunity, much less to make it. He was an accomplished soldier, but lacked that downright common sense which is only another name for genius with its coat off for actual work in hand.[3]

Bryant helps Lincoln, who is looking for a general, by eliminating at least one candidate.

We have suffered long enough from inaction and over-caution. Henceforth we must have action. . . . If it be asked who is the best man, we can only say that it is Mr. Lincoln's business to know, but bitter experience has taught us that Gen. McClellan is not.[4]

17   A War of Personalities

Whitman appraises Sherman, Sheridan and Grant.

Have you ever seen Sherman? It is necessary to see him in order to realize the Norse makeup of the man—the hauteur, yet democratic. . . . Try to picture Sherman—seamy, sinewy in style—a bit of stern open air made up in the image of a man. The best of Sherman was best in the war. . . .

I can see Sherman now, at the head of the line, on Pennsylvania Avenue, the day the army filed before Lincoln—the silent Sherman riding beyond his aides. Yes, Sherman is all very well! I respect him. But after all, Sheridan was the Napoleonic figure of the war—not subjected to the last tests (though I am sure he would have been equal to them), but adequate, it seemed, to whatever duty arose. That is where I place Sheridan—among Napoleonic things.

The real military figure of the war, counting the man in, was Grant, whose homely manners, dislike for military frippery—for every form of ostentation in war and peace—amounted to genius.

. . . Grant was the typical Western man—the plainest, the most efficient; was the least imposed upon by appearances; was most impressive in the severe simplicity of his flannel shirt and his utter disregard for formal military etiquette.[1]

Emerson hobnobbed with a number of the leaders of the government during his visit to Washington in January, 1862.

Mr. Stanton . . . made a good impression, as of an able, determined man, very impatient of his instruments, and, though he named nobody, I thought he had McClellan in mind.

As Judge Chase had invited us to dine with him at 5 o'clock, we went thither and saw his pretty daughter Kate, who alone with her father did the honours of the house. . . . . He and Sumner appeared to agree entirely in their counsels. They both held that as soon as a State seceded, it gave up its State organization, but did not thereby touch the National Government. The moment Arkansas or Mississippi seceded, they would have said, "Certainly, if you do not like your State Government, surrender it, and you lapse instantly into United States territory, again"; and they would have sent immediately a territorial governor to the first foot of that land which they could reach, and have established United States Power in the old form.

I breakfasted at Mr. Robbin's, with Mr. Sherman of the Senate, and Mr. Colfax of the House. In talking with the last, he said that Congress had not yet come up to the point of confiscating slaves of rebel masters, no, but only such as were engaged in military service. I said, "How is it possible Congress can be so slow?" He replied, "It is owing to the great social power here in Washington of the Border States. They step into the place of the Southerners here, and wield the same power."

When I told Sumner what Seward had said to me about England . . . he replied, "He has not been frank with you. I have heard him utter the most hostile sentiments to England."

Sumner showed me several English letters of much interest which he had just received . . . . all relating to our politics, and pressing Emancipation. Bright writes that, thus far, the English have not suffered from the war, but rather been benefited by stopping manufacturing and clear-

ing out their old stocks and bringing their trade into a
more healthy state. But, after a few months, they will be
importunate for cotton.

I spent Sunday evening at the house of Charles
Eames, late Minister to Venezuela. . . . At his house I
found many new and some old acquaintances, Governor
Fish, Governor Andrew, N. P. Willis, Gurowski, Mr. Nico-
lay, the President's private secretary, and another young
gentleman, who shares I believe, the same office [Ed. note:
John Hay], and is also, I am told, a contributor to the *Atlantic Monthly,* but whose name I have forgotten. Young
Robert Lincoln, the President's son, was also there, and
Leutze, the painter, who invited me to see his pictures
which he is painting for a panel in the Capitol, ''The
Emigration to the West.'' No military people, I think,
were present. And when I went home at a late hour I was
vexed to have forgotten that Mr. Secretary Stanton had
invited me to call on him at his house this evening.[2]

*Hawthorne is impressed by the painter Leutze and then by
the personal appearance of Secretary of State Seward.*

It was an absolute comfort, indeed, to find Leutze so
quietly busy at this great national work, which is destined
to glow for centuries on the walls of the Capitol, if that
edifice shall succeed in subverting it with the Union which
it represents. It was delightful to see him so calmly elabo-
rating his design, while other men doubted and feared, or
hoped treacherously, and whispered to one another that
the nation would exist only a little longer, or that, if a
remnant still held together, its centre and seat of government would be far northward and westward of Washington.

But the artist keeps right on, firm of heart and hand,
drawing his outlines with an unwavering pencil, beautify-
ing and idealizing our rude, material life, and thus mani-
festing that we have an indefeasible claim to a more enduring national existence. In honest truth, what with the hope-

inspiring influence of the design, and what with Leutze's undisturbed evolvement of it, I was exceedingly encouraged, and allowed these cheerful auguries to weigh against a sinister omen that was pointed out to me in another part of the Capitol. The freestone walls of the central office are pervaded with great cracks, and threaten to come thundering down, under the immense weight of the iron dome—an appropriate catastrophe enough, if it should occur on the day when we drop the Southern stars out of our flag.

Everybody seems to be at Washington, and yet there is a singular dearth of imperatively noticeable people there. I question whether there are half a dozen individuals, in all kinds of eminence, at whom a stranger, wearied with the contact of a hundred moderate celebrities, would turn around to snatch a second glance. Secretary Seward, to be sure—a pale, large-nosed, elderly man, of moderate stature, with a decided originality of gait and aspect, and a cigar in his mouth—etc., etc.[3]

Whitman gives his opinion of Jefferson Davis many years after the war clouds had vanished and follows it up with an anecdote about Stonewall Jackson.

. . . I still hold to my opinion formed at the time—Davis was representative, he must bear the onus of that. Besides, Davis is alive; he has perfect freedom; he goes where he wills; every now and then we read accounts of new speeches by him; he is everywhere down South warmly received, applauded to the echo—the echo itself echoes. What more could he have? This has been paralleled almost nowhere in the world—in any other country on the globe the whole batch of the Confederate leaders would have had their heads cut off. . . .

. . . There's the story of Lige—it plays the dickens with the character of Stonewall Jackson, taking him down (whipping him off) the pedestal he has decorated by general consent.

Everybody in Washington wanted to think well of Jackson—I with the rest—and we were inclined to the very last to distrust the many stories which seemed to reflect upon his glory. But Lige's tale was so modestly told that I could not doubt it; and was told so entirely without brag, bad temper, without any desire for revenge—in fact without any consciousness that Jackson had done anything but what was usual and right.

Lige had been captured. Jackson subjected him to an inquisition; wanted information; would have it—would, would, would—whether or no. Lige only said and kept on saying: "I'm a Union soldier and can't do it." Finding he could get nothing from Lige, Jackson punished him by making him walk the ten miles to Richmond, while the others were conveyed.

I could never think the same of Jackson after hearing that—after seeing how he resented in Lige what was a credit to him—what Lige would not have given and what Jackson could not have taken, and either remain honest. And think of it, too! Jackson was such a praying man—going off into the woods, flopping on his knees everywhere and anywhere to pray.[4]

Lanier, in letters and reminiscences, sketches portraits of some of the Confederate generals, especially Robert E. Lee.

Your "come, come, to your child," nigh broke my heart—For I *cannot* come—I had based my hopes of a furlough upon the friendship of Gen French, and the confidence which I knew he reposes in me— In my absence from Petersburg, however, Gen. F. has been ordered to assume command of a Division at Vicksburg; and has been succeeded here by Gen. D. H. Hill, a tyrannical old curmudgeon.

Yet, I rejoice in the Peace party, not because of any results which I expect directly from its operations in favor of our independence, but simply because it is an infallible indication of a wide-spreading belief in the ability of the South to win its independence *by force of arms*— The true and effective Peace party is led, not by Mr. Long, but by

Gen. Lee. This noble fugleman, with his ragged constituency, who combine filth with heroism, in such a way as the world has not before seen, who vote by bullet and not by ballot, who thunder from the Earthworks and not from this Hustings; this innovating politician who discards bribery, who spreads not soft-soap, who pulls not the concealed wires, who confers no lucrative positions, who makes no shoddy contracts, who rejects all the old and well-established "mechanical appliances" of Party, that is the man, these are the voters, who are to give us peace and to establish our independence.

Gen. Lee held services at his Hd Q'rs. about two hundred yards from our station, on last Sunday— Gen. Pendleton preached; Gen. A. P. Hill was present, and some other officers— The table which held the simple paraphernalia of our worship, a Bible and a prayer book, was placed under a noble tree; the sky was serene: the sunlight was warm and beautiful on the green grass; a shell shrieked occasionally; a bird flew into the tree over the Preacher's head and sat and sang; my dog Flag, trotted composedly around and through the assemblage, rubbing himself sometimes against Gen. Lee, anon against Gen. Hill—and then seating himself in the circle to stare at everybody, this being the first time that Flag ever attended Divine Service; the Preacher preached peace on earth and good–will towards men, dressed in a uniform which was trimmed with bloodred;—all of which incongruous elements set me into a reverie upon the illimitable mystery of the World, the end of which has not yet come— —Gen. Pendleton is a noble, dignified man of large stature, and reminds me forcibly of a picture of Oliver Cromwell which I have seen somewhere— Gen. Lee has the commander in every lineament of his face, and motion of his body; his dignity is graceful and simple, and his firmness which declares itself at first glance to be impregnable, is relieved by intelligence and charity which one discovers in his eyes presiding over it.[5]

The last time I saw (Lee) with mortal eyes . . . the scene was so beautiful, the surroundings were so rare, nay,

time and circumstance did so fitly frame him as it were,
that I think the picture should not be lost. There was nothing melodramatic in the circumstances, nothing startling,
nothing sensational; which was all the more particularly in
accord with his character, for this was one of those grand
but modest, sweet souls that love simplicity and shrink
from all that is loud and vulgar.

It was at fateful Petersburg on one glorious Sunday
morning, whilst the armies of Grant and Butler were in-
vesting our last stronghold there. It had been announced to
those who happened to be stationed in the neighborhood of
General Lee's headquarters that religious service would be
conducted on that morning, by Major General Pendleton,
of the Artillery.

At the appointed time I strolled over to Dunn's Hill,
where General Lee's tent was pitched, and found General
Pendleton ensconced under a magnificent tree, and a small
party of soldiers with a few ladies from the dwellings
nearby, collected about him. In a few moments General Lee
appeared, with his camp chair, and sat down. The services
began.

That terrible battery number five, was firing, very
slowly, each report of the great guns making the otherwise
profound silence still more profound. Even Hoke's line
was quiet.

I sat down on the grass, and gazed with such reverence
as I had never given to mortal man before, upon the grand
face of General Lee. He had been greatly fatigued by the
loss of sleep. As the sermon progressed, and the immortal
words of Christian doctrine came to our hearts and comforted us, sweet influences born of the liberal sunlight that
lay warm upon the grass, of the waving leaves and trembling flowers, seemed to steal over the general's soul. Presently his eyelids gradually closed, and he fell gently asleep.

Not a muscle of him stirred, not a nerve of his grand
countenance twitched, there was no drooping of the head,
nor bowing of the figure, and I could not have been sure
that he really slept had I not observed that a venturesome
fly crawled unheeded upon his chest in an attitude of

majestic repose such as I never saw assumed by mortal man before; as the large and comfortable words fell from the preacher's lips; as the lazy cannon of the enemy anon hurled a screaming shell to within a few hundred yards of where we sat, as finally a bird flew into the tree overhead and sat and piped small blissful notes in unearthly contrast with the roar of the war engines; it seemed to me as if the present earth floated off through the sunlight, and the antique earth returned out of the past, and some majestic god sat on a hill, sculptured in stone, and presided over a terrible yet sublime contest of human passions.[6]

Whittier writes to Jessie Fremont, the wife of General John C. Fremont, October 24, 1863.

It was very thoughtful on thy part to inform me of thy unexpected Hegira southward. I would to see thee and the general in your own quiet 'Anchorage,' but am not certain that I should have been well enough to do so. But I must thank thee heartily for thy little visit at our home. We have in some sort known and loved thee and thine for a long time, and seeing thee has confirmed our impressions. . . . I am very happy to know that my word of encouragement was not wholly in vain, during your trials in Missouri. I sent the lines to thee in St. Louis, but thee was absent at the time, and perhaps did not receive them. The villagers have complained sadly because I did not let them know Jessie Fremont was in the place. Our young men and women wanted to see Colonel Zagonyi, the hero of the Body Guard. When thee comes again we will have the bells rung and satisfy them. . . . Remember me kindly to the general. Would that he were at Washington, commander-in-chief. That God may bless you both abundantly is the sincere desire of thy friend.[7]

Bierce is critical of Grant and Halleck in their conduct of the campaign in the West during the early years of the war.

The enemy, defeated in two days of battle at Pittsburg Landing, had sullenly retired to Corinth, whence he had come. For manifest incompetence, Grant, whose beaten army had been saved from destruction and capture by Buell's soldierly activity and skill, had been relieved of his command, which nevertheless had not been given to Buell, but to Halleck, a man of unproved powers, a theorist, sluggish, irresolute.

Foot by foot his troops, always deployed in line–of–battle to resist the enemy's bickering skirmishers, always entrenching against columns that never came, advanced across thirty miles of forest and swamp toward an antagonist prepared to vanish at contact, like a ghost at cock-crow. It was a campaign of "excursions and alarums," of reconnaissances and countermarches, of cross–purposes and countermanded orders. For weeks the solemn farce held attention, luring distinguished civilians from fields of political ambition to see what they could of the horrors of war.[8]

Holmes makes some post-war appraisals of Grant, Stanton, Admiral Farragut and Major Anderson.

I had a good deal of talk with Grant, whom I met twice. He is one of the simplest, stillest men I ever saw. He seems torpid at first, and requires a little management to get much talk out of him. Of all the considerable personages I have seen, he seems to be the least capable of the emotion of vanity. He can be drawn out and will tell his habits and feelings.

I have been very shy of repeating all he said to me, for every word of his is snapped up with great eagerness, and the most trivial of his sayings, if mentioned in the hearing of a gossip, would run all through the press of the country. His entire sincerity and homely truthfulness of manner and speech struck me greatly. He was not conscious, he said, of ever having acted from any personal motive during his public service. We (of the West), he said, were terribly in earnest. The great crisis was the Battle of Shiloh; that he would not lose; he would have fought as long as any men were left to fight with. If that had been lost the war would have dragged on for years longer. The North would have lost its *prestige*. Did he enjoy the being followed as he was by the multitude? "It was very painful." This answer is singularly characteristic of the man. They call on him for speeches, which he cannot and will not try to make.

One trait, half physiological, half moral, interested me. He said he was a good sleeper; commonly slept eight hours. He could go to sleep under almost any circumstances; could set a battle going, go to sleep as if nothing were happening, and wake up by and by, when the action had got along somewhat. Grant has the look of a plain business man, which he is. I doubt if we have had any ideal so completely realized as that of the republican soldier in him. I cannot get over the impression he made on me. I have got something like it from women sometimes, hardly ever from men—that of entire loss of selfhood in a great aim which made all the common influence which stir up other people as nothing to him.

I don't think you have met Stanton. I found him a very mild, pleasant person to talk with, though he is an ogre to the rebels and their Northern friends. Short, with a square head, broad not high, full black beard turned gray; a dark, strong–looking man; he talks in a very gentle tone, protruding his upper lip in rather an odd way. Nothing could be more amiable than the whole man. It was a pleasant chat, mainly, that we had together. One thing he said which I could not forget. Speaking of the campaign of the Wilderness: "It was the bloodiest swath ever made on this globe." Perhaps a little *hasardé,* this statement, but coming from the Secretary of War it has its significance.

Old Farragut, whom I foregathered with several times, is the lustiest *gaillard* of sixty–something, one will meet with in the course of a season. It was odd to contrast him and Major Anderson. I was with them both on one occasion. The Major General, I should say—is a conscientious, somewhat languid, rather bloodless-looking gentleman, who did his duty well, but was overtasked in doing it. Nothing would have supported him but, etc., etc.; but the old Admiral—bona fide accident—let it stand—is full of hot red blood, jolly, juicy, abundant, equal to anything, and an extra dividend of life left ready for payment after the largest expenditure. I don't know but he is as much the ideal seaman as Grant the ideal general; but the type is not so rare. He talks with everybody, merry, twinkling-eyed, up to everything, fond of telling stories, tells them well; the gayest, heartiest, shrewdest old boy you ever saw in your life.[9]

18   Secesh Prisoners

Hawthorne describes his encounter with Confederate prisoners during a visit to Harpers Ferry.

. . . My Yankee heart stirred triumphantly when I saw the use to which John Brown's fortress and prison-house has now been put. What right have I to complain of any other man's foolish impulses, when I cannot possibly control my own? The engine house is now a place of confinement for Rebel prisoners.

A Massachusetts soldier stood on guard, but readily permitted our party to enter. It was a wretched place. A room of perhaps twenty-five feet square occupied the whole interior of the building, having an iron stove in its centre, whence a rusty funnel ascended towards a hole in the roof, which served the purposes of ventilation, as well as for the exit of smoke. We found ourselves right in the midst of the Rebels, some of whom lay on heaps of straw, asleep, or, at all events, giving no sign of consciousness; others sat in the corners of the room, huddled close together, and staring with a lazy kind of interest at the visitors; two were astride of some kind of planks, playing with the dirtiest pack of cards that I ever happened to see.

There was only one figure in the least military among these twenty prisoners of war—a man with a dark, intelligent, mustached face, wearing a shoddy cotton uniform, which he had contrived to arrange with a degree of sol-

dierly smartness, though it had evidently borne the brunt
of a very filthy campaign. He stood erect, and talked freely
with those who addressed him, telling them his place of
residence, the number of his regiment, the circumstances of
his capture, and such other particulars as their Northern
inquisitiveness prompted them to ask. I liked the manliness
of his deportment, he was neither ashamed, nor afraid, nor
in the slightest degree sullen, peppery, or contumacious,
but bore himself as if whatever animosity he had felt
towards his enemies was left upon the battlefield, and
would not be resumed till he had again a weapon in his
hand.

Neither could I detect a trace of hostile feeling in the
countenance, words, or manner of any prisoner there. Almost to a man, they were simple, bumpkin–like fellows,
dressed in homespun clothes with faces singularly vacant
of meaning, but sufficiently good humored: a breed of men,
in short, such as I did not suppose to exist in this country,
although I have seen their like in some other parts of the
world.

They were peasants, and of a very low order: a class
of people with whom our Northern rural population has
not a single trait in common. They were exceedingly respectful—more so than a rustic New Englander ever
dreams of being towards anybody, except perhaps his minister; and had they worn any hats, they would probably
have been self–constrained to take them off, under the
unusual circumstance of being permitted to hold conversation with well-dressed persons.

It is my belief that not a single bumpkin of them all
(the mustached soldier always excepted) had the remotest
comprehension of what they had been fighting for, or how
they had deserved to be shut up in that dreary hole; nor,
possibly, did they care to inquire into this latter mystery,
but took it as a godsend to be suffered to lie here in a heap
of unwashed human bodies, well foddered to-day, and without the necessity of bothering themselves about the possible hunger and cold of to-morrow. Their dark prison life

may have seemed to them the sunshine of all their lifetime.

There was one poor wretch, a wild beast of a man, at
whom I gazed with greater interest than at his fellows; although I know not that each one of them, in their semi-
barbarous moral state, might not have been capable of the
same savage impulse that made this particular individual a
horror to all beholders. At the close of some battle or
skirmish, a wounded Union soldier had crept on hands and
knees to his feet, and besought his assistance—not dreaming that any creature in human shape, in the Christian land
where they had so recently been brethren, could refuse it.
But this man (this fiend, if you prefer to call him so,
though I would not advise it) flung a bitter curse at the
poor Northerner, and absolutely trampled the soul out of
his body, as he lay writhing beneath his feet.

The fellow's face was horribly ugly; but I am not
quite sure that I would have noticed it if I had not known
his story. He spoke not a word, and met nobody's eye, but
kept staring upward into the smoky vacancy towards the
ceiling, where, it might be, he beheld a continual portrai-
ture of his victim's horror-stricken agonies. I rather fancy,
however, that his moral sense was yet too torpid to trouble
him with such remorseful visions, and that, for his own
part, he might have had very agreeable reminiscences of the
soldier's death, if other eyes had not been bent reproachfully upon him and warned him that something was amiss.

It was this reproach in other men's eyes that made
him look aside. He was a wild beast, as I began with
saying—an unsophisticated wild beast—while the rest of
us are partially tamed, though still the scent of blood excites some of the savage instincts of our nature. What this
wretch needed, in order to make him capable of the degree
of mercy and benevolence that exists in us, was simply
such a measure of moral and intellectual development as
we have received; and, in my mind, the present war is so
well justified by no other consideration as by the probability that it will free this class of Southern whites from a

thraldom in which they scarcely begin to be responsible
beings. So far as the education of the heart is concerned,
the Negroes have apparently the advantage of them; and
as to other schooling, it is practically unattainable by black
or white.

Looking around at these poor prisoners, therefore, it
struck me as an immense absurdity that they should fancy
us their enemies; since, whether we intend it or no, they
have a far greater stake on our success than we can possibly have. For ourselves, the balance of advantages between defeat and triumph may admit of question. For
them, all truly valuable things are dependent on our complete success; for thence would come the regeneration of a
people—the removal of a people—the removal of a foul
scurf that has overgrown their life, and keeps them in a
state of disease and decrepitude, one of the chief symptoms of which is, that, the more they suffer and are de-
based, the more they imagine themselves strong and
beautiful.[1]

*Holmes is confronted with a wounded Rebel officer dur-
ing one of his hospital visits, and later, while searching for
his son, is admitted to the presence of a group of captured
Rebels in a camp near Harrisburg, Pennsylvania.*

"There are two wounded Secesh," said my compan-
ion. I walked to the bedside of the first, who was an officer,
a lieutenant, if I remember right, from North Carolina. He
was of good family, son of a judge in one of the higher
courts of his State, educated, pleasant, gentle, intelligent.
One moment's intercourse with such an enemy, lying helpless and wounded among strangers, takes away all personal bitterness toward those with whom we or our children have been but a few hours before in deadly strife. The
basest lie with which the murderous contrivers of this
Rebellion have told is that which tries to make a difference
of face in the men of the North and South.

It would be worth a year of battles to abolish this
delusion, though the great sponge of war that wiped it out

were moistened with the best blood of the land. My Rebel was of slight, scholastic habit, and spoke as one accustomed to treat carefully among the parts of speech. It made my heart ache to see him, a man finished in the humanities and Christian culture, whom the sin of his forefathers and the crime of his rulers had set in barbarous conflict against others of like training with his own—a man who, but for the curse which our generation is called on to expiate, would have taken his part in the beneficent task of shaping the intelligence and lifting the moral standard of a peaceful and united people.

There were some heavy hours to get rid of, and we thought a visit to Camp Curtin might lighten some of them. A rickety wagon carried us to the camp. . . . The rustic sentries uncrossed their muskets and let us in. The camp was on a fair plain, girdled with hills, spacious, well kept, apparently. . . . The visit would have been a dull one, had we not happened to get sight of a singular-looking set of human beings in the distance. They were clad in stuff of different hues, gray and brown being the leading shades, but both subdued by a natural tint, such as is wont to harmonize the variegated apparel of travel-stained vagabonds. They looked slouchy, listless, torpid—an ill-conditioned crew, at first sight, made up of such fellows as an old woman would drive away from her henroost with a broomstick. Yet these were strays from the fiery army which has given our generals so much trouble—"Secesh prisoners," as a bystander told us. A talk with them might be profitable and entertaining. But they were tabooed to the common visitor, and it was necessary to get inside of the line which separated us from them.

A solid, square captain was standing near by, to whom we were referred. . . . The captain acceded to my postulate, and accepted my friend as a corollary . . . my new friend . . . must have been in politics at some time or other, for he made orations to all the "Secesh," in which he explained to them that the United States considered and treated them as children, and enforced upon them the ridiculous impossibility of the Rebel's attempting to do anything against such a power as that of the National Government.

Much as his discourse edified them and enlightened me, it interfered somewhat with my little plans of entering into frank and friendly talk with some of these poor fellows, for whom I could not help feeling a kind of human sympathy, though I am as venomous a hater of the Rebellion as one is like to find under the stars and stripes. It is fair to take a man prisoner. It is fair to make speeches to a man. But to take a man prisoner and then make speeches to him while in durance is *not* fair,

I began a few pleasant conversations, which would have come to something but for the reason assigned.

One old fellow had a long beard, a drooping eyelid, and a black clay pipe in his mouth. He was a Scotchman from Ayr, dour enough, and little disposed to be communicative, though I tried him with the "Twa Briggs," and, like all Scotchmen, he was a reader of "Burns." He professed to feel no interest in the cause for which he was fighting, and was in the army, I judged, only from compulsion. There was a wild-haired, unsoaped boy, with pretty, foolish features enough, who looked as if he might be about seventeen, as he said he was. I give my questions and his answers literally.

"What State do you come from?"

"Georgy."

"What part of Georgia?"

"Midway."

"Where did you go to church when you were at home?"

"Never went inside 'f a church b't once in m'life."

"What did you do before you became a soldier?"

"Nothin'."

"What do you mean to do when you get back?"

"Nothin'."

Who could have any other feeling than pity for this poor human weed, this dwarfed and etiolated soul, doomed to an existence but one degree above the idiot?

With this group was a lieutenant, buttoned close in his gray coat—one button gone, perhaps to make a breastpin for some fair traitorous bosom. A short, stocky man, undistinguishable from one of the "subject race" by any obvious meanderings of the *sangre azul* on his exposed surfaces. He did not say much, possibly because he was convinced by the statements and arguments of the . . . captain. He had on strong, iron–heeled shoes of English make, which he said cost him seventeen dollars in Richmond.

I put the question, in a quiet, friendly way, to several of the prisoners, what they were fighting for. One answered, "For our homes." Two or three others said they did not know, and manifested great indifference to the whole matter, at which another of their number, a sturdy fellow, took offence, and muttered opinions strongly derogatory to those who would not stand up for the cause they had been fighting for. A feeble, attenuated old man, who wore the Rebel uniform, if such it could be called, stood by without showing any sign of intelligence. It was cutting very close to the bone to carve such a shred of humanity from the body politic to make a soldier of.

We were just leaving, when a face attracted me, and I stopped the party. "That is the true Southern type," I said to my companion. A young fellow, a little over twenty, rather tall, slight, with a perfectly smooth, boyish cheek, delicate, somewhat high features, and a fine almost feminine mouth, stood at the opening of his tent, and as we turned towards him fidgeted a little nervously with one hand on the loose canvas, while he seemed at the same time not unwilling to talk.

He was from Mississippi, he said, had been at Georgetown College, and was so far imbued with letters that even the name of the literary humility before him was not new to his ears. Of course, I found it easy to come into magnetic relation with him, and to ask him without incivility what he was fighting for. "Because I like the excitement of it," he answered. I know these fighters with women's mouths and boy's cheeks. One such from the circle of my own friends, sixteen years old, slipped away from his nursery. . . .

"Did you ever see a genuine Yankee?" said my Philadelphia friend to the young Mississippian.

"I have shot at a good many of them," he replied, modestly, his woman's mouth stirring a little, with a pleasant, dangerous smile.

The . . . captain here put his foot into the conversation. . . . It deranged the balance of our intercourse; there was no use in throwing a fly where a paving stone had just splashed into the water, and I nodded a good-by to the boy-fighter, thinking how much better it was for my friend the Captain to address him with unanswerable arguments and crushing statements in his own tent than it would be to meet him upon some remote picket station and offer his fair proportions to the quick eye of a youngster who could draw a bead on him before he had time to say *dunder* and *blixum*.[2]

Whitman's firsthand experience with Rebel prisoners was confined to hospital cases he met in his rounds.

. . . Some of my best friends in the hospitals were probably Southern boys. I remember one in particular right off—a Kentucky youngster (a mere youngster), illiterate, extremely—I wrote several letters for him to his parents, friends—fine, honest, ardent, chivalrous. I found myself loving him like a son. . . .

The large ward I am in is used for Secession soldiers exclusively. One man, about forty years of age, emaciated with diarrhoea, I was attracted to, as he lay with his eyes turned up, looking like death. His weakness was so extreme that it took a minute or two every time for him to talk with anything like consecutive meaning, yet he was evidently a man of good intelligence and education. As I said anything, he would lie a moment perfectly still; then, with closed eyes, answer in a low, very slow voice—quiet, correct and sensible—but in a way and tone that wrung my heart.

He had a mother, wife, and child living (or probably living) in his home in Mississippi. It was a long, long time since he had seen them. Had he caused a letter to be sent them since he got here in Washington? No answer. I repeated the question very slowly and soothingly. He could not tell whether he had or not—things of late seemed to him like a dream.

After waiting a moment, I said: "Well, I am going to walk down the ward a moment, and when I come back you can tell me. If you have not written, I will sit down and write." A few moments after I had returned, he said that he remembered now that someone had written for him two or three days before.

The presence of this man impressed me profoundly. The flesh was all sunken on face and arms; the eyes low in their sockets and glassy and with purple rings around them. Two or three great tears silently flowed out from the eyes and rolled down his temples (he was doubtless unused to be spoken to as I was speaking to him). Sickness, imprisonment, exhaustion, etc. had conquered the body, yet the mind held mastery still and called even wandering remembrance back. . . .

Afternoon and evening at Douglas Hospital, . . . went through several wards. In one of them found an old acquaintance transferred here lately, a Rebel prisoner in a dying condition. Poor fellow, the look was already on his face. He gazed long at me. I asked him if he knew me. After a moment he uttered something—but inarticulately.

I have seen him off and on for the last five months. He has suffered very much; a bad wound in the left leg, severely fractured, several operations, cuttings, extractions of bones, splinters, etc. I remember he seemed to me, as I used to talk to him, a fair specimen of the main strata of the Southerners—those without property or education, but still with the stamp which comes from freedom and equality. I liked him—Jonathan Wallace of Hurd Co., Georgia, age thirty (wife, Susan F. Wallace, Houston, Hurd Co., Georgia. If any good soul of that county could see this, I hope he will send her this word). Had a family; had not heard from them since taken prisoner, now six months.

I had written for him, and done trifles for him before he came here. He made no outward show, was mild in his talk and behavior, but I knew he worried much inwardly. But now all would be over very soon. I half sat upon the little stand near the head of the bed. Wallace was somewhat restless. I placed my hand lightly on his forehead and face, just sliding it over the surface. In a moment or two, he fell into a calm, regular–breathing lethargy or sleep, and remained so while I sat there.

It was dark, and the lights were lit. I hardly knew why (death seemed hovering near), but I stayed nearly an hour. A Sister of Charity, dressed in black, with a broad white linen bandage around her head and under her chin, and a black crape overall flowing down her head in long wide pieces, came to him and moved around the bed. She bowed low and solemn to me. For some time she moved around there noiseless as a ghost, doing little things for the dying man. . . .[3]

Lanier tells something of his own capture and imprisonment. First is a letter from the military prison in which he was being held (Camp Hamilton, near Ft. Monroe, Virginia), written to an uncle, a member of the Confederate Congress at Richmond. The second passage is from a letter to a friend more than a year after the war had ended.

After remaining for some days on board the Steamer "Santiago" (my captor), I was sent to the Provost Marshall at Norfolk, who assigned me to confinement in the military prison at this place. The officers of the Santiago, whom I found full of gentlemanly courtesy, invited me into their Wardroom, and during my stay with them, treated me in all respects with the utmost kindness. I have met acquaintances also here, and am as pleasantly situated as I could expect.

See Judge Ould immediately, and arrange a *special exchange* for me—; also write home and inform Mother how well I have been treated.

You will pardon a very laconic epistle I'm limited to one page. Send a thousand kisses to Mother and Sister and Father. . . .

. . . I . . . ran the blockade of Wilmington, successfully, but was captured, in the gulf stream, by the Federal cruiser "Santiago de Cuba," carried to Norfolk, thence to Fortress Monroe, and Camp Hamilton, and at last to Point Lookout, where I spent four months in prison. Some gold, which a friend of mine had smuggled into the prison in his mouth, obtained the release of both of us. I made my way home, by a long and painful journey, and, immediately upon my arrival, losing the stimulus which had kept me going so long, fell dangerously ill and remained so for three months—delirious part of the time. I had but begun to recover, when Gen. Wilson entered and occupied the city (Macon, Georgia).[4]

19   Ships of the War

Hawthorne, during his travels below the Mason-Dixon line, inspects a number of naval vessels.

The waters around Fortress Monroe were thronged with a gallant array of ships of war and transports, wearing the Union flag—"Old Glory," as I hear it called in these days. A little withdrawn from our national fleet lay two French frigates, and in another direction an English sloop, under that manner which always makes itself visible, like a red portent in the air, wherever there is strife.

In pursuance of our official duty (which had no ascertainable limits), we went on board the flagship, and were shown over every part of her, and down into her depths, inspecting her gallant crew, her powerful armament, her mighty engines, and her furnaces, where the fires are always kept burning, as well at midnight as at noon, so that it would require only five minutes to put the vessel under full steam. This vigilance has been felt necessary ever since the "Merrimac" made that terrible dash from Norfolk. Splendid as she is, however, and provided with all but the very latest improvements in naval armament, the "Minnesota" belongs to a class of vessels that will be built no more, nor ever fight another battle—being as much a thing of the past as any of the ships of Queen Elizabeth's time, which grappled with the galleons of the Spanish Armada.

On her quarter deck, an elderly flag officer was pacing

to-and-fro, with a self–conscious dignity to which a touch of the gout or rheumatism perhaps contributed a little additional stiffness. He seemed to be a gallant gentleman, but of the old, slow and pompous school of naval worthies, who have grown up amid rules, forms and etiquette which were adopted full-blown from the British navy into ours, and are somewhat too cumbrous for the quick spirit of today.

This order of nautical heroes will probably go down, along with the ships in which they fought valourously and strutted most intolerably. How can an admiral condescend to go to sea in an iron pot? What space and elbow room can be found for quarter-deck dignity in the cramped lookout of the "Monitor," or even in the twenty-feet diameter of her cheese-box?

All the pomp and splendor of naval warfare are gone by. Henceforth there must come up a race of enginemen and smoke-blackened canoneers, who will hammer away at their enemies under the direction of a single pair of eyes; and even heroism—so deadly a grip is Science laying on our noble possibilities—will become a quality of very minor importance, when its possessor cannot break through the iron crust of his own armament and give the world a glimpse of it.

At no great distance from the "Minnesota" lay the strangest-looking craft I ever saw. It was a platform of iron, so nearly level with the water that the swash of waves broke over it, under the impulse of a very moderate breeze; and, on this platform was raised a circular structure, likewise of iron, and rather broad and capacious, but of no great height. It could not be called a vessel at all; it was a machine—and I have seen one of somewhat similar appearance employed in cleaning out the docks; or for lack of a better similitude, it looked like a gigantic rattrap; it was ugly, questionable, suspicious, evidently mischievous—nay, I will allow myself to call it devilish; for this was the new war fiend, destined, along with others of the same breed, to annihilate whole navies and batter down old supremacies.

The wooden walls of Old England cease to exist, and a whole history of naval renown reaches its period, now that the "Monitor" comes smoking into view; while the billows dash over what seems her deck, and storms bury even her turret in green water, as she burrows and snorts along, oftener under the surface than above. The singularity of the object has betrayed me into a more ambitious vein of description than I often indulge, and, after all, I might as well have contented myself with simply saying that she looked very queer.

Going on board, we were surprised at the extent and convenience of her interior accommodations. There is a spacious ward room, nine or ten feet in height, besides a private cabin, for the commander, and sleeping accommodations on an ample scale; the whole well lighted and ventilated, though beneath the surface of the water. Forward, or aft (for it is impossible to tell stem from stern), the crew are relatively quite as well provided for as the officers. It was like finding a palace, with all its conveniences, under the sea.

The inaccessibility, the apparent impregnability, of this submerged iron fortress are most satisfactory; the officers and crew get down through a little hole in the deck, hermetically seal themselves, and go below; and until they see fit to reappear, there would seem to be no power given to man whereby they can be brought to light. A storm of cannonshot damages them no more than a handful of dried peas. We saw the shot marks made by the great artillery of the "Merrimac" on the outer casing of the iron tower; they were about the breadth and depth of shallow saucers, almost imperceptible dents, with no corresponding bulge on the interior surface. In fact, the thing looked altogether too safe, though it may not prove quite an agreeable predicament to be thus boxed up in impenetrable iron, with the possibility, one would imagine, of being sent to the bottom of the sea, and, even there, not drowned, but stifled.

Nothing, however, can exceed the confidence of the officers in this new craft. It was a pleasure to see their benign exultation in her powers of mischief, and the delight with which they exhibited the circumvolutory movement of the tower, the quick thrusting forth of the immense guns to deliver their ponderous missiles, and then the immediate recoil, and the security behind the closed portholes. Yet even this will not long be the last and most terrible improvement in the science of war. Already we hear of vessels the armament of which is to act entirely beneath the surface of the water; so that, with no other external symptoms than a great bubbling and foaming, and gush of smoke, and belch of smothered thunder out of the yeasty waves, there shall be a deadly fight going on below—and, by and by, a sucking whirlpool, as one of the ships goes down.

The "Monitor" was certainly an object of great interest; but on our way to Newport News, whither we went next, we saw a spectacle that affected us with far profounder emotion. It was the sight of the few sticks that are left of the frigate "Congress," stranded near the shore —and still more, the masts of the "Cumberland" rising midway out of the water, with a tattered rag of a pennant fluttering from one of them. The invisible hull of the latter ship seems to be careened over, so that the three masts stand slantwise; the rigging looks quite unimpaired, except that a few ropes dangle loosely from the yards. The flag (which never was struck, thank Heaven!) is entirely hidden under the waters of the bay, but is still doubtless waving in its old place, although it floats to and fro with the swell and reflux of the tide, instead of rustling on the breeze. A remnant of the dead crew still man the sunken ship, and sometimes a drowned body floats up to the surface.

That was a noble fight. When was ever a better word spoken than that of Commodore Smith, the father of the "Congress," when he heard that his son's ship was surrendered? "Then Joe's dead!" said he; and so it proved. Nor can any warrior be more certain of enduring renown than the gallant Morris, who fought so well the final battle of the old system of naval warfare, and won glory for his country and himself out of inevitable disaster and defeat.

That last gun from the "Cumberland," when her deck was half submerged, sounded the requiem of many sinking ships. Then went down all the navies of Europe, and our own, "Old Ironsides" and all, and Trafalgar and a thousand other fights became only a memory, never to be acted over again; and thus our brave countrymen come last in that long procession of heroic sailors that includes Blake and Nelson, and so many mariners of England, and other mariners as brave as they, whose renown is our native inheritance.

There will be other battles, but no more such tests of seamanship and manhood as the battles of the past; and, moreover, the Millennium is certainly approaching, because human strife is to be transferred from the heart and personality of man into cunning contrivances of machinery, which by and by will fight out our wars with only the clank and smash of iron, strewing the field with broken engines, but damaging nobody's little finger, except by accident. Such is the tendency of modern improvement,

But, in the meanwhile, so long as manhood retains any part of its pristine value, no country can afford to let gallantry like that of Morris and his crew, any more than that of the brave Worden, pass unhonored and unrewarded. If the Government do nothing, let the people take the matter into their own hands, and cities give him swords, gold boxes, festivals of triumph, and, if he needs it, heaps of gold. Let poets brood upon the theme, and make themselves sensible how much of the past and future is contained within its compass, till its spirit shall flash forth in the lightning of a song! [1]

Lanier recounts some of his experiences as a signal officer on a blockade-runner sailing between Wilmington, N.C., and the West Indies.

Ten or twelve blockade-runners came into Port within a day or two after our arrival here, and were immediately placed in strict quarantine, it being reported that the Yellow Fever was raging in Bermuda, and even that there were cases on board of some of the vessels. This proceeding somewhat damped our hopes at first, as we did not like the prospect of being assigned to duty in the Forts protecting this harbor, and awaiting the coming of Frost before we could proceed on our voyages. But the vessels having developed no serious cause of alarm after riding out a quarantine-term of fifteen days, are being released and allowed to discharge cargo and reload. The "Lilian" went out last night; and to-morrow two of our party, Richardson and Langhorn, go out as passengers on the "Mary Celeste," to bring in two new steamers now ready at Bermuda. It is reported that there are a number of new blockaders in foreign ports awaiting Signal Operators to bring them in; and it is probable that, in the course of two or three weeks, a large majority of our party will sail from the Port for that purpose.

. . . Send us about a Thousand Dollars wherewith to relieve our nakedness— When we get to running the Blockade, we shall be able to fix ourselves up in the clothing line together with you and the rest— I am told our pay will amount to two Hundred dollars a trip, in Gold—

We could have been assigned to blockading vessels some time ago, but the prevalence of Yellow Fever at all the Ports to which our blockaders run determined me to await the coming of Frost before accepting the position —The Fever is now said to have nearly subsided at Nassau: and I shall endeavor to obtain a Ship running to that port— But three or four weeks will probably elapse yet before we sail— It is, on the other hand, quite possible that we will not go at all: inasmuch as there seems to be indications that the Yanks will attack this place soon, in which event I presume that the blockading-business would be nearly or quite closed up—

. . . I cannot see how the enemy, straining every nerve at Petersburg and Atlanta and St. Louis, can assemble the force sufficient to make any serious attempt upon a well-fortified position like that of Wilmington— The popular

apprehensions of an attack here seem to be based principally upon the fact that Farragut has been ordered to relieve Lee in charge of the blockading fleet now off this
Port: but I do not think that this change contemplates any
other purpose than the employment of Farragut's well-
known energy, in the work of capturing and destroying the
Confederate blockading vessels and privateers which have
recently been flocking into our Harbor— At any rate, we
will be found, I think, ready, in any emergency: and the
enemy will find it a serious undertaking either to stop the
Blockaders or to capture Wilmington,—

I do not know what time I shall leave here. The imminent prospect of an attack on this place by the Yankees
will probably induce the blockading firms to keep their
vessels in port on the other side of the water, as far as
possible. Were it not for this, I should get out very soon, in
a week or so; since large numbers of new vessels are waiting at Nassau, Halifax and Bermuda for Pilots and Signal
Officers.

My brother and I . . . were assigned to duty on blockading steamers as Signal Officers; Clifford on the "Talis-
man," I on the "Lucy." Cliff made three delightful and
adventurous trips: from Nassau to Wilmington: was
wrecked on the last voyage, and just saved his life, getting
on a Federal schooner just in time to see his steamer go
down. He went then to Bermuda, and was on the point of
sailing for Wilmington as Sig. Off. of the "St'r. Maude
Campbell," when, hearing of the capture of Wilmington,
he went to Havana, thence, after a pleasant time of a
month with friends in Cuba, to Galveston, Texas, *whence*
he *walked to Macon, Ga.:* . . . I, meanwhile, ran the blockade of Wilmington, successfully, but was captured, in the
gulf stream, by the Federal cruiser "Santiago de
Cuba." . . .[2]

*Emerson, in Washington, visits Lincoln's Secretary of the
Navy, Gideon Wells.*

. . . I ought not to omit that, when Sumner introduced me to Mr. Wells, Secretary of the Navy, and asked him if there were anything new, Mr. Wells said, "No, nothing of importance," and then remarked that "he observed the journals censured him for sending vessels drawing too much water, in the Burnside expedition." Now, he said, that was not the fault of his department. "We (the Navy) only sent seventeen (I think) vessels in all the hundred sail; and the War Department sent all the rest; he had nothing to do with them, and the overdrawing vessels were all storeships and transports, etc., of the War Department's sending."[3]

Lowell's comment serves as a warning to the Union Navy that it had better keep up-to-date if it expects to win victories. The date is March 10, 1862.

As I write, comes the news of our disaster at Hampton Roads. I do not understand the supineness which, after fair warning, leaves wood to an unequal conflict with iron. It is not enough merely to have the right on our side, if we stick to the old flintlock of tradition. I have observed in my parochial experience (*haud ignarus mali*) that the Devil is prompt to adopt the latest inventions of destructive warfare. . . . It is curious, that, as gunpowder made armour useless on shore, so armour is having its revenge by baffling its old enemy at sea; and that, while gunpowder robbed land warfare of nearly all its picturesqueness to give even greater stateliness and sublimity to a sea-fight, armour bids fair to degrade the latter into a squabble between two iron–shelled turtles.[4]

20   *The Negro in Uniform*

Longfellow makes an enthusiastic entry in his journal for May 28, 1863.

In town saw the first regiment of blacks march through Beacon Street. An imposing sight, with something wild and strange about it, like a dream. At last the North consents to let the Negro fight for freedom.[1]

Emerson makes a note on a newspaper report.

The *Herald's* correspondence from Washington, North Carolina (General Forster commanding), speaks of the Negroes lying behind the breastworks, with a musket in one hand and a spelling-book in the other.[2]

Whittier writes two successive letters to a friend in South Carolina.

Our old friend and former neighbor, Colonel T. W. Higginson, commands the 1st Regiment of South Carolina Volunteers. I hope thee will see and know him. He is a rare man, a gentleman, scholar, and true friend of the slave.

I am glad thee has met Colonel Higginson, and to know him is to like him. He is a worthy coadjutor of General Saxton. I read General Saxton's Thanksgiving Proclamation with the deepest emotion. It is the most touching and beautiful official paper I ever saw. God bless him! "The bravest are the tenderest." I am a peace man, but nevertheless I am rejoiced that the 1st Regiment of South Carolina Volunteers have behaved so bravely and manfully in the late expedition. Twenty such regiments, under twenty such men as Higginson and Dr. Rogers, would soon give a new aspect to the struggle. . . .[3]

Whitman appraises the qualities of Negro troops.

 . . . At Milliken's Bend, at Vicksburg, at Port Hudson, on Morris Island, and wherever tested, they have exhibited determined bravery, and compelled the plaudits alike of the thoughtful and thoughtless soldiery. During the siege of Port Hudson, the question was often asked those who beheld their resolute charges, how the "niggers" behaved under fire; and without exception the answer was complimentary to them. "O, tiptop!" "First rate!" "Bully!" were the usual replies.

 . . . After reaching this island . . . Mason's (otherwise Analostan) Island . . . we get presently in the midst of the camp of the 1st Regiment U.S.C.T. The tents look clean and good; indeed, altogether, in locality especially, the pleasantest camp I have yet seen.

 . . . Now the paying is to begin. The major (paymaster), with his clerk, seat themselves at a table; the rolls are before them; the money box is opened; they are packages of five, ten, twenty–five cent pieces. Here comes the first company (B), some 82 men, all blacks. Certes, we can find no fault with the appearance of this crowd—Negroes though they be. They are manly enough, bright enough, look as if they had the soldier stuff in them, look hardy, patient, many of them real handsome fellows.

The paying, I say, has begun. The men are marched up in close proximity. The clerk calls off name after name, and each walks up, receives his money, and passes along out of the way. It is a real study, both to see them come close, and to see them pass away, stand counting their cash (nearly all this company gets $10.03 each). The clerk calls "George Washington." That distinguished personage steps from the ranks, in the shape of a very dark man, good sized and shaped, and aged about thirty, with a military mustache; he takes his "ten three," and goes off, evidently well pleased. . . . The regiment numbers today about one thousand men (including officers, the only whites).

Now another company. These get $5.36 each. The men look well. They, too, have great names; besides the Washingtons—John Quincy Adams, Daniel Webster, Calhoun, James Madison, Alfred Tennyson, John Brown. . . . The men step off aside, count their money with a pleased, half-puzzled look. Occasionally, but not often, there are some thoroughly African physiognomies—very black in color, large, protruding lips, low forehead, etc. But I have to say that I do not see one revolting face.

Then another company, each man of this getting $10.03 also. The pay proceeds very rapidly. . . . Then some trouble. One company, by the rigid rules of official computation, gets only 23 cents each man. The company (K) is indignant, and after two or three are paid, the refusal to take the paltry sum is universal, and the company marches off to quarters unpaid.

Another Company (I) got only 70 cents. The sullen, lowering, disappointed look is general. Half refuse it in this case. Company G, in full dress, with brass scales on shoulders, looked perhaps as well as any of the companies—the men had an unusually alert look.

These then are the black troops—or the beginning of them. Well, no one can see them, even under these circumstances—their military career in its novitiate—without feeling well pleased with them.[4]

Emerson urges Negroes to join the colors.

Negro Soldiers. If the war means Liberty to you, you should enlist. It does mean Liberty to you in the opinion of the South, for the South says, We fight to plant Slavery as our foundation; and, of course, we who resist the South are forced to make liberty of the Negro our foundation.

I speak for the forces above us, those issues which are made for us, over our heads, under our feet, paramount to our wills. If you will not fight for your liberty, who will? If you will not, why then, take men as they are, and the universe of men will say you are not worth fighting for; go and be slaves forever, and you shall have our aid to make you such. You had rather be slave than freemen; go to your own place.[5]

Miss Alcott is at work on the home front in the fall of 1864.

Sewed for Wheeler's colored company and sent them comfort–bags, towels, books, and bed–sacks.[6]

Thomas Wentworth Higginson, commander of the First Regiment of South Carolina Volunteers (the first Negro regiment in the Union Army), gives the most complete picture of the Negro as a soldier.

. . . I did not seek the command of colored troops, but it sought me. And . . . under these circumstances, I naturally viewed the new recruits rather as subjects for discipline than for philanthropy. . . . And unless these men could be brought tolerably near . . . a high standard of drill and discipline . . . the fact of their extreme blackness would afford me, even as a philanthropist, no satisfaction. Fortunately, I felt perfect confidence that they could be so trained—having happily known, by experience, the qualities of their race, and knowing also they had home and household and freedom to fight for, besides that abstraction of "the Union." I had been an abolitionist too long, and known and loved John Brown too well, not to feel a thrill of joy on finding myself in the position where he merely wished to be.

Of discipline, as it proved, there was great need—that is, of order and regular instruction. Some of the men had already been under fire, but they were very ignorant of drill and camp duty.

A battalion of black soldiers, a spectacle since so common, seemed then the most daring of innovations, and the whole demeanor of this particular regiment was watched with microscopic scrutiny by friends and foes. The slightest camp incidents sometimes came back to us, magnified and distorted, in letters of anxious inquiry from remote parts of the Union. It was no pleasant thing to live under such constant surveillance; but it guaranteed the honesty of any success, while fearfully multiplying the penalties had there been a failure. A single mutiny—such as had happened in the infancy of a hundred regiments, a single miniature Bull Run, a stampede of desertions, and it would have been all over with us; the party of distrust would have got the upper hand, and there might not have been, during the whole contest, another effort to arm the Negro.

The first few days on duty with a new regiment must be devoted almost wholly to tightening reins; in this process one deals chiefly with the officers, and I have as yet had but little personal intercourse with the men. They concern me chiefly in bulk, as so many consumers of rations, wearers of uniforms, bearers of muskets. But as the machine comes into shape, I am beginning to decipher the individual parts.

At first, of course, they all look just alike; the variety comes afterwards, and they are just as distinguishable . . . as so many whites. Most of them are wholly raw, but there are many who have already been for months in camp. . . . I notice that some companies, too, look darker than others, though all are purer African than I expected. This is said to be partly a geographical difference between the South Carolina and Florida men. When the Confederates evacuated this region, they probably took with them the house servants, including most of the mixed blood, so that the residuum seems very black.

It needs but a few days to show the absurdity of distrusting the military availability of these people. They have quite as much average comprehension as whites of the need of the thing, as much courage (I doubt not), as much previous knowledge of the gun, and, above all, a readiness of ear and of imitation, which, for purposes of drill, counterbalances any defect of mental training.

As to camp life, they have little to sacrifice; they are better fed, housed, and clothed than ever in their lives before, and they appear to have few inconvenient vices. They are simple, docile, and affectionate almost to the point of absurdity. The same men who stood fire in open field with perfect coolness on the late expedition, have come to me blubbering in the most irresistibly ludicrous manner on being transferred from one company in the regiment to another.

In noticing the squad drills I perceive that the men learn less laboriously than whites that "double, double, toil and trouble," which is the elementary vexation of the drill master—that they more rarely mistake their left for their right—and are more grave and sedate while under instructions. The extremes of jollity and sobriety, being greater with them, are less liable to be intermingled; these companies can be driven with a looser rein than my former one [Higginson's first army experience was as captain of a white company], for they restrain themselves; but the moment they are dismissed from drill every tongue is relaxed and every ivory tooth visible.

This morning I wandered about where the different companies were target–shooting, and their glee was contagious. Such exalting shouts of "Ki! ole man," when some steady old turkey–shooter brought his gun down for an instant's aim, and then unerringly hit the mark; and then, when some unwary youth fired his piece into the ground at half-cock, such infinite guffawing and delight, such rolling over and over on the grass, such dances of ecstasy, as made the "Ethiopian minstrelsy" of the stage appear a feeble imitation.

Today, for the first time, I marched the whole regiment through Beaufort and back. . . . They did march splendidly; this all admit. M——'s prediction was fulfilled: "Will not —— be in bliss? A thousand men, every one as black as a coal!" I confess it. To look back on twenty broad double ranks of men (for they march by platoons) —every polished musket having a polished face beside it, and every face set steadily to the front—a regiment of freed slaves marching on into the future—it was something to remember. . . .

I had cautioned the men, before leaving camp, not to be staring about them as they marched, but to look straight to the front, every man; and they did it with their accustomed fidelity, aided by the sort of spontaneous eye for effect which is in all their melodramatic natures. One of them was heard to say exultingly afterwards, "We didn't look to de right nor to de leff. I didn't see notin' in Beaufort. Eb'ry step was worth a half a dollar."

Some of these men have splendid memories. One sergeant, who cannot read, calls the roll from memory. One of our ablest sergeants, a carpenter, paid his master $365 a year for his time for several years; think of it! He used to make $2.50 a day, erected buildings on contract, etc. He would never learn to read, because it exposes them to so much more suspicion and watching.

. . . There is something so plaintive about the whole condition of these grown–up children, at any time . . . whether they laugh or cry; there is a sort of mute appeal about them unknown to themselves. It is very hard to punish them; they seem like dumb or blind babies, or maimed animals. There is infinitely less of the defiant or dangerous element about them than I expected; very few *devils* in the regiment; but the same soft texture which nothing but the contact with gunpowder seems to harden.

Have I ever said what is the favorite reading primer of our drummer boys? McClellan's Bayonet Exercises. Large type, short words, subject intelligible, pictures fascinating; it contains all merits. "Ad-vance, retreat, leap to de front, leap to de rear," and so on. Think of the great dethroned idol, banished from all other temples, still reigning in the primary schools of the Ethiopians!

Corporal Robert Sutton was . . . the wisest man in our ranks. As large, as powerful, and as black as our good–looking color sergeant, but more heavily built and with less of personal good looks, he had a more massive brain and a far more meditative and systematic intellect. Not yet grounded even in the spelling book, his modes of thought were nevertheless strong, lucid, and accurate; and he yearned and pined for intellectual companionship beyond all ignorant men whom I have ever met. His comprehension of the whole problem of Slavery was more thorough and far–reaching than that of any abolitionist, so far as its social and military aspects went; in that direction I could teach him nothing, and he taught me much. But it was his methods of thought which always impressed me chiefly; superficial brilliancy he left to others, and grasped at the solid truth.

Of course his interest in the war and in the regiment was unbounded; he did not take to drill with especial readiness, but he was insatiable of it, and grudged every moment of relaxation. Indeed, he never had any such moments; his mind was at work all the time, even when he was singing hymns, of which he had endless store. He was not, however, one of our leading religionists, but his moral code was solid and reliable, like his mental processes. Ignorant as he was, the "years that bring the philosophic mind" had yet been his, and most of my young officers seemed boys beside him.

He was a Florida man, and had been chiefly employed in lumbering and piloting on the St. Mary's River, which divides Florida from Georgia. Down this stream he had escaped in a "dug out," and after thus finding the way, had returned (as had not a few of my men in other cases) to bring away wife and child. "I wouldn't have leff my child, Cunnel," he said, with an emphasis that sounded the depths of his strong nature. And up this same river he was always imploring to be allowed to guide an expedition.

. . . The first time that the men had been seriously exposed to artillery fire—a danger more exciting to the ignorant mind than any other, as this very war has shown.
. . . I watched them anxiously. Fortunately there were deep trenches on each side of the railway, with many stout, projecting roots, forming very tolerable bomb–proofs for those who happened to be near them. The enemy's gun was a sixty–four pound Blakeley, as we afterwards found, whose enormous projectiles moved very slowly and gave ample time to cover—insomuch that, while the fragments of shell fell all around and amongst us, not a man was hurt. This soon gave the men the most buoyant confidence, and they shouted with childish delight over every explosion.

The point of inferiority that I always feared, though I never had occasion to prove it, was that they might show less fibre, less tough and dogged resistance, than whites, during a prolonged trial—a long, disastrous march, for instance, or the hopeless defence of a besieged town. I should not be afraid of their mutinying or running away, but of their drooping and dying. It might not turn out so; but I mention it for the sake of fairness, and to avoid overstating the merits of these troops.

As to the simple general fact of courage and reliability, I think no officer in our camp ever thought of there being any difference between black and white. And certainly the opinions of these officers, who for years, risked their lives every moment on the fidelity of their men, were worth more than those of all the world beside.

No doubt there were reasons why this particular war was an especially favorable test of the colored soldiers. They had more to fight for than the whites. They fought with ropes round their necks; and when the Confederate orders were issued that the officers of colored troops should be put to death on capture, they took a grim satisfaction. It helped their *esprit de corps* immensely. With us at least, there was to be no play–soldier. Though they had begun with a slight feeling of inferiority to the white troops, this compliment substituted a peculiar sense of self-respect. And, even when the new colored regiments began to arrive from the North, my men still pointed out this difference—that, in case of ultimate defeat, the Northern troops, black or white, would go home, while the First South Carolina must fight it out or be re-enslaved.

We who served with the black troops have this peculiar satisfaction, that, whatever dignity or sacredness the memories of the war may have to others, they have more to us. In that contest, all the ordinary ties of patriotism were the same, of course, to us as to the rest; they had no motives which we had not, as they have now no memories which are not also ours. But the peculiar privilege of associating with an outcast race, of training it to defend its rights, and to perform its duties, this was our especial need.

The vacillating policy of the Government sometimes filled other officers with doubt and shame; until the Negro had justice, they were but defending liberty with one hand and crushing it with the other. From this inconstancy, we were free. Whatever the Government did, we at least were working in the right direction. If this was not recognized on our side of the lines, we knew that it was admitted on the other. Always knowing ourselves to be denied the ordinary courtesies of war till we ourselves compelled their concession, we could at least turn this outlawry into a compliment. We had touched the pivot of the war. Whether this vast and dusky mass should prove the weakness of the nation, or its strength, must depend in great measure, we knew, upon our efforts. Till the blacks were armed, there was no guarantee of their freedom. It was their demeanor under arms that shamed the nation into recognizing them as men.[7, 8]

21 Copperheadism

Whitman summarizes the extent of secessionist feeling in the North.

. . . If at the opening of the contest the abstract dual-ity question of *slavery* and *quiet* could have been submitted to a direct popular vote, as against their opposite, they would have triumphantly carried the day in a majority of the Northern States—in large cities, leading off with New York and Philadelphia, by tremendous majorities.

The events of '61 amazed everybody North and South, and burst all prophecies and calculations like bubbles. But even then, and during the whole war, the stern fact remains that not only did the North put it down, but *the Secession cause had numerically just as many sympathizers in the Free, as in the Rebel, States.*[1]

Bryant confronts those who would accommodate the South, in an editorial written three months after the beginning of hostilities.

The community is thrown into astonishment by a rumor of offers to compromise the quarrel between the Government and the rebels—between the violators of the law and those who obey it—between those who seek to overthrow the Constitution by violence and those who up-hold it. We wonder not at the astonishment; we only wonder at those who in the present state of things can talk of compromise.

The question of compromise has been fully debated and settled. Both the North and the South, before the breaking out of hostilities, have rejected the idea of accommodating the quarrel by compromise. What we would not yield in a peaceable conference, shall we yield to those who have assembled a numerous army, threatening the seat of Government and overhanging the frontier of the free States? Grant anything that looks like a compromise, agree to anything that has the slightest resemblance to a concession, and you only minister to the arrogance of the rebels.

"See," they will exclaim, "what we have extorted from the cowardly North! We have forced from their fears and their interests what we could not obtain from their love of justice. The resort to arms is the only way of dealing with the free States. When they hold the power, we have only to rebel, and they come to our terms."

In the present state of things, therefore, compromise is only an encouragement to rebellion. Those who ask us to make concessions ask that treason be permitted to dictate to the lawful authorities of the land. We cannot yield anything to the rebels without bringing the Government into discredit for its weakness, both at home and abroad. We shall give the different States of the Union to understand that if any of them is dissatisfied with the Government, the proper remedy is a resort to arms. Still worse will be the consequence in our dealings with other countries. If traitors within our own limits can obtain what they desire by taking up arms, foreign governments will presume on our want of spirit and make war upon us whenever they have a demand to make which we are not prepared to concede.

The one thought of the vast majority of the people of the Union now is to enforce the laws. All classes, persons of all ages, the gentler as well as the rougher sex, are inspired with a feeling of loyalty to the Union which partakes of the sublimity of religion. All hasten to lend their aid; all pour out their means; parents send their children to the war; the young men freely offer their lives; the aged and the women their prayers, and zealously occupy themselves in providing for the comfort and health of our armies. The Government is surrounded by a greater number of willing defenders than it can find arms for. Never did men flock with such enthusiasm to a war since the time of the Crusades.

And now that we have hemmed in the rebels by sea and land; now that we have cut off their supplies of arms, ammunitions, and provisions; now that we have deprived them of their resources, while our own are constant, abundant, and beyond their power to diminish; now that we have made them feel their own weakness and helplessness, and the overwhelming strength of the loyal population—their abettors and friends call for a compromise. Now that it is in our power to enforce the laws and vindicate the Constitution, they ask us to give way. We are to beat a retreat the moment victory is in our grasp.

Are, then, all the sacrifices which we have made in support of public order made to no end? Are all these preparations to maintain the majesty of the laws to be countermanded the moment they are likely to prove ineffectual? Is all this noble enthusiasm wasted? Was the blood of those men of Massachusetts who were murdered in the streets of Baltimore shed in vain?

By making terms with the rebels we abandon the friends of the Union in the rebel States whom we have promised to protect and defend, and to reinstate in the power which has been wrested from them by terror and violence. Are we ready to act so base and cowardly a part as this? Are we ready to leave West Virginia to her fate, after having engaged to vindicate her rights against the traitors? Are we willing to see Missouri again governed by Jackson? In Kentucky, in Tennessee, in North Carolina, are we prepared to deprive of their last hopes the friends of the Union, who have long anxiously looked to us for deliverance from the tyranny which crushes them in the dust?

We cannot do any act which acknowledges those who now hold the power in those States as the legitimate civil authority without delivering up the friends of the Union to their mercy. Nothing short of the unconditional submission of the rebels to the authority which they have cast off, the flight or punishment of their leaders, and the installation of a new order of things, with the friends of the Union at its head, can make the slave States safe either for a citizen from the North or a loyal citizen of the South. That the commercial men of this city should desire a settlement of the present unhappy quarrel, and a return of the relations of trade between the North and the South, is most natural. Let them have a little patience. They will not be obliged to wait long. The Southern ports are already ours, except that the time to occupy them has not quite arrived. We shall enter and possess them with the frosts and the healthful gales of winter. With the ports of Charleston, Savannah, Mobile, and New Orleans in the occupation of the Federal forces, with the custom houses re–established and harbors opened, we shall have a trade with the South as active and as profitable as could be obtained by any compromise, and more certain, since it would be a trade beyond the power of the malcontents to interrupt.

The rebel leaders, it is said, desire a suspension of hostilities. If that be what they want, they have only to disband their forces, and hostilities will cease. There can be no hostilities where there is no opposition. It was they who began the war, and, if they desire that it should cease, they have only to desist from it to make its further prosecution impossible.[2]

Emerson is critical of the young men of the North.

The difficulty with the young men is not their opinion and its consequences, not that they are Copperheads, but that they lack idealism. A man for success must not be pure idealist—then he will practically fail; but he must have ideas, he must obey ideas or he is a brute.

A man does not want to be dazzled with a blaze of sunlight—he will be sun-blind; but every man must have glimmer enough to keep him from knocking his head against the walls and posts. And it is in the interests of civilization, and good society, and friendship, that I hate to hear of well-born and gifted and amiable men, that they have this low tendency, this despair. Their death is no loss to their country—skeptical as felons.[3]

Holmes condemns Southern sympathizers in a letter to Motley.

As I am in the vein of saying things that ought to please you, let me say that my heart always swells with pride, and a glitter comes over my eyes, when I read or hear your denunciations of the enemies of liberty at home and abroad, and your noble pleas for the great system of self-government now on its trial in a certain sense—say rather, now putting our people on trial, to see whether they are worthy of it. . . . You know better than I do the contrivances of that detested horde of mercenary partisans who would in a moment accept Jeff Davis, the slavetrader, and a Southern garrison in Boston, to get back their post offices and their custom houses, where the bread they have so long eaten was covered with slime, like that of their brother serpents, before it was swallowed.

The mean sympathizers with the traitors are about in the streets under many aspects. You can generally tell the more doubtful ones by the circumstance that they have a great budget of complaints against the government, that their memory is exceedingly retentive of every reverse and misfortune, and that they have the small end of their opera glasses towards everything that looks encouraging. I do not think strange of this in old men; they wear their opinions like their old clothes, and we need them as standards of past thought which we may reckon our progress by, as the ship wants her stationary log to tell her headway. But to meet *young* men who have breathed this American air without taking the contagious fever of liberty, whose hands lie as cold and flabby in yours as the fins of a fish, on the morning of a victory—this is the hardest thing to bear.

Oh, if the bullets would only go to the hearts that have no warm human blood in them! But the most generous of our youth are the price we must pay for the new heaven and the new earth which are to be born of this fiery upheaval. I think one of the most trying things of a struggle like this is the painful revelation of the meanness which lies about as unsuspected. Perhaps I am harder than you would be in my judgment, but it does seem to me that the essential elements of the armed debate now going on are so evident, that it is a shame for any man, woman, or child in the land of school houses and colleges not to know which is the civilized side—though the youth at Cambridge, in England, may settle it in their debating society that God and all his holy angels are with the slavebreeders.[4]

Bryant takes issue with the Copperhead press and then points out the weakness of a peace purchased without the emancipation of the slaves.

It certainly is remarkable how unable the newspapers of the country, even those of the largest circulation, have been to divert the public mind from a fixed determination to put down the rebellion by every possible means and to allow no pause in the war until the integrity of the Union is assured. One class of journals has labored to show that the war for the Union is hopeless; the people never believed them. One class has called for a revolutionary leader; the call has only excited a little astonishment, the people being satisfied to prosecute the war under the legal and constitutional authorities.

A peace purchased by receding from the policy of emancipation will be but a hollow truce, in the womb of which would lurk other insurrections and rebellions, ready to break out in civil war whenever an occasion like that of 1861 should arise. Suffer the rebel states to return to the Union with the right of slavery acknowledged, and you proclaim to them that they can at any time rebel at their good pleasure, and, if unsuccessful in their revolt, take their old place in the Union until a more auspicious moment shall arrive for forming a new confederacy.

You restore to their old station a class of man whose sole occupations are politics and the use of firearms and the lash; a restless, ambitious, overbearing, arbitrary class, with whom we have never lived in harmony except by submitting to their will, and with whom we can never live in peace hereafter, except by new submissions, a class of men bent on embroiling our country with foreign nations, except when a quarrel with a foreign government might bring the institution of slavery into danger.

By continuing the slaveholding class in existence, we shall keep alive the vexed question of slavery, the curse of our politics, the cause of infinite national disgrace, the source of indescribable barbarities, the occasion of this dreadful Civil War with all its calamities and all its crimes. By adhering to the policy of the proclamation we blot out this fierce controversy forever, and put in its place eternal peace.

On questions of expenditure, of trade, internal improvements, of foreign policy, we may differ, we may dispute, we may form parties; but on this great, gloomy, fearful question, which, after many years of stormy discussion, has been submitted to the frightful arbitrament of war, we shall have perpetual silence. We shall then be a homogeneous people—a people with the same interests and institutions as well as origin, from the Atlantic to the Pacific, and from our northernmost to our southernmost limit. Our parties will no longer be local and geographical, but, as in other countries, formed upon difference of opinion as to the proper province and powers of legislation.[5, 6]

22   *Malevolent England*

*Emerson vents his spleen against English critics of the
Union cause.*

The English journals are flippant and spiteful in their
notices of American politics and society, but mean abuse
cannot be answered.

It is mortifying that all events must be seen, by wise
men even, through the diminishing lens of a petty interest.
Could we have believed that England should have disappointed us thus?—that no man in all that civil, reading,
brave, cosmopolitan country, should have looked at our
revolution as a student of history, as philanthropist, eager
to see what new possibilities for humanity were to begin—what the inspirations were: what new move on the
board the Genius of the World was preparing?

No, but every one squinted—like Borrow's Gypsies
when he read St. John's Gospel. *Edinburgh Quarterly, Saturday Review,* Gladstone, Russell, Palmerston, Brougham,
nay, Tennyson; Carlyle—I blush to say it; Arnold. Everyone forgot his history, his poetry, his religion, and looked
only at his shop till, whether his salary, whether his small
investment in the funds, would not be less; whether the
stability of the English order might not be in some degree
endangered. No Milton, no Berkeley, no Montesquieu, no
Adam Smith was there to hail a new dawn of hope and

culture for men, to see the opportunity for riddance of this filthy pest which dishonored human nature; to cry over to us, "Up, and God with you! and for this Slavery—off with its head! We see and applaud; the world is with you; such occasion does not come twice; Strike for the Universe of man!"

No; but, on the other hand, every poet, every scholar, every great man, as well as the rich, thought only of his pocketbook, and, to our astonishment cried, *"Slavery forever! Down with the North! Why does not England join with France to protect the slaveholder?"*

I thought they would have seized the occasion to forgive the Northerner every old grudge; to forget their dislike of his rivalry, of his social shortcomings; forget, in such a moment, all petty disgusts and would see in him the honored instrument of Heaven to destroy this rooted poison tree of five thousand years.

We shall prosper, we shall destroy slavery, but by no help of theirs. They assailed us with mean cavils, they sneered at our manners, at our failures, at our shifts, at the poverty of our treasury, at our struggles, legal and municipal, and the irregularities in the presence of mortal dangers. They cherished our enemies, they exalted at the factions which crippled us at home; whenever the allies of the rebels obstructed the great will and action of the government, they danced for joy.

They ought to have remembered that great actions have mean beginnings; poor matters point to rich ends.

Alas, for England; she did not know her friends. 'Tis a bad omen for England, that, in these years, her foreign policy is ignominious, that she plays a sneaking part with Denmark, with France, with Russia, with China, with America.

America makes its own precedents. The imperial voice of the Age cannot be heard for the tin horns and charivari of the varlets of the hour, such as the *London Times*, *Blackwood's* and the *Saturday Review*. But already these *claquers* have received their cue—I suppose it was hinted to them that the American People are not always to be trifled with; they are ending their home war, and are exasperated at English bad behaviour, and are in force to destroy English trade. Speak them fair—and *The Times* has just discovered what "temper, valour, constancy, the Union has shown in the War," and what a noble "career of honour and prosperity lies before her," etc.[1]

Bryant is not only concerned over England's attitude but is critical of Napoleon III's desire to intervene in behalf of peace.

It is some satisfaction to me to know that, if you and I took the same view of the facts, we should not differ so much in our conclusions as you suppose. The British newspaper press has not given all the facts to its readers. In all the States in which the civil war was raging, at the date of your letter to me, there was an ascertained majority in favor of remaining in the Union. These States are Virginia, North Carolina, Kentucky, Tennessee, and Missouri. These States the rebellion attempted to wrest from us. You will agree that the war on behalf of the majority of their citizens was a just one on our part.

We claim, also, that there is a majority in favor of the Union in Arkansas, Louisiana and Texas; in Alabama, Georgia, and Florida, and perhaps in Mississippi; in short, that there is no state in which the secessionists possess a clear majority, except it be South Carolina. In none of the slave States was the question whether they desired to remain in the Union submitted to the people. We of the North said to them: First show that your own citizens are in favor of separating from the Union. Make that clear, and then bring the matter before Congress, and agitate for a change in the Constitution, releasing you in a peaceful and regular way from your connection with the free States.

There is no hurry; you have lived a great many years in partnership with us, and you can certainly now wait till the matter is thoroughly discussed. They refused to do anything of this nature; they had for the most part got their own creatures into the State legislatures, and into the governors' seats; they rushed the vote for separation through these legislatures; they lured troops; they stole arms from the Government arsenals, and money from the Government mints; they seized upon the Government navy yards and Government forts; in short, they made war upon the Government. Taking the whole of the Southern States together, this was done by a minority of people.

You see, then, the entire groundlessness of the unfavorable conclusions formed in England. As for the Trent affair, that will be settled, and I will not say what I might concerning it, except to remark that the preparations for war with which your government accompanied its demand have left a sense of injury and insult which, I fear, will not soon pass away.

Your view of the proposal of the French government that there shall be a suspension of arms for six months, to give the great powers of modern Europe an opportunity to mediate between the acknowledged governments, as to the rebellion, is the one which almost universally prevails here. Everybody sees that it is neither more or less than asking us to give up what we are fighting for.

The most favorable construction that can be put upon it makes it a device to give the rebel government an opportunity to get on its legs again, to breathe, recruit, and take a new start. That is, on the supposition that the interference is to end with the procuring of an armistice, which is not probable. The top of the wedge being once inserted, the rest would be driven in after it. An interference of the nature proposed once allowed, would draw after it interferences of the most decided and domineering character, and transfer to our continent the system of dictation by which three or four sovereigns give law to Europe.

I do not think the French ministry will be much pleased with the manner in which the project is received here. The most blatant of the Peace Party would not even venture upon the unpopularity of proposing a cessation of

hostilities. You put the case strongly against England.
. . . Notwithstanding the expression of the French Emperor's desire to interfere, and the refusal of his proposal
by Great Britain, the feeling of dissatisfaction with Great
Britain is much stronger than against France. It pervades
all classes; the old British party, who looked at everything
British through a prism, are reached by it, give up their
old prejudices, and scold vehemently against England. At
least this is the case with very many of them. The English
have lost more ground in public opinion in America within
the past year and a half than they can redeem in a century.

I am glad, and so is Frances, to see that your feelings
are with our country in this calamitous war. You have
seen, I suppose, enough to convince you that our Government and people are resolved that it shall end in but one
way—the absolute submission of those who are in arms
against them. We think we see this conclusion of the war at
no very great distance. The news of our country, when cir-
culated in England, is, in many instances, much discolored
by passing through unfriendly channels. One of the worse
consequences of this distortion of facts, and of the hostile
comments so often made by your press upon almost every
event of our war, is a growing animosity toward Great
Britain. Some of us take great pains to distinguish the
British nation, so far as relates to this matter, from
the British government, and the British aristocracy from
the British people; but it is not the great majority of newspaper readers who will attend to these distinctions.[2]

*Emerson attempts to set his friend Carlyle on the right
track as to American affairs.*

I have in these last years lamented that you had not
made the visit to America, which in earlier years you
projected or favored. It would have made it impossible
that your name should be cited for one moment on the side
of the enemies of mankind. Ten days' residence in this
country would have made you the organ of the sanity of

England and of Europe to us and to them, and have shown you the necessities, and aspirations which struggle up in our Free States, which, as yet, have no organ to others, and are ill and unsteadily articulated here. In our today's division of Republican and Democrat, it is certain that the American nationality lies in the Republican party (mixed and multiform though that party be); and I hold it not less certain, that, viewing all the nationalities of the world, the battle for Humanity, is, at this hour, in America. A few days here would show you the disgusting composition of the Party which within the Union resists the national action.

Take from it the wild Irish element, imported in the last twenty-five years into this country, and led by Romish Priests, who sympathize, of course, with despotism, and you would bereave it of all its numerical strength. A man intelligent and virtuous is not to be found on that side. Ah! how gladly I would enlist the wise, thoughtful, efficient pens and voices of England! We want England and Europe to hold our people stanch to their best tendency. Are English of this day incapable of a great sentiment? Can they not leave cavilling at petty failures, and bad manners, and at the dunce part (always the largest part in human affairs), and leap to the suggestions and fingerpointings of the gods, which, above the understanding, feed the hopes and guide the wills of men?

This war has been conducted over the heads of all the actors in it; and the foolish terrors, "What shall we do with the Negro?" "The entire black population is coming North to be fed," &c., have strangely ended in the fact that the black refuses to leave his climate; gets his living *and* the living of his employers there, as he has always done; is the natural ally and soldier of the Republic, in that climate; now takes the place of two hundred thousand white soldiers; and will be, as the conquest of the country proceeds, its garrison, till peace, without slavery, returns.

Slaveholders in London have filled English ears with their wishes and perhaps beliefs; and our people, generals, and politicians have carried the like, at first, to the war, until corrected by irresistible experience. I shall always respect War hereafter. The cost of life, the dreary havoc of comfort and time, are overpaid by the vistas it opens of Eternal Law, reconstructing and uplifting Society—breaks up the old horizon, and we see through the rifts a wider. The dismal Malthus, the dismal DeBow, have had their night.

Our Census of 1860, and the War, are poems, which will, in the next age, inspire a genius like your own. I hate to write you a newspaper, but, in these times 'tis wonderful what sublime lessons I have once and again read on the Bulletin-boards in the streets. Everybody has been wrong in his guess, except good women, who never despair of an Ideal right.[3]

Lowell adds his criticism of England on the heels of the Mason and Slidell affair.

. . . I am old enough to have heard those who talk of England who still, even after the unhappy estrangement, could not unschool their lips from calling her the Mother Country. But England has insisted on ripping up old wounds, and has undone the healing work of fifty years. . . .

The sore points on both sides have been skillfully exasperated by interested and unscrupulous persons, who saw in a war between the two countries the only hope of profitable return for their investment in Confederate stock, whether political or financial. The always supercilious, often insulting, and sometimes even brutal tone of British journals and publick men has certainly not tended to soothe whatever resentment might exist in America.

We have no reason to complain that England, as a necessary consequence of her clubs, has become a great society for the minding of other people's business, and we can smile good–naturedly when she lectures other nations on the sins of arrogance and conceit; but we may justly consider it a breach of the political *convenances* which are expected to regulate the intercourse of one well–bred government with another, when men holding places in the ministry allow themselves to dictate our domestic policy, to instruct us in our duty, and to stigmatize as unholy a war for the rescue of whatever a high–minded person should hold most vital and most sacred. Was it in good taste, that I may use the mildest term, for Earl Russell to expound our own Constitution to President Lincoln, or to make a new and fallacious application of an old phrase for our benefit, and tell us that the Rebels were fighting for independence and we for empire.

And now all respectable England is wondering at our irritability, and sees a quite satisfactory explanation of it in our national vanity.

It is time for Englishmen to consider whether there was nothing in the spirit of their press and of their leading public men calculated to arouse a just indignation, and to cause a permanent estrangement on the part of any nation capable of self–respect, and sensitively jealous, as ours then was, of interference. Was there nothing in the indecent haste with which belligerent rights were conceded to the Rebels, nothing in the abrupt tone assumed in the Trent case, nothing in the fitting out of Confederate privateers, that might stir the blood of a people already overcharged with doubt, suspicion, and terrible responsibility? . . . Every sensible American knew, that the moral support of England was equal to an army of two hundred thousand men to the Rebels, while it insured us of another year or two of exhausting war.

Because the door of the old homestead had been once slammed in our faces, shall we in a huff reject all further advances of conciliation, and cut ourselves foolishly off from any share in the humanizing influences of the place, with its ineffable riches in association, its heirlooms of immemorial culture, its historic monuments, ours no less than theirs, its noble gallery of ancestral portraits?

We have only to succeed, and England will not only

respect, but, for the first time, begin to understand us. And let us not, in our justifiable indignation at wanton insult, forget that England is not the England only of snobs who dread the democracy they do not comprehend, but the England of history, of heroes, statesmen, and poets, whose names are dear, and their influence as salutary to us as to her.[4]

Mrs. Stowe sets out to prove to English women (thousands of whom, eight years before, had petitioned their American sisters to use their influence to end slavery) that right is on the side of the North (January, 1863).

. . . Sisters of England, in this solemn, expectant hour, let us speak to you of one thing which fills our hearts with pain and solicitude.

It is an unaccountable fact, and one which we entreat you seriously to ponder, that the party which has brought the cause of Freedom thus far on its way, during the past eventful year, has found little or no support in England. Sadder than this, the party which makes Slavery the chief cornerstone of its edifice finds in England its strongest defenders.

The voices that have spoken for us who contend for Liberty have been few and scattering. God forbid that we should forget those few noble voices, so sadly exceptional in the general outcry against us! They are, alas, too few to be easily forgotten. False statements have blinded the minds of your community, and turned the most generous sentiments of the British heart against us. The North are fighting for supremacy and the South for independence, has been the voice. Independence? for what? to do what? To prove the doctrine that all men are *not* equal. To establish the doctrine that the white may enslave the Negro?

It is natural to sympathize with people who are fighting for their rights; but if these prove to be the right of selling children by the pound and trading in husbands and wives as merchantable articles, should not Englishmen think twice before giving their sympathy? A pirate ship on the high seas is fighting for independence! Let us be consistent.

It has been said that we have been over-sensitive, thin-skinned. It is one inconvenient attendant of love and respect, that they do induce sensitiveness. A brother or father turning against one in the hour of trouble, a friend sleeping in the Gethsemane of our mortal anguish, does not always find us armed with divine patience. We loved England; we respected, revered her; we were bound to her by ties of blood and race. Alas! must all these declarations be written in the past tense?

In the beginning of our struggle, the voices that reached us across the water said, "If we were only sure you were fighting for the abolition of slavery, we should not dare to say whither our sympathies for your cause might not carry us."

Such, as we heard, were the words of the honored and religious nobleman who draughted this very letter which you signed and sent us, and to which we are now replying.

When these words reached us, we said, "We can wait, our friends in England will soon see whither this conflict is tending." A year and a half have passed; step after step has been taken for Liberty; chain after chain has fallen, till the march of our armies is choked and clogged by the glad flocking of emancipated slaves; the day of final emancipation is set; the Border States begin to move in voluntary consent; universal freedom for all draws like the sun in the distant horizon: and still no voice from England.

No voice? Yes, we have heard on the high seas the voice of a war steamer, built for a man–stealing Confederacy with English gold in an English dockyard, going out of an English harbor, manned by English sailors, with the full knowledge of English Government officers, in defiance of the Queen's proclamation of neutrality. So far has English sympathy overflowed. We have heard of other steamers, iron–clad, designed to furnish to a Slavery–defending Confederacy their only lack—a navy for the high seas. We have heard that the British Evangelical Alliance refuses to express sympathy with the liberating party, when requested to do so by the French Evangelical Alliance. We find in English religious newspapers all those sad degrees in the downward sliding scale of defending and apologizing for slaveholders and slaveholding with which we have so many years contended in our own country. We find the President's Proclamation of Emancipation spoken of in those papers only as an incitement to servile insurrection. Nay more—we find in your papers, from thoughtful men, the admission of rapid decline of anti-slavery sentiments in England.

Alas, then, England! is it so? In this day of great deeds and great heroisms, this solemn hour when the Mighty Redeemer is coming to break every yoke, do we hear such voices from England?

This very day the writer of this has been present at a solemn religious festival in the national capitol, given at the home of a portion of those fugitive slaves who have fled to our lines for protection—who, under the shadow of our flag, find sympathy and succor. The national day of thanksgiving was there kept by over a thousand redeemed slaves, and for whom Christian charity had spread an ample repast. Our Sisters, we wish *you* could have witnessed the scene. We wish you could have heard the prayer of a blind old Negro, called among his fellows John the Baptist, when, in touching, broken English, he poured forth his thanksgivings. We wish you could have heard the sound of that strange rhythmical chant which is now forbidden to be sung on Southern plantations—the psalm of this modern exodus—which combines the barbaric fire of the "Marseillaise" with the religious fervor of the old Hebrew prophet.

As we were leaving, an aged woman came and lifted up her hands in blessing. "Bressed be de Lord dat brought me to see dis first happy day of my life! Bressed be de Lord!" In all England, is there no Amen?

We have been shocked and saddened by the question asked in an association of Congregational ministers in England, the very blood–relations of the liberty–loving Puritans, "Why does not the North let the South go?"

What! give up the point of emancipation for these four million slaves? Turn our backs on them, and leave them to their fate? What! leave our white brothers to run a career of oppression and robbery, that, as sure as there is a God that ruleth in the armies of heaven, will bring a day of wrath and doom?

We have sealed our devotion by desolate hearth and darkened homestead—by the blood of sons, husbands and brothers. In many of our dwellings the very light of life has gone out; and yet we accept the life–long darkness as our own part in this great and awful expiation, by which the bonds of wickedness shall be loosed, and abiding peace established on the foundation of righteousness. Sisters, what have *you* done, and what do you mean to do?

In view of the decline of the whole anti–slavery fire in England, in view of all the facts and admissions recited from your own papers, we beg leave in solemn sadness to return to you your own words:—

"A common origin, a common faith, and, we sincerely believe, a common cause, urge us, at the present moment, to address you on the subject" of that fearful encouragement and support which is being afforded by England to a slaveholding Confederacy.[5]

23 *These Were Men*

Emerson consoles bereaved parents.

I have waited a week since I heard the heavy news
from Port Hudson—fearing to disturb you—but do not
like to wait longer. I believe I have read every syllable
which the journals contain of William's heroic behavior
[Lieut. Col. William L. Rodman, killed in the Union attack
on Port Hudson, La., May 27, 1863] & death at the head of
his regiment, & with entire sympathy for, & I fear, too true
knowledge of the desolation the tidings will have brought
to your house, however, consoled by the cordial testimony
which the Army sends home of the love & honor which
attached to him in life & in death.

I had kept up by frequent inquiries some knowledge of
his whereabouts, & read the New Orleans correspondence
with hope of quite happier news.—But this sacrifice which
he has finished, I am sure, could not be a surprise to his
thoughts, nor to yours. The soldier & the soldier's father &
mother must have rehearsed this dread contingency to
themselves quite too often not to know its face when it
arrived.—And yet there can be no sufficient preparation.

His life, so fair & amiable from the childhood which I
remember—his manly form & qualities, promised a solid
character & fortune. I dread to think how the change will
darken your house—hitherto the home of every friendly influence. Neither perhaps can any considerations of duty to

country and mankind for a long time reconcile to this devastation in the family. And yet who dare say, amid all the greatness the war has called out, in the privatest & obscurest, as well as in eminent persons, that these calamities do not suddenly teach self–renouncement, & raise us to the force they require. I am sure your son's own devotion will arm you to surrender him.

I think daily that there are crises which demand nations, as well as those which claim the sacrifices of single lives. Ours perhaps is one—and that one whole generation might well consent to perish, if, by their fall, political liberty & clean & just life could be made sure to the generations that follow. As you suffer, all of us may suffer, before we shall have an honest peace—

—I have seen Mrs. Anna Lowell, not long since . . . mother of Capt. James J. Lowell who fell on the peninsula—and found in her not so much grief, as devotion of herself & all her family to the public service.

My kindest remembrances & best thoughts to both your daughters. Susan at home will miss her brother most & love him best.—One of these days, I shall seek an opportunity of learning all you know & think in these hours.[1]

Bierce portrays the lurid aftermath of the battle of Chickamauga.

They were men. They crept upon their hands and knees. They used their hands only, dragging their legs. They used their knees only, their arms hanging idle at their sides. They strove to rise to their feet, but fell prone in the attempt. They did nothing naturally, and nothing alike, save only to advance foot by foot in the same direction.

Singly, in pairs, and in little groups, they came on through the gloom, some halting now and again while others crept slowly past them, then resuming their movement. They came by dozens and by hundreds; as far on either hand as one could see in the deepening gloom they ex-

tended and the black wood behind them appeared to be in-
exhaustible. The very ground seemed in motion toward the
creek. Occasionally one who had paused did not again go
on, but lay motionless. He was dead. Some, pausing, made
strange gestures with their hands, erected their arms and
lowered them again, clasped their heads; spread their
palms upward, as men are sometimes seen to do in public
prayer.

. . . These were men, yet crept like babies. Being men,
they were terrible, though unfamiliarly clad. . . . All
their faces were singularly white and many were streaked
and gouted with red. . . . But on and ever on they crept,
these maimed and bleeding men. . . . one of the crawling
figures . . . turned . . . a face that lacked a lower jaw—
from the upper teeth to the throat was a great red gap
fringed with hanging shreds of flesh and splinters of bone.
The unnatural prominence of nose, the absence of chin, the
fierce eyes, gave this man the appearance of a great bird of
prey crimsoned in throat and breast by the blood of its
quarry. . . .

And so the clumsy multitude dragged itself slowly and
painfully along in hideous pantomime—moved forward
down the slope like a swarm of great black beetles with
never a sound of going—in silence profound, absolute.

Instead of darkening, the haunted landscape began to
brighten. Through the belt of trees beyond the brook shone
a strange red light, the trunks and branches of the trees
making a black lacework against it. It struck the creeping
figures and gave them monstrous shadows, which carica-
tured their movements on the lit grass. It fell upon their
faces, touching their whiteness with a ruddy tinge, accen-
tuating the stains with which so many of them were
freaked and maculated. It sparkled on buttons and bits of
metal in their clothing.

Scattered about upon the ground now slowly narrow-
ing by the encroachment of this awful march to the water,
were certain articles . . . : an occasional blanket, tightly
rolled lengthwise, doubled and the ends bound together

with a string; a heavy knapsack here, and there a broken rifle—such things, in short, as are found in the rear of retreating troops, the "spoor" of men flying from their hunters. Everywhere near the creek, which here had a margin of lowland, the earth was trodden into mud by the feet of men and horses . . . footprints pointed in both directions; the ground had been twice passed over—in advance and in retreat. A few hours before, these desperate, stricken men, with their more fortunate and now distant comrades, had penetrated the forest in thousands. Their successive battalions, breaking into swarms and reforming in lines. . . . They had fought a battle. . . .

The fire beyond the belt of woods on the farther side of the creek, reflected to earth from the canopy of its own smoke, was now suffusing the whole landscape. It transformed the sinuous line of mist to the vapor of gold. The water gleamed with dashes of red, and red, too, were many of the stones protruding above the surface. But that was blood; the less desperately wounded had stained them in crossing. . . .

The advance was arriving at the creek. The stronger had already drawn themselves to the brink and plunged their faces into the flood. Three or four who lay without motion appeared to have no heads. . . . After slaking their thirst these men had not the strength to back away from the water, nor to keep their heads above it. They were drowned. In the rear of these, the open spaces of the forest showed . . . many formless figures . . . ; but not nearly so many were in motion.

. . . He now entered the belt of woods, passed through it easily in the red illumination . . . and so approached the blazing ruin of a dwelling. Desolation everywhere! In all the wide glare not a living thing was visible.

Shifting his position, his eyes fell upon some outbuildings which had an oddly familiar appearance, as if he had dreamed of them. He stood considering them with wonder, when suddenly the entire plantation, with its enclosing forest, seemed to turn as if upon a pivot. His little world swung half around. . . . He recognized the blazing building as his own home!

For a moment he stood stupefied by the power of the revelation, then ran with stumbling feet, making a half–circuit of the ruin. There, conspicuous in the light of the conflagration, lay the dead body of a woman—the white face turned upward, the hands thrown out and clutched full of grass, the clothing deranged, the long dark hair in tangles and full of clotted blood. The greater part of the forehead was torn away, and from the jagged hole the brain protruded, overflowing the temple, a frothy mass of gray, crowned with clusters of crimson bubbles—the work of a shell.

The child moved his little hands, making wild, uncertain gestures. He uttered a series of inarticulate and indescribable cries—something between the chattering of an ape and the gobbling of a turkey—a startling, soulless, unholy sound, the language of a devil.

Then he stood motionless, with quivering lips, looking down upon the wreck.[2]

Lowell writes to the mother of Robert Gould Shaw who was killed while leading his Negro regiment in an attack against Battery Wagner near Charleston.

Not a day has passed since I heard the dreadful news that I have not thought tenderly of you and yours; but I could not make up my mind to write you, and the longer I put if off the harder it grew. I have tried several times, and broken down. I knew you would be receiving all manner of consolation, and as I know that consolation is worse than nothing, I would not add mine. There is nothing for such a blow as that but to bow the head and bear it. We may think of many things that in some measure make up for such a loss, but we can think of nothing that will give us back what we have lost. The best is that, so far as he was concerned, all was noble and of the highest example.

I have been writing something about Robert, and if, after keeping it a little while, it should turn out to be a

poem, I shall print it; but not unless I think it some way
worthy of what I feel; however the best verse falls short of
noble living and dying such as his.

I would rather have my name known and blest, as his
will be, through all the hovels of an outcast race, than blar-
ing from all the trumpets of repute. . . .

If the consolation of the best is wearisome, it is yet
something to have the sympathy of everyone, as I know
you and Frank have. God bless and sustain you![3]

Whittier aims a barb at the home front.

God only knows whether we deserve success in this
terrible war. When I think of the rapacity of contractors
and officeholders, and of the brutal and ferocious prejudice
against the poor blacks, as evinced at Detroit and Port
Royal, I almost despair, so far as we, the whites of the
North, are concerned. God's will be done, whatever becomes of us.[4]

Bryant joins in happy tidings to the parents of a soldier.

I wish I had written to you as was becoming, and as my
wife more than once suggested to me, the moment I had received your letter, to tell you how glad we all were that
Charles had come out of the battle of which you speak,
unhurt.

To be engaged in a bloody conflict like that, and to be
alive at the end of it, is like going to the gate of death
knocking defiantly, and being allowed after that affront to
return. . . . I hope there will not be many more such
battles; but who can say? I feel that the rebel cause is on a
decline that must put an end to it sooner or later. . . .

. . . The rebellion . . . is like a dying man kept alive
from day to day by stimulants, to the wonder of everybody. When it goes, I expect to see it go all at once; life
will not linger in some of the members after the rest are
lifeless. After the head is cut off, there will be no wriggling
in the limbs.[5]

24 The Many Needless Dead

Bierce describes an act of soldierly courage.

A breezy day and a sunny landscape. An open country to right and left and forward; behind, a wood. In the edge of this wood, facing the open, but not venturing into it, long lines of troops halted. The wood is alive with them, and full of confused noises—the occasional rattle of wheels as a battery of artillery goes into position to cover the advance; the hum and murmur of the soldiers talking; a sound of innumerable feet in the dry leaves that strew the interspaces among the trees; hoarse commands of officers.

Detached groups of horsemen are well in front—not altogether exposed—many of them intently regarding the crest of a hill a mile away in the direction of the interrupted advance. For this powerful army, moving in battle order through a forest, has met with a formidable obstacle—the open country. The crest of that gentle hill a mile away has a sinister look; it says, Beware! Along it runs a stone wall extending to left and right a great distance. Behind the wall is a hedge; behind the hedge are seen tops of trees in rather straggling order. Among the trees—what? It is necessary to know.

Yesterday, and for many days and nights previously, we were fighting somewhere; always there was cannonad-

ing, with occasional keen rattlings of musketry, mingled
with cheers, our own or the enemy's, we seldom knew,
attesting some temporary advantage. This morning at day-
break the enemy was gone. We have moved forward across
the earthworks, across which we have so often vainly attempted to move before, through the debris of his abandoned camps, among the graves of his fallen, into the
woods beyond.

How curiously we had regarded everything! how odd
it all had seemed! Nothing had appeared quite familiar;
the most commonplace objects—an old saddle, a splintered
wheel, a forgotten canteen—everything had related something of the mysterious personality of those strange men
who had been killing us. The soldier never becomes wholly
familiar with the conception of his foes as men like himself; he cannot divest himself of the feeling that they are
another order of beings, differently conditioned, in an environment not altogether of the earth. The smallest ves-
tiges of them rivet his attention and engage his interest.
He thinks of them as inaccessible; and, catching an unexpected glimpse of them, they appear farther away, and
therefore larger, than they really are—like objects in a
fog. He is somewhat in awe of them.

From the edge of the wood leading up the acclivity are
the tracks of horses and wheels—the wheels of cannon. The
yellow grass is beaten down by the feet of infantry. Clearly
they have passed this way in thousands; they have not
withdrawn by the country roads. This is significant—it is
the difference between retiring and retreating.

That group of horsemen is our commander, his staff
and escort. He is facing the distant crest, holding his field
glass against his eye with both hands, his elbows needlessly
elevated. It is a fashion; it seems to dignify the act; we are
all addicted to it.

Suddenly he lowers the glass and says a few words to
those about him. Two or three aides detach themselves
from the group and canter away into the woods, along the
lines in each direction. We did not hear his words, but we

know them: "Tell General X. to send forward the skirmish line."

Those of us who have been out of place resume our positions; the men resting at ease straighten themselves and the ranks are reformed without a command. Some of us staff officers dismount and look at our saddle girths; those already on the ground remount.

Galloping rapidly along in the edge of the open ground comes a young officer on a snow–white horse. His saddle blanket is scarlet. What a fool! No one who has ever been in action but remembers how naturally every rifle turns toward the man on the white horse; no one but has observed how a bit of red enrages the bull of battle. That such colors are fashionable in military life must be accepted as the most astonishing of all the phenomena of human vanity. They would seem to have been devised to increase the death rate.

This young officer is in full uniform, as if on parade. He is all agleam with bullion—a blue and gold edition of the Poetry of War. A wave of derisive laughter runs abreast of him all along the line. But how handsome he is!—with what careless grace he sits his horse!

He reins up within a respectful distance of the corps commander and salutes. The old soldier nods familiarly; he evidently knows him. A brief colloquy between them is going on; the young man seems to be preferring some request which the older one is indisposed to grant. Let us ride a little nearer. Ah! too late—it is ended. The young officer salutes again, wheels his horse, and rides straight toward the crest of the hill.

The thin line of skirmishers, the men deployed in six paces or so apart, now pushes from the wood into the open. The commander speaks to his bugler, who claps his instrument to his lips. *Tra–la–la! Tra–la–la!* The skirmishers halt in their tracks.

Meantime the young horseman has advanced a hundred yards. He is riding at a walk, straight up the long slope, with never a turn of the head. How glorious! Gods!

What would we not give to be in his place—with his soul!
He does not draw his sabre; his right hand hangs easily at
his side. The breeze catches the plume in his hat and flut-
ters it smartly. The sunshine rests upon his shoulder
straps, lovingly, like a visible benediction. Straight on he
rides. Ten thousand pairs of eyes are fixed upon him with
an intensity that he can hardly fail to feel; ten thousand
hearts keep quick time to the inaudible hoof-beats of his
snowy steed. He is not alone—he draws all souls after him.
But we remember that we laughed! On and on, straight for
the hedge–lined wall, he rides. Not a look backward. O, if
he would but turn—if he could but see the love, the adora-
tion, the atonement!

Not a word is spoken; the populous depths of the
forest still murmur with their unseen and unseeing swarm,
but all along the fringe is silence. The burly commander is
an equestrian statue of himself. The mounted staff officers,
their field glasses up, are motionless all. The line of battle
in the edge of the wood stands at a new kind of "attention," each man in the attitude in which he was caught by
the consciousness of what is going on.

All these hardened and impatient mankillers, to whom
death in its awfulest forms is a fact familiar to their
everyday observation; who sleep on hills trembling with
the thunder of great guns, dine in the midst of streaming
missiles, and play at cards among the dead faces of their
dearest friends—all are watching with suspended breath
and beating hearts the outcome of an act involving the life
of one man. Such is the magnetism of courage and devotion.

If now you should turn your head you would see a
simultaneous movement among the spectators—a start, as
if they had received an electric shock—and looking forward again to the now distant horseman you would see
that he has in that instant altered his direction and is riding at an angle to his former course. The spectators suppose the sudden deflection to be caused by a shot, perhaps
a wound; but take this field glass and you will observe that

he is riding toward a break in the wall and hedge. He means, if not killed, to ride through and overlook the country beyond.

You are not to forget the nature of this man's act; it is not permitted to you to think of it as an instance of bravado, nor, on the other hand, a needless sacrifice of self. If the enemy has not retreated he is in force on that ridge. The investigator will encounter nothing less than a line-of-battle; there is no need of pickets, videttes, skirmishers, to give warning of our approach; our attacking lines will be visible, conspicuous, exposed to an artillery fire that will shave the ground the moment they break from cover, and for half the distance to a sheet of rifle bullets in which nothing can live.

In short, if the enemy is there, it would be madness to attack him in front; he must be manoeuvred out by the immemorial plan of threatening his line of communication, as necessary to his existence as to the diver at the bottom of the sea his air tube. But how ascertain if the enemy is there?

There is but one way—somebody must go and see. The natural and customary thing to do is to send forward a line of skirmishers. But in this case they will answer in the affirmative with all their lives; the enemy crouching in double ranks behind the stone wall and in cover of the hedge will wait until it is possible to count each assailant's teeth. At the first volley a half of the questioning line will fall—the other half before it can accomplish the predestined retreat. What a price to pay for gratified curiosity! At what a dear rate an army must sometimes purchase knowledge! "Let me pay all," says this gallant man—this military Christ!

There is no hope except the hope against hope that the crest is clear. True, he might prefer capture to death. So long as he advances the line will not fire—why should it? He can safely ride into the hostile ranks and become a prisoner of war. But this would defeat his object. It would not answer our question; it is necessary either that he return unharmed or be shot to death before our eyes. Only so shall we know how to act. If captured—why, that might have been done by a half–dozen stragglers.

Now begins an extraordinary contest of intellect between a man and an army. Our horseman, now within a quarter of a mile of the crest, suddenly wheels to the left and gallops in a direction parallel to it. He has caught sight of his antagonist; he knows all. Some slight advantage of ground has enabled him to overlook a part of the line. If he were here he could tell us in words. But that is now hopeless; he must make the best use of the few minutes of life remaining to him, by compelling the enemy himself to tell us as much and as plainly as possible— which, naturally, that discreet power is reluctant to do.

Not a rifleman in those crouching ranks, not a cannoneer at those masked and shotted guns, but knows the needs of the situation, the imperative duty of forbearance. Besides, there has been time enough to forbid them all to fire. True, a single rifle shot might drop him and be no great disclosure.

But firing is infectious—and see how rapidly he moves, with never a pause except when he wheels his horse about to take a new direction, never directly backward toward us, never directly forward toward his executioners. All this is visible through the glass; it seems occurring within pistol–shot; we see all but the enemy, whose presence, whose thoughts, whose motives we infer. To the unaided eye there is nothing but a black figure on a white horse, tracing slow zigzags against the slope of a distant hill—so slowly they seem almost to creep.

Now—the glass again—he has tired of his failure, or sees his error, or has gone mad; he is dashing directly forward at the wall, as if to take it at a leap, hedge and all! One moment only and he wheels right about and is speeding like the wind straight down the slope—toward his friends, toward his death! Instantly the wall is topped with a fierce roll of smoke for a distance of hundreds of yards to right and left. This is as instantly dissipated by the wind, and before the rattle of the rifle reaches us he is down. No, he recovers his seat; he has pulled his horse upon its haunches. They are up and away! A tremendous cheer bursts from our ranks, relieving the insupportable tension of our feelings.

And the horse and its rider? Yes, they are up and away. Away, indeed—they are making directly to our left, parallel to the now steadily blazing and smoking wall. The rattle of the musketry is continuous, and every bullet's target is that courageous heart.

Suddenly a great bank of white smoke pushes upward from behind the wall. Another and another—a dozen roll up before the thunder of the explosions and the humming of the missiles reach our ears and the missiles themselves come bounding through clouds of dust into our covert, knocking over here and there a man and causing a temporary distraction, a passing thought of self.

The dust drifts away. Incredible!—that enchanted horse and rider have passed the ravine and are climbing another slope to unveil another conspiracy of silence, to thwart the will of another armed host. Another moment and that crest too is in eruption. The horse rears and strikes the air with its forefeet. They are down at last.

But look again—the man has detached himself from the dead animal. He stands erect, motionless, holding his sabre in his right hand straight above his head. His face is toward us. Now he lowers his hand to a level with his face and moves it outward, the blade of the sabre describing a downward curve. It is a sign to us, to the world, to posterity. It is a hero's salute to death and history.

Again the spell is broken; our men attempt to cheer; they are choking with emotion; they utter hoarse, discordant cries; they clutch their weapons and press tumultuously forward into the open. The skirmishers, without orders, against orders, are going forward at a keen run, like hounds unleashed. Our cannons speak and the enemy's now open in full chorus; to right and left as far as we can see, the distant crest, seeming now so near, erects its towers of clouds and the great shot pitch roaring down among our moving masses. Flag after flag of ours emerges from the wood, line after line sweeps forth, catching the sunlight on its burnished arms. The rear battalions alone are in obedience; they preserve their proper distance from the insurgent front.

The commander has not moved. He now removes his field glass from his eyes and glances from right to left. He sees the human current flowing on either side of him and his huddled escort, like tide waves parted by a rock. Not a sign of feeling in his face; he is thinking. Again he directs his eyes forward; they suddenly traverse that malign and awful crest. He addresses a calm word to his bugler. *Tra-la-la! Tra-la-la!* The injunction has an imperiousness which enforces it. It is repeated by the bugles of all the subordinate commanders; the sharp metallic notes assert themselves above the hum of the advance and penetrate the sound of the cannon. To halt is to withdraw. The colors move slowly back; the lines face about and sullenly follow, bearing their wounded; the skirmishers return gathering up the dead.

Ah, those many, many needless dead! That great soul whose beautiful body is lying over yonder, so conspicuous against the sere hillside—could it not have been spared the bitter consciousness of a vain devotion? Would one exception have marred too much the pitiless perfection of the divine, eternal plan? [1]

Melville writes a footnote to a poem on General James B. McPherson, who was killed on the outskirts of Atlanta.

The late Major General McPherson, commanding the Army of the Tennessee, a native of Ohio and a West Pointer, was one of the foremost spirits of the war. Young, though a veteran; hardy, intrepid, sensitive in honor, full of engaging qualities, with manly beauty; possessed of genius, a favorite with the army, and with Grant and Sherman. Both Generals have generously acknowledged their professional obligations to the able engineer, and admirable soldier, their subordinate and junior.

In an informal account written by the Achilles to this Sarpedon, he says, "On that day we avenged his death. Nearly twenty–two hundred of the enemies' dead remained on the ground when night closed upon the scene of action."

It is significant of the scale on which the war was waged, that the engagement thus written of goes solely . . . under the vague designation of one of the battles before Atlanta.[2]

Lanier, from his Virginia post, finds it difficult to get letters through to his people in Georgia.

I have unexpectedly found an opportunity to get a note through the Yankee lines, by a scout who goes up to Petersburg today—

You need have no anxiety about Cliff and me, if you should receive no letters from us— Our communications with the Railroad has been cut off so far as *regular* mails are concerned: but we will probably have frequent chances of sending letters to you by our scouts, who find no difficulty at all in penetrating the weak line of the enemy—.

Cliff, and I, having received no orders to leave, are going to remain in our present locality, which I do not name for obvious reasons— Somewhat to our discomfiture, we are probably in the *safest* place in the Southern Confederacy.[3]

Melville has words of admiration for an acquaintance.

Dear General:

When I read of you at Cold Harbor, I recalled your hospitality at Fairfax, and the agreeable evening I spent with you there, in company with my cousin, Col. Gansevoort, and would have written you, had I known how to address the note.

Though I hope I *am* patriotic—enthusiastically so—yet I will not congratulate you, General, upon your wound, but will reserve that for the scar, which will be equally glorious and not quite so irksome. —I am glad it is no worse with you, and rejoice to learn that you are in a promising way. I trust that you are in a condition to enjoy your book and your cigar, also (but this should have gone before) the sweet eyes of the sympathetic ladies, who, you know, have a natural weakness for heroes. How they must hover over you—the angels!—and how must your dreams be mingled of love and glory. I don't know but that I ought to congratulate you at once, after all.

But me thinks I heard somebody say, Don't bore him with too long a yarn.

Of course I shall not look for any reply to this note, or that you will trouble yourself any further about it than to receive it as an expression of respect and good-feeling.[4]

25   *The War Drags On*

Bryant makes a prediction concerning the end of the war, and then, on May 21, 1863, in an Evening Post *editorial, warns of Lee's intended invasion of Pennsylvania.*

How this war drags on! Yet I cannot help believing that it will end suddenly, almost unexpectedly. . . . We have all along, in my opinion, conducted the war on a false principle, weakened our forces by the loosest dispersion, and strengthening the rebels by keeping them in a compact body, when there was no necessity for all this. I think I see symptoms of a disposition to depart from this policy; and, when we do, I shall then conclude the war is near an end.[1]

There are unmistakeable indications that Davis is quietly withdrawing troops from the outlying camps along the seacoasts to reinforce Lee, which movement will be continued, we think, until the general has a command of 150,000 to 200,000 men. As soon as it is ready, Lee will move, we conjecture, not in the direction of Washington, but of the Shenandoah Valley, with a view to crossing the Potomac somewhere between Martinsburg and Cumberland. It will be easy for him . . . to defend his flanks . . . and to maintain also uninterrupted communications with Staunton and the Central Virginia railway. The valley itself is filled with rapidly ripening harvests, and once upon the river supplies may be got from Pennsylvania.[2]

Whittier chaffs a school teacher friend over Jeb Stuart's raids in the North.

I take it you are not expecting Stuart and his rebel scaramouches at your school. Think what a fluttering in your dovecote such a visit would occasion! I am half inclined to believe that the rascals will reach Philadelphia; and amidst all my anxieties and regrets, I cannot help smiling to think of the drab-colored panic among the staid and quiet people of that city.[2, 3]

Bierce enumerates his principal duties as an officer in the Union army.

Whether in camp or on the march, in barracks, in tents, or *en bivouac,* my duties as topographical engineer kept me working like a beaver—all day in the saddle and half the night at my drawing–table, plotting my surveys. It was hazardous work; the nearer to the enemy's lines I could penetrate, the more valuable were my field notes and the resulting maps. It was a business in which the lives of men counted as nothing against the chance of defining a road or sketching a bridge. Whole squadrons of cavalry escort had sometimes to be sent thundering against a powerful infantry outpost in order that the brief time between the charge and the inevitable retreat might be utilized in sounding a ford or determining the point of intersection of two roads.

. . . Our frequent engagements with the Confederate outposts, patrols, and scouting parties had . . . educating value; they fixed in my memory a vivid and apparently imperishable picture of the locality—a picture serving instead of accurate field notes, which, indeed, it was not always convenient to take, with carbines cracking, sabers clashing, and horses plunging all about. These spirited encounters were observations entered in red.[4]

Longfellow makes a brief reference to Lincoln's Gettysburg Address, in a letter to George W. Curtis.

We are all well here in this old house; mainly waiting and watching the tides of the great war. This morning's paper (Nov. 19, 1863) brings the report of Lincoln's brief speech at Gettysburg, which seems to me admirable.[5]

Melville writes to his cousin telling him how much he enjoyed visiting him at his camp in Virginia.

My dear Henry:

I embrace the earliest opportunity afforded by my recovery from an acute attack of neuralgia in the eyes, to thank you for your hospitality at the camp, and make known the fact that I have not forgotten you. I enjoyed my visit very much, & would not have missed it on any account, and can only regret that you happened to be away when we arrived. But as when the sun reappears after being hidden; so—&c. &c &c. Your imagination and modesty will supply the rest.

I missed seeing the Dr. at Washington, though I sought him at Willard's. I trust he got rid of his temporary disfigurement. When in your tent you introduced him to Gen. Tyler, you should have said:—General, let me make you acquainted with my friend here. Don't be frightened. This is not his face, but a masque. A horrible one, I know, but for God's sake don't take it to be the man. General, that horrible masque, my word for it, hides a noble and manly countenance. &c &c &c. Your wit & invention render further strumming on this string idle.

—How is Captain Brewster? Coke on Lyttleton, and Strap on the Shoulder. My friendly regards & best wishes to the Captain & say to him that I hear the neigh of his war–horse in my dreams, likewise that I have a flannel shirt of his in my keeping; which I hope one day to exhibit as the identical shirt worn by that renowned soldier shortly after his entrance into the army. —Edwin Lansing—remember him. Tell him I frequently think of him & his tent & there is pleasure in the thought. Tell him to tell

Dr. Wolf (savage name, but sweet man) that my prayers ascend for him.

And Gen. Tyler, too. Pray, give my respects to him, & say that I agree with him about "titan." The worst thing I can say about it is that it is a little better than "Mardi." The Terence I highly value; indeed both works, as memorials of the hospitalities of an accomplished general & jolly Christian.

And now, Col. Gansevoort of the 13th N. Y. Cavalry, conceive me to be standing some paces from you, in an erect attitude and with manly bearing, giving you the military salute. Farewell. May two small but choice constellations of stars alight on your shoulders. May your sword be a lesson to the despicable foe, & your name in after ages be used by Southern matrons to frighten their children by. And after death (which God long avert, and bring about after great battles, quietly, in a comfortable bed, with wife & children around) may that same name be transferred to heaven—bestowed upon some new planet or cluster of stars of the first magnitude. Farewell, my hero

Col. Gansevoort.
Lizzie wishes to be remembered to you.[6]

Emerson expresses his confidence in ultimate victory for the North.

The War On the whole, I know that the cosmic results will be the same, whatever the daily events may be. The Union may win or lose battles, win or lose in the first treaties and settlement; sutlers and pedlars may thrive on some abuse, but Northwest trade and Northeastern production, and Pennsylvania coal mines, and New York shipping, and white labour, though not idealists, gravitate in the ideal direction. Nothing less large than justice to them all can keep them in good temper, because in matters of such compass as the interests of a nation, every partial action hurts and offends some party.

If our brothers or children are killed in the battle, we owe to them the same courage and self–renunciation in bearing well their death, which they showed us in sacrificing themselves. They who come to-day to his funeral, to-morrow will tread in his warpath, and show his slayers the way to death.

Boutwell said to me the other day, "It makes no difference whether we gain or lose a battle, except the loss of valuable lives; we gain the advantage from month to month."

There has been no example like ours of the march of a good cause as by gravitation, or rather, by specific levity, against particular defeats. It is like the progress of health in sleep. You have removed the causes of disease (and one of them is your restless doing) and all mends of itself. It is like the replacement of the dislocated bone, as soon as you have removed the obstruction. The vanity of no man is gratified. The Abolitionist would so willingly put in his claim; the sublime God puts him back into the same category of egotism with the Copperhead.[7]

Bryant reports from rural Long Island as to home front conditions.

Meanwhile, we here in Roslyn . . . know little of the war save by rumor. . . . Birds sing, and the cicada sounds his shrill note from the neighboring tree, and the grapes swell, and pears ripen . . . and children are born, and old people and the sick die in their beds, just as if there were no war. I wish you were here a little while to see how peaceful the place is, and how much pleasanter we have made it, and to join in our prayers that every part of our country may soon be as tranquil.[8]

26 *Enforcing Emancipation*

Emerson expresses his belief in absolute emancipation.

I remember when I feared—what one still newly escaped shudders to think of—that a little more success, a
wiser choice of candidates by the Southern Party—say, of
Jefferson Davis, instead of Pierce or Buchanan—had enabled them by a *coup d'etat* to have strained the whole organism of the Government to the behalf of Slavery, to have
insisted, by all the courts, marshalls, and army and navy of
the Union, on carrying into effect a right of transit with
slaves, from State to State. It had then only been necessary for rich Democrats in New York, Pennsylvania, and
Connecticut to buy slaves, and it is not easy to see how the
ardent Abolitionists—always a minority hated by the rich
class—could have successfully resisted. The effect, however, would have been to put the *onus* of resistance on the
North, and, at last, the North would have seceded. We had
been the rebels, and would have had the like difficulty to
put our States into secession as the Southerners had.

The rebels in the effrontery with which, in their failing
fortunes, they adhere to their audacious terms of peace,
have well instructed us; and I rejoice to see we are likely
to plant ourselves with vigour on the condition of absolute
emancipation as the first point with which each rebel state

must comply. Their women, too, have taught our women, who have excellently learned the lesson. It will go hard, but we shall better the instruction.[1]

Bryant opposes bartering freedom for peace.

. . . Gradual emancipation! there is no grosser delusion ever entertained by man. . . . There have been good men, doubtless, who have yielded to the dream that gradual emancipation was the best method of getting rid of slavery, and some wise men have perhaps sanctioned that policy in time past, but the policy is now exploded. Our experience in North Carolina, our experience in Port Royal, and a larger and more decisive experience in Louisiana, have borne testimony against it; have shown that instant emancipation carries with it every advantage.

I have read a letter this very day—a letter from a person whose name, if I were to mention it, would carry authority, assurance, acquiescence, conviction to all that should read it—in which he says all those Negroes who have been made free, who are treated like freemen, paid wages, and allowed to provide for their families, now work better, more to the profit of those from whom they receive wages, and in all respects observe a more respectful deportment than ever before.

He goes on to say that all the planters say this, and that, if things were rightly managed in Louisiana, within a year that State would take her place among the free States of the Union, with the entire consent of all who dwell within her limits. He goes further than this: he says that all over the South, in every part of the slave States, the change, the transition from absolute and universal slavery to universal and instantaneous emancipation, might take place with even less violence and confusion than a tax law could be changed in a Northern State.

. . . Gradual emancipation! Have we not suffered mischief enough from slavery without keeping it any longer? Has not blood enough been shed? My friends, if a child of yours were to fall in the fire, would you pull him out gradually? If he were to swallow a dose of laudanum sufficient to cause speedy death, and a stomach-pump were at hand, would you draw the poison out by degrees? If your house were on fire, would you put it out piecemeal?

And yet there are men who talk of gradual emancipation by force of ancient habit, and there are men in the slave States who make of slavery a sort of idol which they are unwilling to part with; which, if it must be removed, they would prefer to see removed by a lapse of time and tender leave-takings.

Slavery is a foul and monstrous idol, a Juggernaut under which thousands are crushed to death; it is a Moloch for whom the children of the land pass through fire. Must we consent that the number of the victims shall be gradually diminished? If there are a thousand victims this year, are you willing that nine hundred should be sacrificed next year, and eight hundred the next, and so on until after the lapse of ten years it shall cease?

No, my friends, let us hurl this grim image from its pedestal. Down with it to the ground. Dash it to fragments; trample it in the dust. Grind it to a powder, as the prophets of old commanded that the graven images of the Hebrew idolators should be ground, and in that state scatter it to the four winds, and strew it upon the waters, that no human hand shall ever again gather up the accursed atoms and mould them into an image to be worshipped again with human sacrifices.[2]

An Evening Post *editorial, undated—''Peace but not Without General Freedom'' (probably some time in the summer of 1863).*

There is but one way of ending the war. Blow upon blow, battle after battle, conquest upon conquest, the capture of all the rebel seaports, the occupation of all the rivers in the rebel territory, no delay, no pause in the course of victory, till everyone of their strongholds, and every one of their towns, from Manassas to Fort Pickens, and from the Potomac to the Sabine, is ours. Then, when we have subdued the insurrection, we will make our own terms—terms such as shall seem to us just and fair, and so devised as best to avoid the danger of a future insurrection of the class who have caused all this strife and bloodshed.[3]

Longfellow's letter to Sumner suggests that Emancipation was to be only a beginning.

Your report on the rejection of colored testimony I read with a kind of agony, to think what we had been inflicting on those "whose despair is dumb" (in no court of the District of Columbia or any slave state could the testimony of a black man be received). This dreadful stone of Slavery!—whenever you lift it, what reptiles crawl out from under it!

Your speech on the Abolition of Slavery came this morning. I shall read it at once. It is enough for me that you have made it.[4]

27 Lincoln Re-elected

Lowell assures Motley, in July, 1864, that if Lincoln wins in November the war will soon end.

As to the situation here, you are doubtless well informed. My own feeling has always been confident, and it is now hopeful. If Mr. Lincoln is re–chosen, I think the war will soon be over. If not, there will be attempts at negotiation, during which the rebels will recover breath, and then war again with more chances in their favor.

Just now everything looks well. The real campaign is really in Georgia, and Grant has skillfully turned all eyes to Virginia by taking the command there in person. Sherman is a very able man, in dead earnest, and with a more powerful army than that of Virginia.

It is true that the mercantile classes are longing for peace, but I believe the people are more firm than ever. So far as I can see, the opposition to Mr. Lincoln is both selfish and factious, but it is much in favor of the right side that the Democratic party have literally not so much as a single plank of principle to float on, and the sea runs high. They don't know what they are in favor of—hardly what they think it safe to be against. And I doubt if they will gain much by going into an election on negatives.[1]

On the eve of the election, Lowell clarifies the fundamental difference between the two candidates.

General McClellan's election will be understood by the South and by the whole country as an acknowledgement of the right of secession—an acknowledgment which will resolve the United States into an association for insurance against any risk of national strength and greatness by land or sea. Mr. Lincoln, on the other hand, is the exponent of principles vital to our peace, dignity and renown—of all that can save America from becoming Mexico, and insure popular freedom for centuries to come.

The single question is, Shall we have peace by submission or by victory? General McClellan's election insures the one, Mr. Lincoln's gives us our only chance of the other. It is Slavery, and not the Southern people, that is our enemy; we must conquer this to be at peace with them. With the relations of the several States of the Rebel Confederacy to the Richmond government we have nothing to do, but to say that after being beaten as foreign enemies, they are to resume their previous relations to our own government as if nothing had happened, seems to us a manifest absurdity.

From whom would General McClellan, if elected under his plan of conciliation, exact the penalties of rebellion? The States cannot be punished, and the only merciful way in which we can reach the real criminals is by that very policy of emancipation whose efficacy is proved by the bitter opposition of all the allies of the Rebellion in the North. This is a punishment which will not effect the independence of individual states, which will improve the condition of the mass of the Southern population, and which alone will remove the rock of offence from the pathway of democratic institutions.

It is idle, however, to think of allaying angry feeling or appeasing resentment while the war lasts, and idler to hope for any permanent settlement, except in the complete subjugation of the rebellion. There are persons who profess to be so much shocked at the *word* subjugation as to be willing that we should have immediate experience of the *thing,* by receiving back the Rebels on their own conditions. Mr. Lincoln has already proclaimed an amnesty wide enough to satisfy the demands of the most exacting humanity, and they must reckon on the singular stupidity of their hearers who impute ferocious designs to a man who cannot nerve his mind to the shooting of a deserter or the hanging of a spy.

Mr. Lincoln, in our judgment, has shown from the first the considerate wisdom of a practical statesman. If he has been sometimes slow in making up his mind, it has saved him from the necessity of being hasty to change it when once made up, and he has waited till the gradual movement of the popular sentiment should help him to his conclusions and sustain him in them.

To be moderate and unimpassioned in revolutionary times that kindle natures of more flimsy texture to a blaze may not be a romantic quality, but it is a rare one, and goes with those massive understandings on which a solid structure of achievement may be reared. Mr. Lincoln is a long–headed and long–purposed man, who knows when he is ready—a secret General McClellan never learned.[2]

In an editorial dated September 20, 1864, Bryant urges his readers to vote for Lincoln.

He has gained wisdom by experience. Every year has seen our cause more successful; every year has seen abler generals, more skillful leaders, called to the head; every year has seen fewer errors, greater ability, greater energy, in the administration of affairs. The timid McClellan has been superseded by Grant, the do–nothing Buell by Sherman; wherever a man has shown conspicuous merit he has been called forward; political and military rivalries have been as far as possible banished from the field and from the national councils. . . . While Mr. Lincoln stays in power, this healthy and beneficial state of things will continue. . . .[3]

Emerson defines the kind of president a nation like ours must inevitably elect, and congratulates his fellow citizens on their selection of Lincoln.

We must accept the results of universal suffrage, and not try to make it appear that we can elect fine gentlemen. We shall have coarse men, with a fair chance of worth and manly ability, but not polite men, not men to please the English or French.

I congratulate my countrymen on the great and good omens of the hour; that a large portion of mankind dwelling in the United States have given their decision in unmistakeable terms in favor of social and statute order, that a nation shall be a nation, and refuses to hold its existence on the tenure of a casual *rencontre* of passengers, who meet at the corner of a street, or on a railroad, or at a picnic—held by no bond, but meeting and partying at pleasure; that a nation cannot be trifled with, but involves interests so dear and so vast that it is intolerable crime to treat them with levity; they shall be held binding as marriage; binding as contracts of property, binding as laws which guard the life honour of the citizen.

The people, after the most searching discussion of every part of the subject, have decided that the unity of the nation shall be held by force against the forcible attempt of parties to break it. What gives commanding weight to this decision is that it has been made by the people sobered by the calamity of the War, the sacrifice of life, the waste of property, the burden of taxes, and the uncertainties of the result. They protest in arms against the attempt of any small or any numerous minority of citizens or states to dispart a country. They do not decide that if a part of the nation, from geographic necessities or from irreconcilable interests of production and trade, desires separation, no such separation can be. Doubtless it may, because the permanent interest of one part to separate will come to be the interest and good will of the other part.

But, at all events, it shall not be done in a corner, not by stealth, not by violence, but as a solemn act, with all the forms, with all deliberation, and on the declared opinions of the entire population concerned, and with mutual guarantees and compensations.

I need not go over the statistics of the Country: those colossal lines are printed on your brain.[4]

A brief entry in Longfellow's journal for November 10.

Lincoln re–elected beyond a doubt. We breathe freer. The country will be saved.[5]

Emerson expresses his joy in a letter written at about the same time.

I give you joy of the Election. Seldom in history was so much staked on a popular vote. —I suppose never in history. One hears everywhere anecdotes of late, very late, remorse overtaking the hardened sinners & just saving them from final reprobation.[6]

28   *The Union Victorious*

Emerson remarks on the new look of the Army of the Potomac.

Captain O. W. Holmes tells me that the Army of the Potomac is acquiring a professional feeling, and that they have neither panics nor excitements, but more self–reliance.[1]

Lanier, in a series of letters written during the summer and fall of 1864, inadvertently foreshadows the eventual collapse of the Confederacy.

I can scarcely express to you the relief which I experienced on receiving your letter yesterday, written July 25th. It had been two months since I heard from you. . . . The papers of day before yesterday announced a Yankee raiding party at Clinton, Ga., moving on Macon; and I, not knowing what your capabilities for defence were, suppose that you would have the old tale repeated in which "our forces consisting principally of Militia, made a gallant resistance, but were overwhelmed by superior numbers, and routed &c &c," and that our beautiful city would fall to the barbarians. But we have, this morning, the cheering news that Gen'l Iverson has met the enemy near Clinton, defeating him and capturing several hundred of his men.

And so, with our letter from you informing us that

you are comfortably situated . . . we rest content, and for the first time in two long months allow ourselves to think with satisfaction of the dear ones whom we long so much to see—

Affairs are very quiet here along our lines, tho' it is rumored to-day that Grant is again moving forces to his left, threatening the Petersburg & Weldon R.R. The excitement consequent upon the recent springing of the Yankee mine [at Petersburg] has subsided; and, beyond a little picket firing and an occasional shell shrieking into the city, an air of Sabbath calm prevails—I am strong in the hope that the campaign, and, with it, the war, is nearly over. Grant's repeated failures, and the terrible slaughter of his men (we yesterday shovelled six hundred dead Yankees into their own mine, the grave which they had dug for us!) are already beginning to excite in the mind of our erratic enemy that distrust which has always been the inevitable prelude to a change of Commanders.

We received yesterday your letter of Sept. 23rd, from Macon. I regret that the view which you have both of the *public* and *private* situation is so discouraging: but am very strong in the hope that *both* will wear a decidedly more pleasing aspect in a short time.

The appointment of Beauregard to the command of your department, and the threatening position which our army is reported to have assumed have excited a lively sentiment of pleasure, I think, throughout the whole country. It was high time that the people were being relieved from the Sinbad's burden of discouragement which has been hanging about our neck and frustrating all our best endeavors. You know I never set up for a military prophet; but I think the concentration of all our forces at Marietta, superintended by a little Genius would very soon drive Sherman from our State, if it did not annihilate him before he got out.[2]

Longfellow makes a note on Grant's victories in Virginia in the spring of 1864.

News of battles, and victories of General Grant over General Lee in Virginia. If fully confirmed, it is the beginning of the end.[3]

Bryant addresses an open letter to the Union Army on January 1, 1865.

Soldiers of the Union Army: I have been desired by the conductor of the "Soldiers' Friend" to address a few words to you at the opening of a new year. I take the occasion to offer you my warmest congratulations on what you have accomplished in the past year, and what you may expect to accomplish in the year before you.

At the beginning of the year 1864, the rebel generals presented a formidable front to our armies. Lee, at the head of a powerful force, occupied the banks of the Rapidan and the Rappahannock, threatening Washington and Pennsylvania. Early and his rebel cavalry held the wide valley of the Shenandoah. Johnston, with a formidable army, had posted himself at Atlanta, deemed an impregnable position, in which the rebels had stored the munitions of war in vast magazines, and collected the machinery by which they were fabricated.

A glance at the history of the past year will show you how all this state of things has been rapidly changed.

It will show General Grant transferred from the West, and invested with the command of our armies, pressing Lee by a series of splendid and hotly contested victories southward to Richmond, where Grant now holds the first general of the rebel armies and its choicest troops unwilling prisoners.

It will show General Sheridan sweeping down the valley of the Shenandoah, and, by a series of brilliant successes driving Early from the field.

It will show General Sherman leaving his position in Tennessee, and, by a series of able movements, reaching Atlanta, flanking and defeating Hood, capturing Atlanta, giving that stronghold of rebellion to the flames, and then making a triumphant march of three hundred miles through the heart of Georgia down to Savannah, which yields at the first summons, while the troops which held it save themselves from capture by flight.

It will show General Thomas, left in Tennessee by Sherman to deal with Hood, luring that commander from his advantageous position, and then falling upon his troops with an impetuosity which they cannot resist, till, by defeat after defeat, his broken and diminished army has become a mere band of fugitives.

It will show Mobile Bay entered by our Navy, under the gallant Farragut, and held by him until the Federal troops shall be ready to occupy the town from the land side. It will show Wilmington, that principal mart of blockade–runners, menaced both by sea and land, and Charleston trembling lest her fate may be like that of Savannah.

The year closes in these events, which, important as they are in themselves, are no less important in the consequences to which they lead, and which, as the ports of the enemy fall into our hands, as their resources one by one are cut off, their communications broken, and their armies lessened by defeat and desertion, promise the early disorganization of the rebellion, a speedy end of all formidable resistance to the authority of the Government, and the abandonment of the schemes formed by the rebel leaders, in utter despair of their ability to execute them.

Soldiers! This is your work! These are your heroic achievements; for these a grateful country gives you its thanks. Millions of hearts beat with love and pride when you are named. Millions of tongues speak your praise and offer up prayers for your welfare. Millions of hands are doing and giving all they can for your comfort, and that of the dear ones whom you have left at your homes. The history of the present war will be the history of your courage, your constancy, and the cheerful sacrifices you have made to the cause of your country.

I feel that you need no exhortation to persevere as you

have begun. If I did, I would say to the men at the front: Be strong; be hopeful! Your crowning triumph cannot be far distant. When it arrives, our nation will have wiped out a dark stain, which we fear it might yet wear for ages, and will stand in the sight of the world a noble commonwealth of freemen, bound together by ties which will last as long as the common sympathies of our race.

To those who suffer in our hospitals, the wounded and maimed in the war, I would say: The whole nation suffers with you; the whole nation implores Heaven for your relief and solace. A grateful nation will not, cannot, forget you.

The nation has voted to stand by you who have fought, or are fighting its battles. This great Christian nation has signified to the Government its will that the cause, in which you have so generously suffered and bled, shall never be abandoned, but shall be resolutely maintained until the hour of its complete triumph.

Meantime, the salutation of the new year, which I offer you, comes from millions of hearts as well as from mine, mingled in many of them with prayers for your protection in future conflicts, and thanksgiving for your success in those which are past. May you soon witness the glorious advent of that happy new year, when our beloved land, having seen the end of this cruel strife, shall present to the world a union of States with homogeneous institutions, founded on universal freedom, dwelling together in peace and amity, and when you who have fought so well, and triumphed so gloriously, shall return to your homes, amid the acclamations of your countrymen, wiser and more enlightened, and not less virtuous than when you took up arms for your country, with not one vice of the camp to cause regret to your friends.[4]

Emerson is enthusiastic over the onrushing tide of victories —and finally the surrender of Lee to Grant at Appomattox, April 9.

January 9: The public news is excellent. . . .

April 3: Joy to you, in this joy of the land & the world!

April 10: But what a joyful day is this & proud to Allegheny ranges, Northern Lakes, Mississippi Rivers & all lands & men between the two Oceans, between morning & evening stars. Mankind has appeared just now in its best attitude around Mr. Lincoln—in these recent experiences—& will aid him to use sanely the immense power with which the hour has clothed him.[5]

Longfellow echoes Emerson's enthusiasm.

April 3: Great news today, of the evacuation of Richmond.

April 4: . . . the great events that are taking place every hour!

April 5: Grant in pursuit of Lee, who is "turned into the bitter passes of flight."

April 7: In the afternoon comes news that Lee has surrendered. So ends the Rebellion of the slave owners![6]

Bryant greets the surrender with an editorial entitled "Glory to the Lord of Hosts."

The great day, so long and anxiously awaited, for which we have struggled through four years of bloody war, which has so often . . . dawned only to go down in clouds of gloom; the day of the virtual overthrow of the rebellion, of the triumph of constitutional order and of universal liberty, of the success of the nation against its parts, and of a humane and beneficent civilization over a relic of barbarism that had been blindly allowed to remain as a blot on its escutcheon—the day of PEACE has finally come. . . .

Glory, then, to the Lord of Hosts, who hath given us this final victory! Thanks, heartfelt and eternal, to the brave and noble men by land and sea, officers and soldiers, who by their labors, their courage and sufferings, their blood and their lives, have won it for us. And a gratitude no less deep and earnest to that majestic, devoted and glorious American people, who through all these years of trial have kept true to their faith in themselves and their institutions. . . . [7]

Lowell records the good news in a letter to Charles Eliot Norton.

. . . The news, my dear Charles, is from Heaven. I felt a strange and tender exaltation. I wanted to laugh and I wanted to cry, and ended by holding my peace and feeling devoutly thankful. There is something magnificent in having a country to love. It is almost like what one feels for a woman. Not so tender, perhaps, but to the full as self–forgetful. I worry a little about reconstruction, but am inclined to think matters will very much settle themselves. But I must run to my treadmill. Love and joy to all! [8]

29   *Lincoln Assassinated*

Longfellow, shocked, makes an entry in his journal.

April 14: The hideous news comes this morning of the assassination of President Lincoln, and attempt to assassinate Secretary Seward.[1]

Bryant expresses his grief in an editorial.

How awful and solemn the blow which has fallen upon every true heart in the nation! Abraham Lincoln, the man of the people, whom the Providence of God had raised to be "the foremost man of this world," in the flush of his success over the enemies of his country, while the peals of exultation for a great work accomplished were yet ringing in his ears, when his countrymen of all parties, and liberal minds abroad, had just begun to learn the measure of his goodness and greatness, is struck down by the hand of the assassin. All of him that could perish now lies in the cold embrace of death. His warm, kindly, generous heart beats no more; his services to his nation and to mankind are ended; and he has gone to the Rewarder of all sincere, honest, useful endeavors. The tears and lamentations of twenty millions of people, who are stricken as they never were before by the death of a single man, follow him to his bier, as their gratitude and lasting reverence will follow his fame through all time to come.

Mr. Lincoln has earned the love of his countrymen to a greater degree, perhaps, than any other person who filled the President's chair, scarcely excepting the "Father of his Country." For Washington the universal feeling of love was turned to a grave and profound awe by the imperturbable dignity of his character, and the impressive majesty of his presence. No one could approach him, even with those deep and lively sentiments of admiration which the grandeur and disinterestedness of his career always awakened, without being impressed with a certain solemn veneration.

Next to Washington, President Jackson had taken the firmest hold of the popular mind, by the magnanimity of his impulses, the justness of his sentiments, and the inflexible honesty of his purposes. But the impetuosity of Jackson, the violence with which he sometimes pursued his ends, made him as ardent enemies as he had friends.

But Mr. Lincoln, who had none of Washington's elevation or none of Jackson's energy, yet by his kindliness, his integrity, his homely popular humor, and his rare native instinct of the popular will, has won as large a place in the private heart, while history will assign him no less a place in the public history of the nation.

It was the fate of Mr. Lincoln, without solicitation or wish of his own, to become the leader of the people at a time of gigantic disturbance and transition; during four years of convulsive and almost agonizing civil war he has been the centre of the tumult; upon him it has fallen to direct the movement and to give tone to the spirit of the public.

How ably he had managed, the flags upon every housetop at the very moment of his death bore a gay and exultant witness; how skilfully he avoided and postponed needless troubles, the ease and tranquility of our return from a time of passionate conflict to a time of serene repose is a proof; how wisely he had contrived to put off the suggestions of an extreme or fanatical zeal everybody has been ready to acknowledge, for Mr. Lincoln brought to his high office no prejudice of section, no personal resentments, no unkind or bitter feelings of hatred, and throughout the trying time of his administration he has never uttered one rancorous word toward the South, or toward his political opponents. He contemplated the responsibilities of his great charge with the calm desire to do his duty under the light of conscience and truth, and for the best interests of his country.

The whole nation mourns the death of its President, but no part of it ought to mourn that death more keenly than our brothers of the South, who had more to expect from his clemency and sense of justice than from any other man who could succeed to his position. The insanity of the assassination, indeed, if it was instigated by the rebels, appears in the stronger light that we reflect on the generosity and tenderness with which he was disposed to close up the war, to bury its feuds, to heal over its wounds, and to restore to all parts of the nation that good feeling which once prevailed, and which ought to prevail again. Let us pray God that those who come after him may imitate his virtues and imbibe the spirit of his goodness.[2]

Emerson speaks at funeral services held at Concord, April 19.

We meet under the gloom of a calamity which darkens down over the minds of good men in all civil society, as the fearful tidings travel over sea, over land, from country to country, like the shadow of an uncalculated eclipse over the planet. Old as history is, and manifold as are its tragedies, I doubt if any death has caused so much pain to mankind as this has caused, or will cause, on its announcement; and this, not so much because nations are by modern arts brought so closely together, as because of the mysterious hopes and fears which, in the present day, are connected with the name and institutions of America.

In this country, on Saturday, every one was struck dumb, and saw at first only deep below deep, as he meditated on the ghastly blow. And perhaps, at this hour, when the coffin which contains the dust of the President sets foward on its long march through mourning States, on its way to his home in Illinois, we might well be silent, and suffer the awful voices of the time to thunder to us.

Yes, but the first despair was brief: the man was not to be mourned. He was the most active and hopeful of men; and his work had not perished: but acclamations of praise for the task he had accomplished burst out into a song of triumph, which even tears for his death cannot keep down.

The President stood before us as a man of the people. He was thoroughly American, had never crossed the sea, had never been spoiled by English insularity or French dissipation; a quite native, aboriginal man, as an acorn from the oak; no aping of foreigners, no frivolous accomplishments, Kentuckian born, working on a farm, a flatboat man, a captain in the Black Hawk war, a country lawyer, a representative in the rural legislature of Illinois—on such modest foundations the broad structure of his fame was laid.

How slowly, and yet by happily prepared steps, he came to his place. All of us remember—it is only a history of five or six years—the surprise and disappointment of the country at his first nomination by the Convention at Chicago. Mr. Seward, then in the culmination of his good fame, was the favorite of the Eastern States. And when the new and comparatively unknown name of Lincoln was announced (notwithstanding the report of the acclamations of that Convention) we heard the result coldly and sadly. It seemed too rash, on a purely local reputation, to build so grave a trust in such anxious times; and men naturally talked of the chances in politics as incalculable. But it turned out not to be chance. The profound good opinion which the people of Illinois and of the West had conceived of him, and which they had imparted to their colleagues that they also might justify themselves to their constituents at home, was not rash, though they did not begin to know the riches of his worth.

A plain man of the people, an extraordinary fortune attended him. He offered no shining qualities at the first encounter; he did not offend by superiority. He had a face and manner which disarmed suspicion, which inspired confidence, which confirmed goodwill. He was a man without vices. He had a strong sense of duty, which it was very easy for him to obey. Then, he had what farmers called a long head; was excellent in working out the sum for himself; in arguing his case and convincing you fairly and firmly.

Then, it turned out that he was a great worker; had prodigious faculty of performance; worked easily. A good worker is so rare; everybody has some disabling quality. In a host of young men that start together and promise so many brilliant leaders for the next age, each fails on trial; one by bad health, one by conceit, or by love of pleasure, or lethargy, or an ugly temper—each has some disqualifying fault that throws him out of the career. But this man was sound to the core, cheerful, persistent, all right for labor, and liked nothing so well.

Then, he had a vast good–nature, which made him tolerant and accessible to all; fair–minded, leaning to the claim of the petitioner; affable, and not sensible to the affliction which the innumerable visits paid to him when President would have brought to anyone else. And how his good–nature became a noble humanity, in many a tragic case which the events of the war brought to him, every one will remember; and with what increasing tenderness he dealt when a whole race was thrown on his compassion. The poor Negro said of him, on an impressive occasion, "Massa Linkum am eberywhere."

Then his broad good humor, running easily into jocular talk, in which he delighted, and in which he excelled, was a rich gift to this wise man. It enabled him to keep his secret; to meet every kind of man and every rank in society; to take off the edge of the severest decisions; to mask his own purpose and sound his companion; and to catch with true instinct the temper of every company he addressed. And, more than all, it is to a man of severe labor, in anxious and exhausting crises, the natural restorative, good as sleep, and is the protection of the ever-driven brain against rancor and insanity.

He is the author of a multitude of good sayings, so disguised as pleasantries that it is certain they had no reputation at first but as jests; and only later, by the very acceptance and adoption they find in the mouths of millions, turn out to be the wisdom of the hour.

I am sure if this man had ruled in a period of less facility of printing, he would have become mythological in a very few years, like Aesop or Pilpay, or one of the Seven Wise Masters, by his fables and proverbs. But the weight and penetration of many passages in his letters, messages and speeches, hidden now by the very closeness of their application to the moment, are destined hereafter to wide fame.

What pregnant definitions; what unerring common sense; what foresight; and, on great occasion, what lofty, and more than national, what humane tone! His brief speech at Gettysburg will not easily be surpassed by words on any recorded occasion. This, and one other American speech, that of John Brown to the court that tried him, and a part of Kossuth's speech at Birmingham, can only be compared with each other, and with no fourth.

His occupying the chair of State was a triumph of the good sense of mankind, and of the public conscience. This middle class country had got a middle class President, at last. Yes, in manners and sympathies, but not in powers, for his powers were superior. This man grew according to the full need. His mind mastered the problem of the day; and, as the problem grew, so did his comprehension of it.

Rarely has a man so fitted to the event. In the midst of fears and jealousies, in the Babel of counsels and parties, this man wrought incessantly with all his might and all his honesty, laboring to find out what the people wanted, and how to obtain that.

It cannot be said there is any exaggeration of his worth. If ever a man was fairly treated, he was. There was no lack of resistance nor of slander, nor of ridicule. The times have allowed no state secrets; the nation has been in such ferment, such multitudes had to be trusted, that no secret could be kept. Every door was ajar, and we know all that befell.

Then, what an occasion was the whirlwind of the war! Here was place for no holiday magistrate, no fair-weather sailor; the new pilot was hurried to the helm in a tornado. In four years—four years of battle-days—his endurance, his fertility of resources, his magnanimity, were sorely tried and never found wanting. There, by his courage, his justice, his even temper, his fertile counsel, his humanity, he stood a heroic figure in the centre of a heroic epoch. He is the true history of the American people of his time. Step by step he walked before them; slow with their slowness, quickening his march by theirs, the true representative of his continent; an entirely public man; father of his country, the pulse of twenty millions throbbing in his heart, the thought of their minds articulated by his tongue.

Adam Smith remarks that the axe, which in Houbraken's portraits of British kings and worthies is engraved under those who have suffered at the block, adds a certain lofty charm to the picture. And who does not see, even in this tragedy so recent, how fast the terror and rain of the massacre are already burning into glory around the victim? Far happier this fate than to have lived to be wished away; to have watched the decay of his own faculties; to have seen—perhaps even he—the proverbial ingratitude of statesmen; to have seen mean men preferred. Had he not lived long enough to keep the greatest promise that ever man made to his fellow-men—the practical abolition of slavery? He had seen Tennessee, Missouri and Maryland emancipate their slaves. He had seen Savannah, Charleston and Richmond surrendered; he had seen the main army of the rebellion lay down its arms. He had conquered the public opinion of Canada, England and France. Only Washington can compare with him in fortune.

And what if it should turn out, in the unfolding of the web, that he had reached the term; that this heroic deliverer could no longer serve us; that the rebellion had touched its natural conclusion, and what remained to be done required new and uncommitted hands—a new spirit born out of the ashes of the war; and that Heaven, wishing to show the world a completed benefactor, shall make him serve his country even more by his death than by his life?[3]

30   Reconstruction

With the end of the war clearly in sight, Lowell tackles the important question of reconstruction.

With the end of the war the real trial of our statesmanship, our patriotism, and our patience will begin. The passions excited by it will, no doubt, subside in due time, but meanwhile it behooves the party in possession of the government to conciliate patriotic men of all shades of opinion by a liberal, manly and unpartisan policy. Republicans must learn to acknowledge that all criticisms of their measures have not been dictated by passion or disloyalty, that many moderate and modest men, many enlightened ones, have really found reason for apprehension in certain arbitrary stretches of authority, nay, may even have been opposed to the war itself, without being in love with slavery, and without deserving to be called Copperheads. Many have doubted the wisdom of our financial policy, without being unpatriotic. It is precisely this class, dispassionate and moderate in their opinions, whose help we shall need in healing the wounds of war and giving equanimity to our counsels. We hope to see a course of action entered upon which shall draw them to its support.[1]

Whittier's optimism is stronger than are his doubts.

. . . I am more and more inclined to think we have got a strong man in Andrew Johnson; he has a good deal of the old Jackson strength of will. There is no fear that slavery is not to be utterly annihilated, and ground into powder under his heel. What I fear is that he is not quite democratic enough to give the black man the suffrage, or rather give his aid and influence in that direction.

But the safety of the Negro is in the fact, more and more apparent, that there is no possibility of a safe reconstruction of the States without his vote. This will be perceived; and we shall be compelled, as a matter of self-interest, to do justice to the loyal black man. . . .

I am glad to know thy views about capital punishment. I almost feared that like some others of my friends the events of the last four years had changed thy views. I hope we shall have no unnecessary hanging to gratify an evil desire for revenge.[2]

Emerson discourses on the nature of war.

It is commonly said of the War of 1812 that it made the nation honourably known; it enlarged our politics, extinguished narrow sectional parties. But the states were young and unpeopled. The present war, on a prodigiously large scale, has cost us how many valuable lives; but it has made many lives valuable that were not so before, through the start and expansion it has given. It has fired selfish old men to an incredible liberality, and young men to the last devotion.

The journals say it has demoralized many rebel regiments, but it has *moralized* many of our regiments, and not only so, but *moralized* cities and states. It added to every house and heart a vast enlargement. In every house and shop, an American map has been unrolled, and daily studied, and now that peace has come, every citizen finds himself a skilled student of the condition, means, and future of this continent.

I think it a singular and marked result that the War has established a conviction in so many minds that the right will get done; has established a chronic hope for a chronic despair.

This victory is the most decisive. This will stay put. It will show your enemies that what has now been so well done will be surely better and quicker done, if need be, again.

I think it is not in man to see, without a feeling of pride and pleasure, a tired soldier, the armed defender of the right. I think that in these last years all opinions have been affected by the magnificent and stupendous spectacle which Divine Providence has offered us of the energies that slept in the children of this country—that slept and have awakened. I see thankfully those that are here, but dim eyes in vain explore for some who are not.

The old Greek Heraclitus said, "War is the Father of all things." He said it no doubt, as science, but we of this day can repeat it as political and social truth. War passes the power of all chemical solvents, breaking up the old adhesions and allowing the atoms of society to take a new order. It is not the Government, but the War, that has appointed the good generals, sifted out the pedants, put in the new and vigorous blood. The War has lifted many other people besides Grant and Sherman into their true places. Even Divine Providence, we may say, always seems to work after a certain military necessity. Every nation punishes the General who is not victorious. It is a rule in games of chance that the cards beat all the players, and revolutions disconcert and outwit all the insurgents.

The revolutions carry their own points, sometimes to the ruin of those who set them on foot. The proof that war also is within the highest right, is a marked benefactor in the hands of Divine Providence, is its *morale*. The war gave back integrity to this erring and immoral nation. It charged with power, peaceful, amiable men, to whose life war and discord were abhorrent. What an infusion of character went out from this and other colleges! What an infusion of character down to the ranks!

The experience has been uniform that it is the gentle

soul that makes the firm hero after all. It is easy to recall the mood in which our young men, snatched from every peaceful pursuit, went to the war. Many of them had never handled a gun. They said, "It is not in me to resist. I go because I must. It is a duty which I shall never forgive myself if I decline. I do not know that I can make a soldier. I may be very clumsy. Perhaps I shall be timid; but you can rely on me. Only one thing is certain, I can well die, but I cannot afford to misbehave."

In fact the infusion of culture and tender humanity from these scholars and idealists who went to the war in their own despite—God knows they had no fury for killing their old friends and countrymen—had its signal and lasting effect. It was found that enthusiasm was a more potent ally than science and munitions of war without it.

"It is a principle of war," said Napoleon, "that when you can use the thunderbolt you must prefer it to the cannon." Enthusiam was the thunderbolt. Here in this little Massachusetts, in smaller Rhode Island, in this little nest of New England republics it flamed out when the guilty gun was aimed at Sumter.[3]

Bryant makes some observations about reconstruction.

I have for some time past thought of writing to you, by way of congratulating you on the suppression of the rebellion and the close of our bloody Civil War. And yet I have nothing to say on the subject which is not absolutely commonplace. All that can be said of the terrible grandeur of the struggle which we have gone through, of the vastness and formidable nature of the conspiracy against the life of our republic, of the atrocious crimes of the conspirators, of the valor and self-sacrificing spirit and unshaken constancy of the North, and of the magnificent result which Providence has brought out of so much wickedness and so much suffering, has been said over and over again.

Never, I think, was any great moral lesson so powerfully inculcated by political history. What the critics call poetic justice has been as perfectly accomplished as it could have been in any imaginary series of events.

When I think of this great conflict, and its great issues, my mind reverts to the grand imagery of the Apocalypse. . . .

. . . The legislatures of the Southern States should not be suffered to repeal their ordinances of secession. To repeal an ordinance implies that until its repeal it is in force. The government of the States in revolt are mere revolutionary organizations, which the Federal Government can no more recognize than it can the government of which Jefferson Davis is the head. They have all, I believe, altered their constitutions so as to conform them to their state of separation from the Federal Government, and they must all be recognized under new constitutions.

. . . This matter of restoring the Union is one in regard to which it is, I think easy to go wrong. There are three parties in regard to it—those who are concerned in the rebellion, those who are for punishing almost everybody, and those who are for punishing nobody. If no example should be made, and the men who took the lead in the rebellion—and they are not very few in number—should be allowed to go at large, I could by no means feel sure that the people would not be moved to take them in hand, and execute justice upon them in their rude way, which we ought, if possible to prevent.

I am strongly in favor of Negro suffrage. Our government ought to confer it upon the colored people in the District of Columbia, as an example to the whole of the Union and as an act of simple justice. Equally just is it that the colored race should be allowed the right of suffrage in every State, and I wish to see our Government take measures which will ultimately secure it to them without danger to the public peace, or violence to the structure of our Government—measures of which Negro suffrage will be the natural consequence, or which will persuade the late rebel States to concede it.

The Freedmens' Bureau should be continued in existence for a time to protect the Negroes in the helplessness arising from their present poverty and ignorance, and to reconcile the two races.

The wise provision in Mr. Trumbull's bill, renting them homesteads on the public lands in the South, and giving them a right to purchase these homesteads, should become law.

Then, I think, Mr. Conkling's proposed amendment should be adopted, which directs in substance that, until the colored race receive the right of suffrage, it shall not be counted to any State as a basis of representation.

With these measures, if the blacks are ill–treated in any part of the United States, they will settle on public lands in communities, and then suffrage will be a necessity, for they must elect their local officers. Consider also the natural effect of a state of freedom. The Negroes are laborious, orderly, temperate; the Southern whites are indolent, proud, disorderly, with constitutions tainted by a hereditary thirst for whiskey. The blacks are eager to be educated; the poor white, which are the majority, indifferent to the advantages of education. The blacks have already their schools, and are advancing rapidly in intelligence; they will soon have their schools everywhere, and in a very few years, their educated men, their professional men, even their politicians and public orators and journals, asserting their rights.

The wealth of the South—that great source of power and influence, unless a great change shall take place in the character of the whites of the South, not to be looked for in this generation—must inevitably pass into the hands of the blacks, since they have the qualities by which wealth is acquired.

The South has always been greedy of political power. Adopt the Conkling amendment, which Mr. Sumner, unfortunately, I think, opposed, and which the Democrats also seek to decry, and South Carolina loses half her political importance, half her representation in Congress, half her vote in the choice of President. This makes it the interest of the South to concede suffrage to the blacks.

These are peaceful methods; to me they seem sure to bring about the desired result quite as soon as the Negroes will be able to exercise the right of suffrage intelligently. It will be conceded to them cheerfully, and then it will be exercised without molestation.

Mr. Sumner's plan is to force Negro suffrage upon the whites of the South, and to keep the late insurgent States under the arbitrary rule of the Federal Government until they submit to this change.

I apprehend the worst consequences from this—a bitter hatred of the North, a fiercer and more brutal contempt of the rights of the Negro, the necessity of a large standing army, disturbances, turmoils, and perhaps bloodshed; a vast and corrupting executive patronage, twelve millions of people under the direct rule of the central Government, without a voice in its legislation, and the republic converted into an empire.

This is what may be expected if the party of which Mr. Sumner is the principal leader prevails and retains the power.

But the tide may turn, and the Democratic party—the meanest and narrowest of all the parties at the North, whose main principle is contempt for the equal rights of the Negro, and which opposes the plan I have sketched as vehemently as it does that of Mr. Sumner—may, in consequence of the division in the Republican party, obtain, sooner than we could imagine, the ascendency. Then the moderate, pacific measures of which I have spoken will be wrecked, and nothing will be done by the Government to aid the Negro in the acquisition of political rights. Even then I should not despair of his acquiring them, such faith have I in liberty and the progress of civilization, though I should deeply lament what had happened.

. . . I have long foreseen that this difference would

arise among the friends of the Union—the effect of a difference in political training. May God overrule it in the interest of universal liberty.[4]

Whitman offers a grand vision for the future of the country.

It is certain to me that the United States, by virtue of that war and its results—and through that and them only—are now ready to enter, and most certainly enter, upon their genuine career in history, as no more torn and divided in their spinal requisites, but a great homogeneous Nation—free states all—a moral and political unity in variety, such as Nature shows in her grandest physical works, and as much greater than the merely physical.

Out of that war not only has the Nationality of the States escaped from being strangled, but, more than any of the rest and in my opinion more than the North itself, the vital heart and breath of the South have escaped as from the pressure of a general nightmare, and are henceforth to enter on a life, development, and active freedom whose realities are certain in the future, notwithstanding all the Southern vexations of the hour—a development which could not possibly have been achieved on any less terms or by any other means than that grim lesson or something equivalent to it. And I predict that the South is yet to outstrip the North.[5]

Melville lays down a plan for reconstruction in the epilogue to his book of Civil War poems, Battle-Pieces and Other Aspects of the War.

It is more than a year since the memorable surrender, but events have not yet rounded themselves into completion. Not justly can we complain of this. There has been an upheaval affecting the basis of things; to altered circumstances complicated adaptations are to be made; there are difficulties great and novel. But is Reason still waiting for Passion to spend itself? We have sung of the soldiers and sailors, but who shall hymn the politicians?

In view of the infinite desirableness of Re-establish-
ment, and considering that, so far as feeling is concerned,
it depends not mainly on the temper in which the South
regards the North, but rather conversely; one who never
was a blind adherent feels constrained to submit some
thoughts, counting on the indulgence of his countrymen.

And, first, it may be said that, if among the feelings
and opinions growing immediately out of a great civil convulsion, there are any which time shall modify or do away,
they are presumably those of a less temperate and charitable cast.

There seems no reason why patriotism and narrowness should go together, or why intellectual fairmindedness
should be confounded with political trimming, or why serviceable truth should keep cloistered because not partisan.
Yet the work of Reconstruction, if admitted to be feasible
at all, demands little but common sense and Christian
charity, little but these? These are much.

Some of us are concerned because as yet the South
shows no penitence. But what exactly do we mean by this?
Since down to the close of the war she never confessed any
for braving it, the only penitence now left her is that which
springs solely from the sense of discomfiture; and since
this evidently would be a contrition hypocritical, it would
be unworthy in us to demand it. Certain it is that penitence, in the sense of voluntary humiliation, will never be
displayed. Nor does this afford just ground for unreserved
condemnation.

It is enough, for all practical purposes, if the South
have been taught by the terrors of civil war to feel that
Secession, like Slavery, is against Destiny; that both now
lie buried in one grave; that her fate is linked with ours;
and that altogether we comprise the Nation.

The clouds of heroes who battled for the Union it is
needless to eulogize here. But how of the soldiers on the
other side? And when of a free community we name the
soldiers, we thereby name the people. It was in subservi-
ency to the slave interest that Secession was plotted; but it

was under the plea, plausibly urged, that certain inestimable rights guaranteed by the Constitution were directly menaced, that the people of the South were cajoled into revolution. Through the arts of the conspirators and the perversity of fortune, the most sensitive love of liberty was entrapped into support of a war whose implied end was the erecting in our advanced century of an Anglo-American empire based upon the systematic degradation of man.

Spite this clinging reproach, however, signal military virtues and achievements have conferred upon the Confederate arms historic fame, and upon certain of the commanders a renown extending beyond the sea—a renown which we of the North could not suppress, even if we would. In personal character, also, not a few of the military leaders of the South enforce forbearance; the memory of others the North refrains from disparaging; and some, with more or less of reluctance, she can respect. Posterity, sympathizing with our convictions, but removed from our passions, may go farther here. If George IV could, out of the graceful instinct of a gentleman, raise an honorable monument in the great fane of Christendom over the remains of the enemy of his dynasty, Charles Edward, the invader of England and victor in the route of Preston Pans—upon whom the king's ancestor but one reign removed had set a price, is it probable that the grandchildren of General Grant will pursue with rancor, or slur by sour neglect, the memory of Stonewall Jackson?

But the South itself is not wanting in recent histories and biographies which record the deeds of her chieftains—writings freely published at the North by loyal houses, widely read here, and with a deep though saddened interest. By students of the war such works are hailed as welcome accessories, and tending to the completeness of the record.

Supposing a happy issue out of present perplexities, then, in the generation next to come, Southerners there will be yielding allegiance to the Union, feeling all their inter-

ests bound up in it, and yet cherishing unrebuked that kind
of feeling for the memory of the soldiers of the fallen Confederacy that Burns Scott and Ettrick Shepherd felt for
the memory of the gallant clansmen ruined through their
fidelity to the Stuarts—a feeling whose passion was tempered by the poetry imbuing it, and which in no wise
affected their loyalty to the Georges, and which, it may be
added, indirectly contributed excellent things to literature.
But, setting this view aside, dishonorable would it be in the
South were she willing to abandon to shame the memory of
brave men who with signal personal disinterestedness
warred in her behalf, though from motives, as we believe,
so deplorably astray.

Patriotism is not baseness, neither is it inhumanity.
The mourners who this summer bear flowers to the mounds
of the Virginian and Georgian dead are, in their domestic
bereavement and proud affection, as sacred in the eye of
Heaven as are those who go with similar offerings of
tender grief and love into the cemeteries of our Northern
Martyrs. And yet in one aspect, how needless to point the
contrast.

Cherishing such sentiments, it will hardly occasion
surprise that, in looking over the Battle–Pieces in the
foregoing collection, I have been tempted to withdraw or
modify some of them, fearful lest in presenting, though but
dramatically and by way of poetic record, the passions and
epithets of civil war, I might be contributing to a bitterness which every sensible American must wish at an end.
So, too, with the emotion of victory as produced on some
pages, and particularly toward the close.

It should not be construed into an exultation mis-
applied—an exultation as ungenerous as unwise, and made
to minister, however indirectly, to that kind of censorious-
ness too apt to be produced in certain natures by success
after trying reverses. Zeal is not of necessity religion,
neither is it always of the same essence with poetry or
patriotism.

There were excesses which marked the conflict, most of

which are perhaps inseparable from a civil strife so intense and prolonged, and involving warfare in some border countries new and imperfectly civilized. Barbarities also there were, for which the Southern people collectively can hardly be held responsible, though perpetrated by ruffians in their name. But surely other qualities, exalted ones— courage and fortitude matchless, were likewise displayed, and largely; and justly may these be held the characteristic traits, and not the former.

In this view, what Northern writer, however patriotic, but must revolt from acting on paper a part any way akin to that of the live dog to the dead lion; and yet it is just to rejoice for our triumphs, so far as it may justly imply an advance for one whole country and for humanity.

Let it be held no reproach to any one that he pleads for reasonable consideration for our late enemies, now stricken down and unavoidably debarred, for the time, from speaking through authorized agencies for themselves. Nothing has been urged here in foolish hope of conciliating those men—few in number, we trust—who have resolved never to be reconciled to the Union. On such hearts everything is thrown away except it be religious commiseration, and the sincerest. Yet let them call to mind that unhappy Secessionist, not a military man, who with impious alacrity fired the first shot of the Civil War at Sumter, and a little more than four years afterwards fired the last into his heart at Richmond.

Noble was the gesture with which patriotic passion surprised the people in a utilitarian time and country; yet the glory of the war falls short of its pathos—a pathos which now at last ought to disarm all animosity.

How many and earnest thoughts still rise, and how hard to repress them. We feel what past years have been, and years, unretarded years, shall come. May we all have moderation; may we all show candor. Though, perhaps, nothing could ultimately have averted the strife, and though to treat of human actions is to deal wholly with second causes, nevertheless, let us not cover up or try to extenuate what, humanly speaking, is the truth—namely, that these unfraternal denunciations, continued through years, and which at last inflamed to deeds that ended in bloodshed, were reciprocal; and that, had the preponderating strength and the prospect of its unlimited increase lain on the other side, on ours might have lain those actions which now in our late opponents we stigmatize under the name of Rebellion.

As frankly let us own—what it would be unbecoming to parade were foreigners concerned—that our triumph was won not more by skill and bravery than by superior resources and crushing numbers; that it was a triumph, too, over a people for years politically misled by designing men, and also by some honestly erring men, who from their position could not have been otherwise than broadly influential; a people who, though, indeed, they sought to perpetuate the curse of slavery, and even extend it, were not the authors of it, but (less fortunate, not less righteous than we) were the fated inheritors; a people who, having a like origin with ourselves, share essentially in whatever worthy qualities we possess. No one can add to the lasting reproach which hopeless defeat has now cast upon Secession by withholding the recognition of these verities.

Surely we ought to take it to heart that this kind of pacification, based upon principles operating equally all over the land, which lovers of their country yearn for, and which our arms, though signally triumphant, did not bring about, and which law-making, however anxious, or energetic, or repressive, never by itself can achieve, may yet be largely aided by generosity of sentiment public and private. Some revisionary legislation and adaptive is indispensable; but with this should harmoniously work another kind of prudence, not unallied with entire magnanimity.

Benevolence and policy—Christianity and Machiavelli—dissuade from penal severities toward the subdued. Abstinence here is as obligatory as considerate care for our unfortunate fellowmen late in bonds, and, if observed, would equally prove to be wise forecast. The great qual-

ities of the South, those attested in the war, we can peril-
ously alienate, or we may make them nationally available
at need.

The blacks, in their infant pupilage to freedom, appeal
to the sympathies of every humane mind. The paternal
guardianship which for the interval government exercises
over them was prompted equally by duty and benevolence.
Yet such kindness should not be allowed to exclude kindliness to communities who stand nearer to us in nature. For
the future of the freed slave we may well be concerned; but
the future of the whole country, involving the future of the
blacks, urges a paramount claim upon our anxiety.

Effective benignity, like the Nile, is not narrow in its
bounty, and true policy is always broad. To be sure, it is
vain to seek to glide, with moulded words, over the difficulties of the situation. And for them who are neither partisans, nor enthusiasts, nor theorists, nor cynics, there are
some doubts not readily to be solved. And there are fears.

Why is not the cessation of war now at length attended with the settled claim of peace? Wherefore in a
clear sky do we still turn our eyes toward the South as a
Neapolitan, months after the eruption, turns his toward
Vesuvius? Do we dread lest the repose may be deceptive?
In the recent convulsion has the crater but shifted? Let us
revere that sacred uncertainty which forever impends over
men and nations. Those of us who always abhorred slavery
as an atheistical iniquity, gladly we join in the exulting
chorus of humanity over its downfall.

But we should remember that emancipation was accomplished not by deliberate legislation; only through
agonized violence could so mighty a result be effected. In
our natural solicitude to confirm the benefit of liberty to
the blacks, let us forbear from measures of dubious constitutional rightfulness toward our white countrymen—measures of a nature to provoke, among other of the last evils,
exterminating hatred of race toward race. In imagination
let us place ourselves in the unprecedented position of the
Southerners—their position as regards the millions of ig-

norant manumitted slaves in their midst, for whom some of us now claim the suffrage. Let us be Christians toward our fellow whites, as well as philanthropists toward the blacks, our fellowmen.

In all things, and toward all, we are enjoined to do as we would be done by. Nor should we forget that benevolent desires, after passing a certain point, cannot undertake their own fulfillment without incurring the risk of evils beyond those sought to be remedied. Something may well be left to the graduated care of future legislation, and to heaven.

In one point of view the coexistence of the two races in the South—whether the Negro be bond or free—seems (even as it did to Abraham Lincoln) a grave evil. Emancipation has rid the country of the reproach, but not wholly of the calamity. Especially in the present transition period for both races in the South, more or less of trouble may not unreasonably be anticipated; but let us not hereafter be too swift to charge the blame exclusively in any one quarter. With certain evils men must be more or less patient. Our institutions have a potent digestion, and may in time convert and assimilate to good all elements thrown in, however originally alien.

But, so far as immediate measures looking toward permanent Re–establishment are concerned, no consideration should tempt us to pervert the national victory into oppression for the vanquished. Should plausible promise of eventual good, or a deceptive or spurious sense of duty, lead us to essay this, count we must on serious consequences, not the least of which would be divisions among the Northern adherents of the Union.

Assuredly, if any honest Catos there be who thus far have gone with us, no longer will they do so, but oppose us, and as resolutely as hitherto they have supported. But this path of thought leads toward those waters of bitterness, from which one can only turn aside and be silent.

But supposing Re–establishment so far advanced that the Southern seats in Congress are occupied and by men qualified in accordance with those cardinal principles of representative government which hitherto have prevailed in the land—what then? Why the congressmen elected by the people of the South will—represent the people of the South. This may seem a flat conclusion; but, in view of the last five years, may there not be latent significance in it? What will be the temper of those Southern members? and confronted by them, what will be the mood of our own representatives?

In private life true reconciliation seldom follows a violent quarrel; but if subsequent intercourse be unavoidable, nice observances and mutual (respect) are indispensable to the prevention of a new rupture. Amity itself can only be maintained by reciprocal respect, and true friends are punctilious equals.

On the floor of Congress North and South are to come together after a passionate duel, in which the South, though proving her valor, has been made to bite the dust. Upon differences in debate shall acrimonious recriminations be exchanged? shall censorious superiority assumed by one section provoke defiant self–assertion on the other? shall Manassas and Chickamauga be retorted for Chattanooga and Richmond?

Under the supposition that the full Congress will be composed of gentlemen, all this is impossible. Yet, if otherwise, it needs no prophet of Israel to foretell the end. The maintenance of Congressional decency in the future will rest mainly with the North. Rightly will more forbearance be required from the North than the South, for the North is victor.

But some there are who may deem these latter thoughts inapplicable, and for this reason: Since the test oath operatively excludes from Congress all who in any way participated in Secession, therefore none but Southerners wholly in harmony with the North are eligible to seats. This is true for the time being.

But the oath is alterable; and in the wonted fluctuations of parties not improbably it will undergo alteration, assuming such a form, perhaps, as not to bar the admission into the National Legislature of men who represent the populations lately in revolt. Such a result would involve no violation of the principles of democratic government. Not readily can one perceive how the political existence of the millions of late Secessionists can be permanently ignored by the Republic. The years of the war tried our devotion to the Union; the time of peace may test the sincerity of our faith in democracy.

In no spirit of opposition, not by way of challenge, is anything here thrown out. These thoughts are sincere ones; they seem natural—inevitable. Here and there they must have suggested themselves to many thoughtful patriots. And, if they be just thoughts, ere long they must have that weight with the public which already they have had with individuals.

For the heroic band—those children of the furnace who, in regions like Texas and Tennessee, maintained their fidelity through terrible trials—we of the North felt for them, and profoundly we honor them. Yet passionate sympathy, with resentments so close as to be almost domestic in their bitterness, would hardly in the present juncture tend to discreet legislation. Were the Unionists and Secessionists but as Guelphs and Ghibellines? If not, then far be it from a great nation to act in the spirit that animated a triumphant town-faction in the Middle Ages. But crowding thoughts must at last be checked; and, in times like the present, one who desires to be impartially just in the expression of his views, moves as among sword points presented on every side.

Let us pray that the great historic tragedy of our time may not have been enacted without instructing our whole beloved country through terror and pity, and may fulfillment verify in the end those expectations which kindle the bards of Progress and Humanity.[6]

Notes

1 Fort Sumter Falls

1. Walter Harding and Carl Bode (eds.), *The Correspondence of Henry David Thoreau* (New York: New York University Press, 1958), p. 378.
2. Samuel Clemens, "The Private History of a Campaign that Failed," *The Portable Mark Twain,* ed. Bernard DeVoto (New York: Viking Press, 1957), pp. 119–120.
3. Samuel Longfellow (ed.), *The Life of Henry Wadsworth Longfellow, With Extracts From His Journals and Correspondence* (Boston: Ticknor & Co., 1886), pp. 363–65.
4. Ralph L. Rusk (ed.), *The Letters of Ralph Waldo Emerson* (New York: Columbia University Press, 1939), V, 246.
5. Walter Lowenfels (ed.), *Walt Whitman's Civil War* (New York: Alfred A. Knopf, 1960), p. 21.
6. Ednah D. Cheney (ed.), *Louisa May Alcott: Her Life, Letters, and Journals* (Boston: Little, Brown & Company, 1914), p. 127.
7. James Russell Lowell, "The Pickens-and-Stealin's Rebellion," *Political Essays,* Vol. V of *The Works of James Russell Lowell* (Boston: Houghton, Mifflin & Company, 1899), pp. 87–91.
8. Samuel T. Pickard (ed.), "The Civil War," *The Life and Letters of John Greenleaf Whittier* (Boston: Houghton, Mifflin & Company, 1894), II, 441.

2 The Civil War Gathers

1. Edward Waldo Emerson and Waldo Emerson Forbes (eds.), *Journals of Ralph Waldo Emerson* (Boston: Houghton, Mifflin & Company, 1913), IX, 324–26.
2. Cheney (ed.), *Louisa May Alcott: Her Life, Letters, and Journals,* 127.
3. Samuel Longfellow (ed.), *Life of Henry Wadsworth Longfellow,* 365–66.
4. Julian Hawthorne, *Hawthorne and His Wife* (Boston: Hough-

ton, Mifflin & Company, 1889), II, 276–77.

5. Harding and Bode (eds.), *The Correspondence of Henry David Thoreau*, 385.

6. Lowenfels (ed.), *Walt Whitman's Civil War*, 22–25.

7. Rusk (ed.), *The Letters of Ralph Waldo Emerson*, 251–53.

8. Thomas H. Johnson (ed.), *The Letters of Emily Dickinson* (Cambridge: The Belknap Press of Harvard University Press, 1958), II, 377.

9. Emerson and Forbes (eds.), *op. cit.*, pp. 330–31.

10. Oliver Wendell Holmes, "The Wormwood Cordial of History," *The Autocrat's Miscellanies*, ed. Albert Mordell (New York: Twayne, 1959), pp. 200–201.

11. *Ibid.*, pp. 206, 208–209.

12. Ambrose Bierce, "The Mockingbird," *The Collected Writings of Ambrose Bierce*, ed. Clifton Fadiman (New York: The Citadel Press, 1946), pp. 99–100.

3 The Battle for Missouri

1. DeVoto (ed.), *The Portable Mark Twain*, 120–21, 123–42.

4 The Spirit Aroused

1. Hawthorne, *Hawthorne and His Wife*, 290–91.

2. Oliver Wendell Holmes, "Bread and the Newspapers," *Pages From an Old Volume of Life: A Collection of Essays, 1857–1881* (Boston: Houghton, Mifflin & Company, 1889), pp. 1–2, 6–7, 8–9, 10–11, 14–15.

3. S Longfellow (ed.), *Life of Henry Wadsworth Longfellow*, 371.

4. John F. Morse, Jr. (ed.), *Life and Letters of Oliver Wendell Holmes* (Boston: Houghton, Mifflin & Company, 1896), II, 157–59.

5. Rusk (ed.), *The Letters of Ralph Waldo Emerson*, 258–59.

6. Emerson & Forbes (eds.), *Journals of Ralph Waldo Emerson*, ix, 344–45.

7. Charles R. Anderson and Aubrey H. Starke (eds.), *Letters 1857–1868* [Vol. VII of the *Centennial Edition of the Works of Sidney Lanier* (Baltimore: Johns Hopkins Press, 1945)], pp. 46–49.

8. Johnson (ed.), *The Letters of Emily Dickinson*, 386.

9. Parke Godwin, *A Biography of William Cullen Bryant With Extracts From His Private Correspondence* (New York: D. Appleton & Company, 1883), II, 164.

5 No Hasty Peace

1. Emerson and Forbes (eds.), *Journals of Ralph Waldo Emerson*, IX, 353–54, 358–59, 362, 363–64, 365, 366, 368.

2. Anderson and Starke (eds.), *Letters 1857–1868*, 51.

3. Ralph Waldo Emerson, "American Civilization," *The Works of Ralph Waldo Emerson* (Boston: Houghton, Mifflin & Company, 1884), I, 277–88, 289–290.

4. Godwin, *A Biography of William Cullen Bryant*, II, 175–76.

6 Sanguine Anticipations

1. Morse (ed.), *Life and Letters of Oliver Wendell Holmes*, II, 159–161, 162–63, 164.
2. Longfellow (ed.), *Life of Henry Wadsworth Longfellow*, II, 375–76.
3. Anderson and Starke (eds.), *Letters 1857–1868*, 51–53.
4. Hawthorne, *Hawthorne and His Wife*, II, 309–310.
5. Johnson (ed.), *The Letters of Emily Dickinson*, II, 397–99.
6. Longfellow (ed.), *op. cit.*, pp. 378–79, 382–83.
7. Merrel R. Davis and William H. Gilman (eds.), *The Letters of Herman Melville* (New Haven: Yale University Press, 1960), p. 215.
8. Anderson and Starke (eds.), *op. cit.*, p. 56.
9. *Ibid.*, p. 226.
10. Charles Eliot Norton (ed.), *Letters of James Russell Lowell* (New York: Harper & Brothers, 1894), I, 321.
11. Rusk (ed.), *The Letters of Ralph Waldo Emerson*, V, 278–79.
12. Godwin, *A Biography of William Cullen Bryant*, II, 176–78.

7 Hawthorne Tours the Battle Areas

1. Nathaniel Hawthorne, "Chiefly About War Matters," *The Atlantic Monthly*, X (July, 1862), 44–45, 48, 49–50, 51, 53–54, 59–60.

8 The Test of Men

1. Emerson and Forbes (eds.), *Journals of Ralph Waldo Emer-*

son, IX, 411–12, 421, 424, 425, 428–29, 432–34, 435–36, 437–38, 441–43.
2. Norton (ed.), *Letters of James Russell Lowell*, I, 322.
3. Newton Arvin (ed.), *The Heart of Hawthorne's Journals* (Boston: Houghton, Mifflin & Company, 1929), pp. 330–31.
4. Rusk (ed.), *The Letters of Ralph Waldo Emerson*, V, 279–80, 282, 283, 286.
5. Morse (ed.), *Life and Letters of Oliver Wendell Holmes*, II, 165–67.
6. Godwin, *A Biography of William Cullen Bryant*, II, 180–81.

9 Search for a Wounded Captain

1. Oliver Wendell Holmes, "My Hunt After the Captain," *Pages From an Old Volume of Life* (Boston: Houghton, Mifflin & Company, 1904), p. 16ff.

10 Emerson's Emancipation Proclamation

1. Emerson and Forbes (eds.), *Journals of Ralph Waldo Emerson*, IX, 451–52.
2. Ralph Waldo Emerson, "The Emancipation Proclamation," *The Works of Ralph Waldo Emerson* (Boston: Houghton, Mifflin & Company, 1884), IV, 293, 294–99, 300–303.

11 Digging Down to the Pan

1. Anderson and Starke (eds.), *Letters 1857–1868*, 61.

2. Lowenfels (ed.), *Walt Whitman's Civil War*, 33–34.
3. Anderson and Starke (eds.), *op. cit.*, pp. 60–61.
4. Emerson and Forbes (eds.), *Journals of Ralph Waldo Emerson*, IX, 449–50, 453, 455–56, 457–60, 461–65, 484–86.

12 Dark Sky

1. Thomas Carlyle and Ralph Waldo Emerson, *The Correspondence of Thomas Carlyle and Ralph Waldo Emerson, 1834–1872* (Boston: John R. Osgood & Company, 1883), II, 278, 280–81.
2. Ambrose Bierce, "The Affair at Coulter's Notch," *The Collected Writings of Ambrose Bierce*, ed. Clifton Fadiman (New York: The Citadel Press, 1946), p. 51. "One Officer, One Man," p. 90.
3. Morse (ed.), *Life and Letters of Oliver Wendell Holmes*, 171–73.
4. Allen Nevins, *The Evening Post, A Century of Journalism* (New York: Boni and Liverwright, 1922), pp. 297–98.
5. Longfellow (ed.), *Life of Henry Wadsworth Longfellow*, II, 390.
6. Rusk (ed.), *Letters of Ralph Waldo Emerson*, V, 311.
7. Johnson (ed.), *The Letters of Emily Dickinson*, II, 423.
8. Rusk (ed.), *op. cit.*, 321–22.

13 Forty Ambulances from Fredericksburg

1. Lowenfels (ed.), *Walt Whitman's Civil War*, 34, 38–39, 29–300.

14 The Hospitals

1. Lowenfels (ed.), *Walt .Whitman's Civil War*, 85–86, 92.
2. Cheney (ed.), *Louisa May Alcott*, 142, 143–44.
3. Louisa May Alcott, "A Night," *Hospital Sketches*, ed. Bessie Z. Jones (Cambridge: The Belknap Press of Harvard University Press, 1960), pp. 42, 44, 45, 45–48, 48–49.
4. Holmes, "My Search for the Captain," *Pages From an Old Volume of Life*, 57, 66.

2. Louisa May Alcott, "The Day," *Hospital Sketches*, ed. Bessie Z. Jones (Cambridge: The Belknap Press of Harvard University Press, 1960), pp. 27–28, 29–30, 30–31, 32–34, 35–36, 36–37, 37–39, 39–40.

15 Old Abe Vis-a-Vis

1. Davis and Gilman (eds.), *The Letters of Herman Melville*, 209–210.
2. Nathaniel Hawthorne, "Chiefly About War Matters," *The Writings of Hawthorne* (Boston: Houghton, Mifflin & Company, 1900), XVII (*Miscellanies*), 372–380.
3. Lowenfels (ed.), *Walt Whitman's Civil War*, 257–58, 260.
4. Emerson and Forbes (eds.), *Journals of Ralph Waldo Emerson*, IX, 375–76, 557.
5. Godwin, *A Biography of William Cullen Bryant*, II, 178–79.

16 General McClellan on Trial

1. Nathaniel Hawthorne, "Chiefly About War Matters," *The Atlantic Monthly,* X (July, 1862), 51–52, 53.
2. Lowenfels (ed.), *Walt Whitman's Civil War,* 248–49, 250.
3. James Russell Lowell, "General McClellan's Report," *Political Essays* (Boston: Houghton, Mifflin & Company, 1899), pp. 94, 96–97, 99–100, 100–102, 103–104, 107, 109, 112–13.
4. Allen Nevins, *The Evening Post,* 289.

17 A War of Personalities

1. Lowenfels (ed.), *Walt Whitman's Civil War,* 247, 250.
2. Emerson and Forbes (eds.), *Journals of Ralph Waldo Emerson,* X, 376, 381–82, 393–94.
3. Hawthorne, "Chiefly About War Matters," XVII (*Miscellanies*), 371.
4. Lowenfels (ed.), *op. cit.,* 251–52.
5. Anderson and Starke (eds.), *Letters, 1857–1868,* 109, 163, 164.
6. Sidney Lanier, "Robert E. Lee: In Memoriam," *Tiger-Lilies and Southern Prose,* ed. Garland Greever and Cecil Abernathy [Vol. V, *Centennial Edition of the Works of Sidney Lanier* (Baltimore: The Johns Hopkins Press, 1945)], pp. 273–74.
7. Pickard (ed.), *The Life and Letters of John Greenleaf Whittier,* II, 464–65.
8. Fadiman (ed.), *The Collected Writings of Ambrose Bierce,* "An Affair of Outposts." 67.
9. Morse (ed.), *Life and Letters of Oliver Wendell Holmes,* II, 174–77.

18 Secesh Prisoners

1. Nathaniel Hawthorne, "Chiefly About War Matters," *The Atlantic Monthly,* X (July, 1862), 52–53.
2. Holmes, "My Hunt After the Captain," *Pages From an Old Volume of Life,* 36–37, 57–61, 61–62.
3. Lowenfels (ed.), *Walt Whitman's Civil War,* 247, 237–39.
4. Anderson and Starke (eds.), *Letters 1857–1868,* 183, 227.

19 Ships of the War

1. Hawthorne, "Chiefly About War Matters," XVII (*Miscellanies*), 57–59.
2. Anderson and Starke (eds.), *Letters 1857–1868,* 170, 171–72, 176–77, 180, 181, 227.
3. Emerson and Forbes (eds.), *Journals of Ralph Waldo Emerson,* IX, 392–93.
4. Horace E. Scudder (ed.), *The Complete Poetical Works of James Russell Lowell* (Boston: Houghton, Mifflin & Company, 1900), p. 249.

20 The Negro in Uniform

1. Longfellow (ed.), *Life of Henry Wadsworth Longfellow,* II, 393.
2. Emerson and Forbes (eds.),

Journals of Ralph Waldo Emerson, IX, 506–07.

3. Pickard (ed.), *The Life and Letters of John Greenleaf Whittier,* II, 472, 473.

4. Lowenfels (ed.), *Walt Whitman's Civil War,* 223, 224–26.

5. Emerson and Forbes (eds.), *op. cit.,* p. 484.

6. Cheney (ed.), *Louisa May Alcott,* 163.

7. Thomas Wentworth Higginson, *Army Life in a Black Regiment* (Cambridge: The Riverside Press, 1900), pp. 4–5, 6–7, 12–13, 13–15, 79–80.

8. Mary Thatcher Higginson, (ed.), *Letters and Journals of Thomas Wentworth Higginson, 1846–1906* (Boston: Houghton, Mifflin & Company, 1921), pp. 206, 209.

21 Copperheadism

1. Lowenfels (ed.), *Walt Whitman's Civil War,* 289.

2. Godwin, *A Biography of William Cullen Bryant,* II, 154–57.

3. Emerson and Forbes (eds.), *Journals of Ralph Waldo Emerson,* IX, 541–42.

4. Morse (ed.), *Life and Letters of Oliver Wendell Holmes,* 168–70.

5. Nevins, *The Evening Post,* 314.

6. Godwin, *op. cit.,* pp. 203–204.

22 Malevolent England

1. Emerson and Forbes (eds.) *Journals of Ralph Waldo Emerson,* X, 15, 56–58, 78.

2. Godwin, *A Biography of William Cullen Bryant,* II, 157–59, 182–83, 210–11.

3. Carlyle and Emerson, *The Correspondence . . . 1834–1872,* II, 283–85.

4. Scudder (ed.), *The Complete Poetical Works of James Russell Lowell,* 230–32.

5. Harriet Beecher Stowe, "A Reply" *The Atlantic Monthly,* XI (January, 1863), 130–31, 132, 133.

23 These Were Men

1. Rusk (ed.), *The Letters of Ralph Waldo Emerson,* V, 331–32.

2. Fadiman (ed.), "Chickamauga," *The Collected Writings of Ambrose Bierce,* 20–23.

3. Norton (ed.), *Letters of James Russell Lowell,* I, 327–28.

4. Pickard (ed.), *Life and Letters of John Greenleaf Whittier,* II, 469–70.

5. Godwin, *A Biography of William Cullen Bryant,* II, 195–96.

24 The Many Needless Dead

1. Fadiman (ed.), "A Son of the Gods," *The Collected Writings of Ambrose Bierce,* 24–29.

2. Howard P. Vincent (ed.), *Collected Poems of Herman Melville* (Chicago: Hendricks House, 1947), p. 454.

3. Anderson and Starke (eds.), *Letters 1857–1868,* 151.

4. Davis and Gilman (eds.), *The*

Letters of Herman Melville, 226–27.

25 The War Drags On

1. Godwin, *A Biography of William Cullen Bryant*, II, 192.
2. Nevins, *The Evening Post*, 299.
3. Pickard (ed.), *Life and Letters of John Greenleaf Whittier*, II, 469.
4. Fadiman (ed.), *The Collected Writings of Ambrose Bierce*, "George Thurston," 95–96.
5. Longfellow (ed.), *Life of Henry Wadsworth Longfellow*, II, 394–95.
6. Davis and Gilman (eds.), *The Letters of Herman Melville*, 224–26.
7. Emerson and Forbes (eds.), *Journals of Ralph Waldo Emerson*, IX, 541, 557, 565.
8. Godwin, *op. cit.*, p. 211.

26 Enforcing Emancipation

1. Emerson and Forbes (eds.), *Journals of Ralph Waldo Emerson*, IX, 565–66, 574.
2. Godwin, *A Biography of William Cullen Bryant*, II, 201–2, 203.
3. Ibid., 203.
4. Longfellow (ed.), *Life of Henry Wadsworth Longfellow*, II, 406.

27 Lincoln Re-elected

1. Norton (ed.), *Letters of James Russell Lowell*, I, 336–37.
2. Lowell, *Political Essays*, 174–75, 175–76, 172–73.

3. Nevins, *The Evening Post*, 313.
4. Emerson and Forbes (eds.), *Journals of Ralph Waldo Emerson*, IX, 556, 82–84.
5. Longfellow (ed.), *Life of Henry Wadsworth Longfellow*, II, 417.
6. Rusk (ed.), *Letters of Ralph Waldo Emerson*, V, 387.

28 The Union Victorious

1. Emerson and Forbes (eds.), *Journals of Ralph Waldo Emerson*, X, 7.
2. Anderson and Starke (eds.), *Letters 1857–1868*, 161–62, 177, 178.
3. Longfellow (ed.), *Life of Henry Wadsworth Longfellow*, II, 406.
4. Godwin, *A Biography of William Cullen Bryant*, II, 221–23.
5. Rusk (ed.), *Letters of Ralph Waldo Emerson*, V, 402, 411, 412.
6. Longfellow (ed.), *op. cit.*, pp. 423, 424.
7. Nevins, *The Evening Post*, 314–15.
8. Norton (ed.), *Letters of James Russell Lowell*, I, 344.

29 Lincoln Assassinated

1. Longfellow (ed.), *Life of Henry Wadsworth Longfellow*, II, 424.
2. Godwin, *A Biography of William Cullen Bryant*, II, 228–230.
3. Ralph Waldo Emerson, "Abraham Lincoln," *The Works of Ralph Waldo Emerson* (Boston: Houghton, Mifflin & Company, 1884), I, 307–314.

30 Reconstruction

1. Lowell, "Reconstruction," *Political Essays,* 233–34.
2. Pickard (ed.), *Life and Letters of John Greenleaf Whittier,* II, 491.
3. Ralph Waldo Emerson, "Harvard Commemoration Speech," *The Works of Ralph Waldo Emerson* (Boston: Houghton, Mifflin & Company, 1884), I, 319–321.
4. Godwin, *A Biography of William Cullen Bryant,* II, 227–28, 231–32, 240.
5. Lowenfels (ed.), *Walt Whitman's Civil War,* 292.
6. Vincent (ed.), *Collected Poems of Herman Melville,* 461–67.

Bibliography

Allen, Gay Wilson. *Walt Whitman As Man, Poet, and Legend*. Carbondale: Southern Illinois University Press, 1961.

Anderson, Charles R., and Starke, Aubrey H. (eds.). *Letters 1857–1862* (Volume VIII of the *Centennial Edition of the Works of Sidney Lanier*). Baltimore: Johns Hopkins Press, 1945.

Arvin, Newton (ed.). *The Heart of Hawthorne's Journals*. Boston: Houghton, Mifflin & Company, 1929.

Atlantic Monthly, The. 1861–1865.

Bennett, Whitman. *Whittier, Bard of Freedom*. Chapel Hill: University of North Carolina Press, 1941.

Carlyle, Thomas, and Emerson, Ralph Waldo. *The Correspondence of Thomas Carlyle and Ralph Waldo Emerson, 1834–1872*. 2 Vols. Boston: John R. Osgood & Company, 1883.

Cheney, Ednah (ed.). *Louisa May Alcott: Her Life, Letters and Journals*. Boston: Little, Brown & Company, 1914.

Davis, Merrel R., and Gilman, William (eds.). *The Letters of Herman Melville*. New Haven: The Yale University Press, 1960.

De Voto, Bernard (ed.). *The Portable Mark Twain*. New York: Viking Press, 1957.

Emerson, Edward Waldo, and Forbes, Waldo Emerson (eds.). *The Journals of Ralph Waldo Emerson*. 10 Vols. Boston: Houghton, Mifflin & Company, 1913.

Emerson, Ralph Waldo. *The Works of Ralph Waldo Emerson: Miscellanies. Natural History of the Intellect*. Boston: Houghton, Mifflin & Company, 1884.

Fadiman, Clifton (ed.). *The Collected Writings of Ambrose Bierce*. New York: The Citadel Press, 1946.

Fields, Annie (Adams). *Life and Letters of Harriet Beecher Stowe*. Cambridge: The Riverside Press, 1897.

Godwin, Parke. *A Biography of William Cullen Bryant*. 2 Vols. New York: D. Appleton & Company, 1883.

Greever, Garland, and Abernathy, Cecil A. (eds.). *Tiger-Lilies and South-*

ern Prose (Vol. V of the *Centennial Edition of the Works of Sidney Lanier*). Baltimore: Johns Hopkins Press, 1945.

Harding, Walter, and Bode, Carl (eds.). *The Correspondence of Henry David Thoreau*. New York: New York University Press, 1958.

Harper's Monthly, 1861–1865.

Harper's Weekly, 1861–1865.

Hawthorne, Julian. *Hawthorne and His Wife.* 2 Vols. Boston: Houghton, Mifflin & Company, 1889.

Hawthorne, Nathaniel. *Miscellanies* (Vol. XVII of *The Works of Hawthorne*). Boston: Houghton, Mifflin & Company, 1900.

Higginson, Mary Thatcher (ed.). *Letters and Journals of Thomas Wentworth Higginson.* Boston: Houghton, Mifflin & Company, 1921.

Higginson, Thomas Wentworth. *Army Life in a Black Regiment.* Cambridge: The Riverside Press, 1900.

Holmes, Oliver Wendell. *The Autocrat's Miscellanies,* ed. Albert Mordell. New York: Twayne, 1959.

————. *Pages From an Old Volume of Life: A Collection of Essays, 1857–1881.* Boston: Houghton, Mifflin & Company, 1904.

Johnson, Thomas H. (ed.). *The Letters of Emily Dickinson.* 2 Vols. Cambridge: The Belknap Press of Harvard University Press, 1958.

Jones, Bessie Z. (ed.). *The Hospital Sketches of Louisa May Alcott.* Cambridge: The Belknap Press of Harvard University Press, 1960.

Longfellow, Samuel (ed.). *Life of Henry Wadsworth Longfellow, With Extracts From His Journals and Correspondence.* Boston: Ticknor & Company, 1886.

Lowell, James Russell. *Political Essays* (Vol. V of *The Works of James Russell Lowell*). Boston: Houghton, Mifflin & Company, 1899.

Lowenfels, Walter (ed.). *Walt Whitman's Civil War.* New York: Alfred A. Knopf, 1960.

Morse, John F. *Life and Letters of Oliver Wendell Holmes.* 2 Vols. Boston: Houghton, Mifflin & Company, 1896.

Mumford, Lewis. *Herman Melville.* New York: Harcourt, Brace & Company, 1929.

Nevins, Allen. *The Evening Post, A Century of Journalism.* New York: Boni and Liverwright, 1922.

Norton, Charles Eliot (ed.). *Letters of James Russell Lowell.* 2 Vols. New York: Harper and Brothers, 1894.

Paine, Albert Bigelow. *Mark Twain; A Biography.* New York: Harper and Brothers, 1912.

Pickard, Samuel T. (ed.). *The Life and Letters of John Greenleaf Whittier.* 2 Vols. Boston: Houghton, Mifflin & Company, 1894.

Rusk, Ralph L. (ed.). *The Letters of Ralph Waldo Emerson.* 6 Vols. New York: Columbia University Press, 1939.

Russell, Phillips. *Emerson: The Wisest American.* New York: Blue Ribbon Books, Inc., 1929.

Scudder, Horace E. (ed.). *The Complete Poetical Works of James Russell Lowell*. Boston: Houghton, Mifflin & Company, 1900.

———. *James Russell Lowell: A Biography*. Boston: Houghton, Mifflin & Company, 1901.

Van Doren, Mark. *Nathaniel Hawthorne*. New York: W. Sloan Associates, 1949.

Vincent, Howard P. (ed.). *Collected Poems of Herman Melville*. Chicago: Hendricks House, 1947.

Wilson, Edmund. *Patriotic Gore: Studies in the Literature of the American Civil War*. New York: Oxford University Press, 1962.

Index